Staff

Key Geography for GCSE

David Waugh

Former Head of Geography
Trinity School
Carlisle

D1331058

Book 1

Stanley Thornes (Publishers)

First published in 1994 by:
Stanley Thornes (Publishers) Ltd
Ellenborough House
Wellington Street
CHELTENHAM GL50 1YD
England

Reprinted 1994 (four times)

A catalogue record for this book is available from the British Library.
ISBN 0 7487 1670 X

Printed in Hong Kong by Dah Hua Printing Co.,Ltd.

Cover photograph: Houston, Texas
Title page photograph: A landsat view of Edinburgh and the surrounding area

Acknowledgements

The author and publishers are grateful to the following for permission to reproduce photographs and other copyright material in this book.

Aerofilms Ltd (pp. 9, F; 27, C; 30, A (right); 94, B); Chris Bentley (p. 122, B); Blenkinsop Studios (p. 139, B); Sue Boulton (p. 126, B); British Petroleum Company plc (p. 108, C); Bruce Coleman Ltd (p. 120, A (centre)); Chorley and Handford Ltd (p. 101, C); Rob Cousins (p. 145, E); Cumbria Library Service, Kendal (p. 154, A); Prodeepta Das (p. 93, E); Environmental Picture Library (pp. 146, A (right); 156, B); European Space Agency (p. 18, B); Eye Ubiquitous (pp. 10, B; 11, D; 33, D; 57, C; 93, D; 147, C); Forest Life Picture Library (p. 152, B (bottom right)); Frank Lane Picture Agency (pp. 120, A (left); 123, D); Geoscience Features (pp. 7, E; 22, B (a); 24, B (a); 38, A; 38, C; 42, B); Sally and Richard Greenhill (p. 144, C); Greenpeace (p. 56, A); Hulton Deutsch (pp. 29, C; 59 C and D); Hutchison Library (pp. 79, E; 111, F (left)); ICCE Photo Library (pp. 124, B; 127, D; 129, D; 135, C; 142, A (bottom); 143, B (bottom); 153, D); Impact (p. 159, C); Intermediate Technology (p. 143, B (top)); Landform (pp. 24, B (b); 25, C; 39, F; 40, B; 41, F; 44, B); Mary Evans Picture Library (p. 98, B); Meadowhall Shopping Centre (p. 148, B); Newcastle Evening Chronicle (p. 103, C (bottom)); North News and Pictures (p. 157, D); Nuclear Electric (p. 133, B); Panos (pp. 74, A; 93, C; 108, B); Picture Point (pp. 120, A (right); 126, A; 152, B (bottom left); 154, C; 158, A); Rex Features (pp. 78, A; 91, E; 91, F); Robert Harding Picture Library (pp. 74, B; 77, D; 79, D; 90, A; 97, D; 98, C; 108, A; 111, F (right); 138, A (top)); Science Photo Library (pp. (i); 8, A; 29, F; 34, C; 44, C; 48, A; 50, A; 51, E; 64, A); Scottish Hydro-Electric (p. 133, C); Sefton Photo Library (pp. 97, C; 144, D; 147, B); Spectrum Colour Library (p. 97, F); Still Pictures (p. 131, C); Syndication International (p. 29, D; 146, A (left)); Telegraph Colour Library (p. 19, D; 51, C; 56, A); Tony Stone Worldwide (pp. cover; 4, C; 7, F; 34, B; 61, B; 63, B; 75, C; 77, C; 90, B; 96, B; 97, G; 107, C; 126, C); Tower Hamlets Local History Library (p. 99, D); University of Cambridge (p. 138, A (top)); Dr A C Waltham (pp. 16, A; 21, C; 22, B (b); 25, D; 29, E; 41, E; 45, F; 46, D; 49, E); Simon Warner (pp. 42, A; 46, A; 46, B; 46, C; 123, C; 124, C; 145, F; 152, B (top left); 153, C; 156, A); David Waugh (pp. 4, B; 6, D; 10, C; 63, C; 87, E, F, G; 97, E; 100, B; 103, C (top and bottom); 109, C (both); 142, A (top); 150, B; 151, D, E; 158, B; 159, D); Eric Whitehead (p. 154, D); Mike Williams (pp. 152, B (top right); 157, C); David Woodfall (pp. 4, A; 5, E; 17, C; 110, C); World Pictures (pp. 150, C; 23, E; 30, A; 40, C)

Figure A, page 112 - the Intercity Route map is reproduced with permission from British Rail (license number TLB/93/1109); figure D, page 115 - the by-pass route is reproduced courtesy of the Department of Transport; figure D, page 33 - adapted extract from 'The Ganges' by Tim McGirk, reproduced from *The Independent on Sunday*, 9 August 1992; figure D, page 149 - the floorplan is reproduced courtesy of the Meadowhall Centre Ltd, Sheffield; figure B, page 114 - map extract from the *Philip's Modern School Atlas (89th edition)* © George Philip.

The map extracts on pages 43, 47, 82-83 and 115 are reproduced from the 1991 Ordnance Survey map of Snowdonia (Landranger 115), the 1989 Ordnance Survey map of Wensleydale and Upper Wharfedale (Landranger 98), the 1992 Ordnance Survey map of Carlisle and Solway Firth (Landranger 85) and the 1991 Ordnance Survey map of Haltwhistle, Bewcastle and Alston (Landranger 86) with the permission of the Controller of HMSO © Crown Copyright.

The author also wishes to thank Gilbert Hitchen for his contribution to pages 122-124.

Every effort has been made to contact copyright holders and we apologise if any have been overlooked.

► Contents ◄

Landforms and natural hazards

1 Rivers - river basins, processes, landforms, flooding   4
2 Coasts - processes, landforms, flooding   22
3 Water pollution - rivers, lakes, seas   32
4 Glaciation, limestone, and rock structure   38
5 Earthquakes and volcanoes   50

Human geography

6 Population - distribution and trends, causes of migration   62
7 Settlement - types, sites and urban growth   80
8 Urban patterns and changes   94
9 Transport - types, problems (including pollution) and solutions   104

Economic geography

10 Employment structures   116
11 Primary activities - farming, energy resources and the environment   120
12 Secondary activities – iron and steel, new technology, distribution and
    location of industry   136
13 Tertiary activities - shops and offices (location and hierarchy);
    tourism and the need to plan and manage certain environments   144

Index   160

▶ What are the main features of a river basin? ◀

A **river** (or **drainage**) **basin** is an area of land drained by a river and its tributaries. The higher land which forms the boundary of the river basin, and which separates two river basins, is called the **watershed**. Most rain falls in mountainous areas. Rain falling on higher land near the watershed will flow slowly downhill either over the surface (photo **A**) or through any topsoil. In time the water will collect in a channel to form a small stream which, as it continues downhill, will increase in size to become a river.

A
The watershed of a river basin above its source in the Pennines. Rainfall is flowing over the land surface, but the water has yet to make a channel for itself.

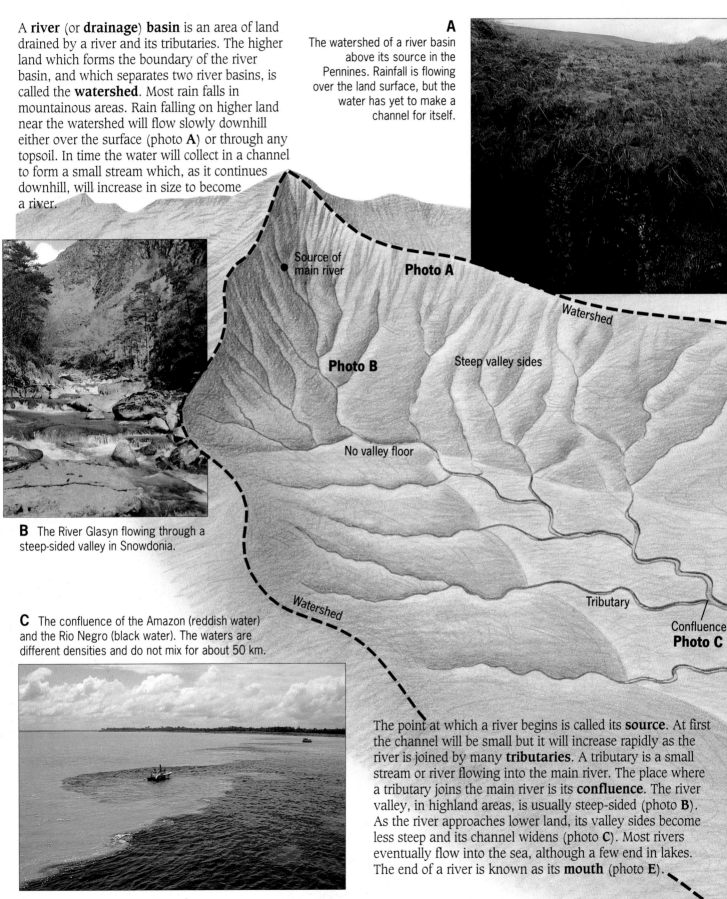

B The River Glasyn flowing through a steep-sided valley in Snowdonia.

C The confluence of the Amazon (reddish water) and the Rio Negro (black water). The waters are different densities and do not mix for about 50 km.

The point at which a river begins is called its **source**. At first the channel will be small but it will increase rapidly as the river is joined by many **tributaries**. A tributary is a small stream or river flowing into the main river. The place where a tributary joins the main river is its **confluence**. The river valley, in highland areas, is usually steep-sided (photo **B**). As the river approaches lower land, its valley sides become less steep and its channel widens (photo **C**). Most rivers eventually flow into the sea, although a few end in lakes. The end of a river is known as its **mouth** (photo **E**).

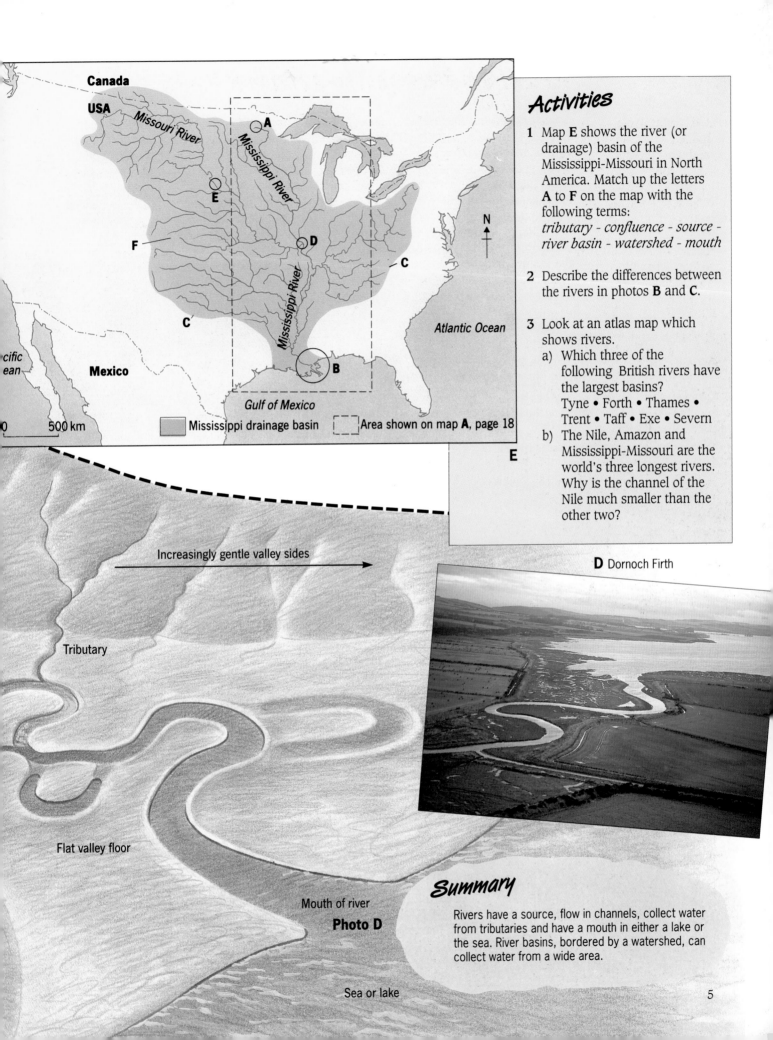

Canada

USA

Missouri River

Mississippi River

A

E

F

D

C

C'

C'

Mississippi River

Mexico

B

Atlantic Ocean

N

Pacific Ocean

Gulf of Mexico

0   500 km

■ Mississippi drainage basin   ⌐ ¬ Area shown on map **A**, page 18

E

Activities

1 Map **E** shows the river (or drainage) basin of the Mississippi-Missouri in North America. Match up the letters **A** to **F** on the map with the following terms:
tributary - confluence - source - river basin - watershed - mouth

2 Describe the differences between the rivers in photos **B** and **C**.

3 Look at an atlas map which shows rivers.
   a) Which three of the following British rivers have the largest basins?
      Tyne • Forth • Thames • Trent • Taff • Exe • Severn
   b) The Nile, Amazon and Mississippi-Missouri are the world's three longest rivers. Why is the channel of the Nile much smaller than the other two?

Increasingly gentle valley sides →

Tributary

Flat valley floor

Mouth of river

Photo D

Sea or lake

D Dornoch Firth

Summary

Rivers have a source, flow in channels, collect water from tributaries and have a mouth in either a lake or the sea. River basins, bordered by a watershed, can collect water from a wide area.

5

▶ *How do rivers shape the land?* ◀

If water flows over the ground surface (photo **A**, page 4) it can pick up fine material. Where valleys have very steep sides (photo **B**, page 4), large rocks can break off and fall downhill under the force of gravity. In both cases the material can end up in the channel of a river. Once in its channel, the river can **transport** this material downstream. As the material is transported, it can cause **erosion**. Erosion is the wearing away of the land. As the rate of erosion increases then more material becomes available for the river to transport. A cycle is created in which erosion depends upon the river transporting material, and transportation depends upon the river producing more material by erosion.

There are four main processes by which a river can cause erosion (figure **A**), and four processes by which a river can transport material (figure **B**). Diagram **C** shows the relationship between the various processes of erosion and transportation.

A Processes of erosion

Attrition - material is moved along the bed of a river, collides with other material, and breaks up into smaller pieces.

Corrasion - fine material rubs against the river bank. The bank is worn away by a sand-papering action called abrasion, and collapses (photo **D**).

Corrosion - rocks forming the banks and bed of a river are dissolved by acids in the water.

Hydraulic action - the sheer force of water hitting the banks of the river.

B Processes of transportation

Traction - large rocks and boulders are rolled along the bed of the river.

Saltation - smaller stones are bounced along the bed of a river in a leap-frogging motion.

Suspension - fine material, light enough in weight to be carried by the river. It is this material which discolours the water.

Solution - dissolved material transported by the river.

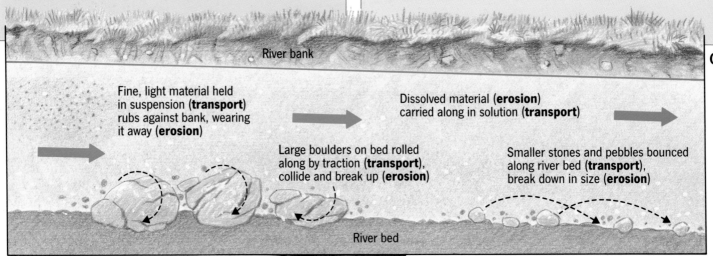

C

River bank

Fine, light material held in suspension (**transport**) rubs against bank, wearing it away (**erosion**)

Dissolved material (**erosion**) carried along in solution (**transport**)

Large boulders on bed rolled along by traction (**transport**), collide and break up (**erosion**)

Smaller stones and pebbles bounced along river bed (**transport**), break down in size (**erosion**)

River bed

D

Most erosion occurs when a river is in flood. It can then carry huge amounts of material in suspension as well as being able to move the largest of boulders lying on its bed. Erosion can both deepen and widen a river valley (photo **D**). The valley deepens as a result of vertical erosion. This is more usual in mountainous areas nearer to the source of the river. Here the river forms a series of characteristic landforms which include a **V-shaped valley** with **interlocking spurs** (diagram **E**) as well as **waterfalls** and **rapids** (diagram **F**).

E   F

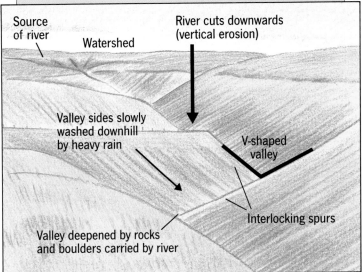

Source of river — Watershed — River cuts downwards (vertical erosion) — Valley sides slowly washed downhill by heavy rain — V-shaped valley — Interlocking spurs — Valley deepened by rocks and boulders carried by river

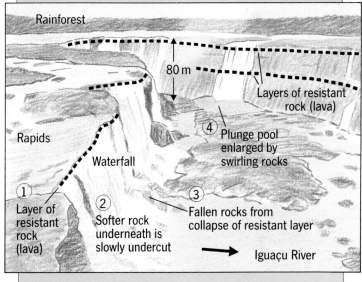

Rainforest — 80 m — Layers of resistant rock (lava) — Rapids — ④ Plunge pool enlarged by swirling rocks — Waterfall — ① Layer of resistant rock (lava) — ② Softer rock underneath is slowly undercut — ③ Fallen rocks from collapse of resistant layer — Iguaçu River

The river, especially when in flood, transports material along its bed. The material cuts downwards (vertical erosion) relatively quickly, deepening the bed of the river. After periods of heavy rain, soil on the valley sides slowly moves downhill under gravity. The valley forms a V-shape as it is deepened faster than it is widened.

The hard resistant surface rock is left unsupported as the underlying softer rock is eroded more quickly by the river. In time the resistant rock will collapse. This material will be swirled around by the river, widening and deepening the plunge pool at the foot of the waterfall. Over a period of time, as more rock collapses, the waterfall will slowly retreat leaving a steep-sided gorge.

Activities

1 Describe four processes by which a river might:
   a) erode its banks and bed;
   b) transport material downstream.

2 a) Describe, with the help of neat and carefully labelled diagrams, how a river might form:
      i) a waterfall;
      ii) a V-shaped valley.
   b) For each answer, explain which processes of erosion and which processes of transportation affect its formation.

Summary

There are several processes by which rivers can erode the land and transport material. Together, these processes can produce a group of distinctive landforms which include V-shaped valleys and waterfalls.

► How do meanders and oxbow lakes form? ◄

A Meander on North Slope River, Alaska

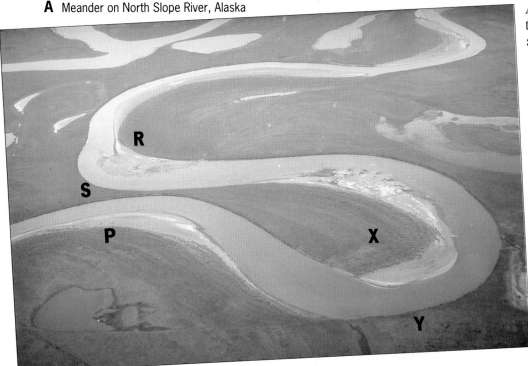

As rivers get nearer to their mouths they flow in increasingly wide, gentle-sided valleys. The channel increases in size to hold the extra water which the river has to receive from its tributaries. As the river gets bigger it can carry larger amounts of material. This material will be small in size, as larger rocks will have broken up on their way from the mountains. Much of the material will be carried in suspension and will erode the river banks by corrasion.

When rivers flow over flatter land, they develop large bends called **meanders** (photo **A**). As a river goes around a bend most of the water is pushed towards the outside causing increased erosion (diagram **C**). The river is now eroding sideways into its banks rather than downwards into its bed, a process called lateral erosion. On the inside of the bend, in contrast, there is much less water. The river will therefore be shallow and slow-flowing. It cannot carry as much material and so sand and shingle will be deposited. Diagram **B** is a cross-section showing the typical shape across a meander bend.

B Cross-section **X–Y** on photo **A**

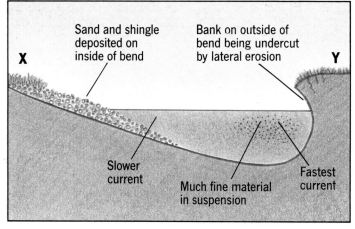

Due to erosion on the outside of a bend and deposition on the inside, the shape of a meander will change over a period of time (diagram **D**). Notice how erosion narrows the neck of the land within the meander. In time, and usually during a flood, the river will cut right through the neck. The river will then take the new, shorter route (diagram **E**). The fastest current will now tend to be in the centre of the river, and so deposition is likely to occur in gentler water next to the banks. Eventually deposition will block off the old meander to leave an **oxbow lake** (photo **F**). The oxbow lake will slowly dry up, only refilling after heavy rain or during a flood.

C
Landsketch based on photo **A**

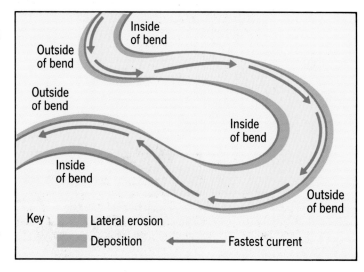

Large rivers like the Mississippi and the Amazon have many oxbow lakes. It is likely that many more oxbows will have been created following the Mississippi floods of mid-1993 (pages 18 and 19).

D Changing shape of a meander

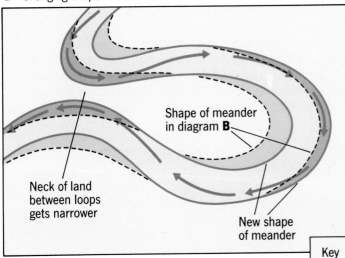

Neck of land between loops gets narrower

Shape of meander in diagram **B**

New shape of meander

E Formation of an oxbow lake

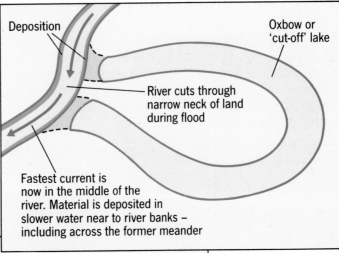

Deposition

Oxbow or 'cut-off' lake

River cuts through narrow neck of land during flood

Fastest current is now in the middle of the river. Material is deposited in slower water near to river banks – including across the former meander

Key

▨	Land lost to the river (eroded)
▧	Land gained from the river (deposited)

◄──── Fastest current

Activities

1 Using photo **A**, draw a cross-section from **P** to **R**. On your cross-section, label:
   a) the areas with the fastest current and the slowest current;
   b) the places where erosion is taking place;
   c) the places where deposition is taking place.

2 Describe, with the help of a diagram, what is likely to happen in the future at point **S** on photo **A**.

3 Diagram **G** is an incomplete cross-section of a meander. Complete the diagram by using the following information:

Distance from left bank in metres	Depth of river in metres
0.5	1.0
0.75	2.0
1.0	3.0
2.0	3.25
3.0	3.0
4.0	2.5
5.0	2.0
6.0	1.0
7.0	0.5
8.0	0.0

4 If there is a small river or stream near to your school, take your own class measurements to produce a cross-section similar to the one in Activity **3**. But remember **to take care**. Serious accidents can occur in even small rivers and streams.

F
Oxbow lake

G

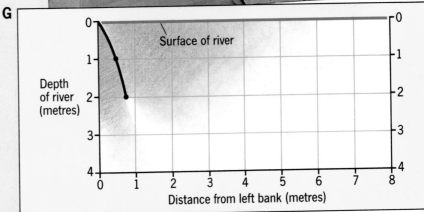

Surface of river

Depth of river (metres)

Distance from left bank (metres)

Summary As most rivers approach the sea they begin to meander and, in some cases, to form oxbow lakes.

▶ What happens to a river as it approaches its mouth? ◀

The flat area of land over which a river meanders is called a **flood plain**. During times of flood, a river will overflow its banks and cover any surrounding flat land. As the speed at which the water flows across the flood plain is less than in the main channel, then the fine material transported in suspension by the river will be deposited. Each time a river floods a thin layer of silt, or alluvium, is spread over the flood plain (diagram **A**). The Egyptians used to rely upon the annual flooding by the River Nile to water their crops and to add silt to their fields until the opening of the Aswan Dam in 1970.

A

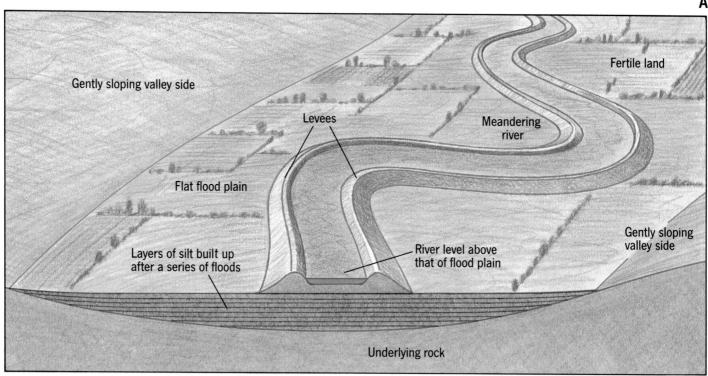

Gently sloping valley side

Levees

Meandering river

Fertile land

Flat flood plain

Gently sloping valley side

Layers of silt built up after a series of floods

River level above that of flood plain

Underlying rock

B Levees on the River Mississippi (these show as white lines beside the river)

C River delta, Kenya

When a river floods, it is the coarsest material which will be deposited first. This coarse material can form small embankments alongside a river which the Americans call **levees**. Large rivers, like the Mississippi, carry tremendous quantities of material in suspension, especially in times of flood. However, during times when the river level falls and its speed is reduced, large amounts of silt will fall out of suspension onto the bed of the river. In time the bed of the river will build up so that, when water levels are high again, the river is more likely to overflow its banks. To try to prevent this happening, large artificial levees are built (photo **B**). The Mississippi now flows at a much higher level than the surrounding flood plain, and cities like New Orleans and St Louis are protected by levees that are up to 16 metres high. The problem is, what happens should these levees break (pages 18 and 19)?

Large rivers transport great amounts of fine material down to their mouths. If a river flows into a relatively calm sea, or lake, then its speed will reduce and the fine material will be deposited. The deposited material will slowly build upwards and outwards to form a **delta** (photo **C**). River deltas provide some of the best soils in the world for farming (e.g. River Nile) but they are also prone to serious flooding as the land is so flat (e.g. Bangladesh). The Mississippi delta (photo **D**) is extending rapidly into the Gulf of Mexico. As in all deltas, deposition blocks the main channel of the river so the Mississippi has to divide into a series of smaller channels called **distributaries**. These channels need constant dredging if they are to be used by ships.

D The Mississippi delta

Activities

1 Diagram **E** shows part of the OS map which appears on page 83. The diagram is incomplete in that it shows only part of the course of the River Eden.
   a) On a copy or a tracing of the diagram, draw in, as accurately as possible, the full course of the River Eden between grid lines 47 and 40 (the river flows from east to west).
   b) Colour in red those parts of the course where erosion is likely to occur.
   c) Colour in yellow those parts of the course where deposition is likely.
   d) Mark in blue the position of the main river current.
   e) Colour in green any flat area next to the river where flooding might occur (Remember that flat land is shown on an OS map by an absence of contours.)
   f) Mark on your map the position of embankments (levees) shown by the map symbol ———.
   g) Write the terms meander and flood plain on an appropriate place on your map.
   h) Make a key for parts b), c), d), e) and f).
   i) Why do you think the land in grid square 4156 is used for a golf course rather than for housing and factories?

E

2 a) Find out the names of six large rivers which have a delta.
   b) Describe fully why some rivers have a delta.
   c) Suggest two advantages and two disadvantages of living by a river delta.

Summary

By the time a large river approaches a lake or the sea it will be carrying large amounts of material. Some of this material may be spread over the flood plain during times of flood, or it may form a delta at the river mouth.

River Eden

River Petteril

60
59
58
57
56
55
40 41 42 43 44 45 46 47

▶ *What is the hydrological cycle?* ◀

Hydrology is the study of water. The **hydrological cycle**, more commonly referred to as the water cycle, is the continuous transfer of water from the oceans into the atmosphere, then onto the land and finally back into the oceans. The cycle is complicated since it involves several processes which include evaporation, transpiration, condensation, precipitation and surface run-off. These processes, together with the various links within the cycle, are shown in diagram **A**.

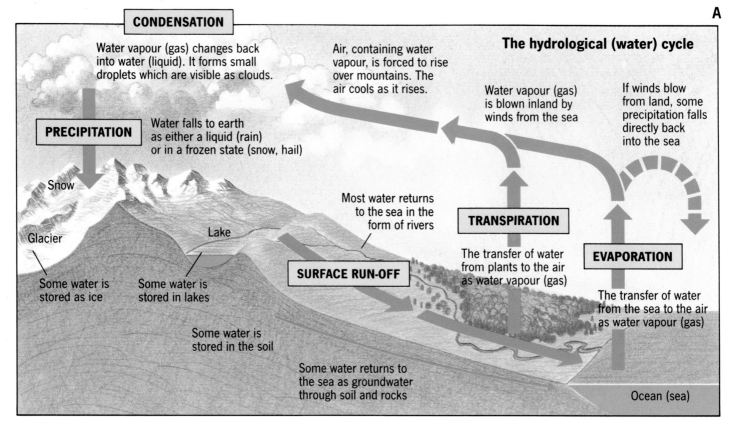

A

The hydrological (water) cycle

CONDENSATION
Water vapour (gas) changes back into water (liquid). It forms small droplets which are visible as clouds.

Air, containing water vapour, is forced to rise over mountains. The air cools as it rises.

Water vapour (gas) is blown inland by winds from the sea

If winds blow from land, some precipitation falls directly back into the sea

PRECIPITATION
Water falls to earth as either a liquid (rain) or in a frozen state (snow, hail)

Snow

Glacier

Lake

Some water returns to the sea in the form of rivers

TRANSPIRATION
The transfer of water from plants to the air as water vapour (gas)

SURFACE RUN-OFF

EVAPORATION
The transfer of water from the sea to the air as water vapour (gas)

Some water is stored as ice

Some water is stored in lakes

Some water is stored in the soil

Some water returns to the sea as groundwater through soil and rocks

Ocean (sea)

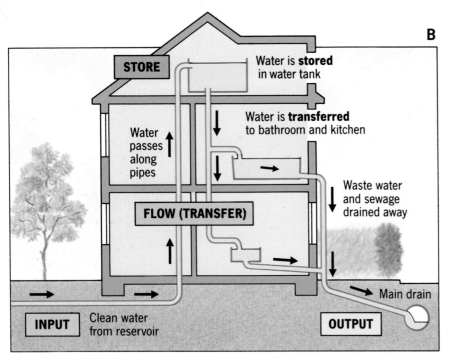

B

STORE
Water is **stored** in water tank

Water is **transferred** to bathroom and kitchen

Water passes along pipes

FLOW (TRANSFER)

Waste water and sewage drained away

Main drain

INPUT Clean water from reservoir

OUTPUT

The recycling of water in the hydrological cycle should mean that water is a sustainable resource. However, at times there are natural interruptions within the cycle. These can either create an extreme surplus of water on the land, resulting in flooding, or an extreme shortage of water, causing drought. Human interference with the natural cycle can also increase the risk of environmental disasters.

How does the river (drainage) basin system work?

The river basin system is that part of the hydrological cycle which operates on the land. Diagram **B** illustrates how a water **system** works in your own home. A system consists of **inputs** (entering the system), **flows** or **transfers** (movement through the system), **stores** (held within the system) and **outputs** (leaving the system). The river basin system is also complicated and is best illustrated as a diagram (diagram **C**).

C

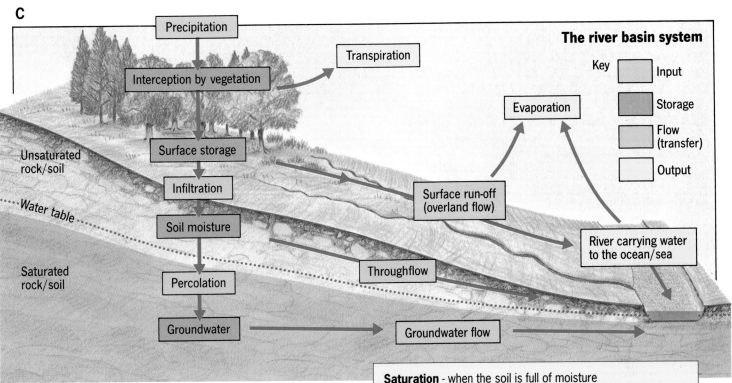

The river basin system

Key
- Input
- Storage
- Flow (transfer)
- Output

Precipitation → Interception by vegetation → Transpiration

Surface storage → Infiltration → Soil moisture → Percolation → Groundwater → Groundwater flow

Evaporation

Surface run-off (overland flow)

River carrying water to the ocean/sea

Throughflow

Unsaturated rock/soil

Water table

Saturated rock/soil

Saturation - when the soil is full of moisture

Water table - the level at which saturation occurs in the ground or soil

Infiltration - movement (transfer) of water into the soil from the surface

Percolation - movement (transfer) of water into underlying rocks.

Groundwater - water stored in rocks following percolation

Activities

1 What is meant by the following terms?
hydrological (water) cycle – condensation - evaporation – precipitation – run-off – transpiration.

2 Make a copy of diagram **D** to show the river basin system. Put the following terms into the correct empty box:
evaporation – infiltration – interception – percolation – precipitation – river run-off – surface run-off – throughflow – transpiration.

3 How will river levels be affected by:
a) a long winter with temperatures below freezing for several weeks;
b) a warm spring following several days of heavy snowfall;
c) a very hot, dry summer;
d) building a dam and creating a reservoir near to the river's source?

Summary

The hydrological cycle is the natural recycling of water between the oceans, atmosphere and land. A river, or drainage basin, system is that part of the cycle which operates on land. It consists of inputs, stores, flows and outputs.

D

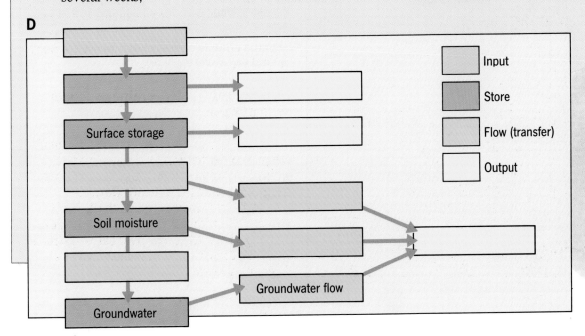

Key
- Input
- Store
- Flow (transfer)
- Output

Surface storage

Soil moisture

Groundwater flow

Groundwater

What is the relationship between precipitation and run-off?

The systems diagram (page 13) showed what happens once water has fallen to the earth as precipitation. Rainwater, or melted snow, will either:

- be lost to the system through **evapotranspiration** (i.e., evaporation and transpiration),
- be held in storage in lakes, the soil or underground, or
- flow into a river to return, eventually, to the sea as run-off.

In other words, the amount of rainwater which will become the run-off of a river will be

Precipitation – (evapotranspiration + storage)

Under normal conditions, therefore, the run-off of a river will be less than precipitation. Precipitation and run-off figures for a year can be plotted graphically as in diagram **A**.

Precipitation and run-off are two variables. They are referred to as variables because the figures used to construct graph **A** are for one particular year. The figures will vary from one year to another. However, although the chances of the same figures being repeated in another year are highly unlikely, the relationship between the two variables is likely to remain similar, e.g. as the amount of precipitation increases so too does run-off.

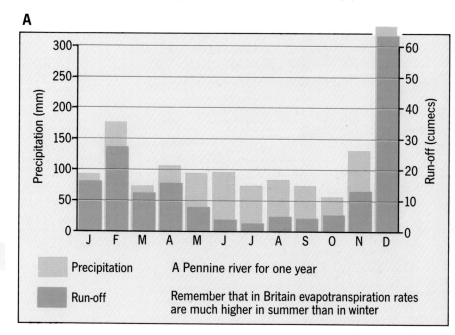

A

Precipitation

Run-off

A Pennine river for one year

Remember that in Britain evapotranspiration rates are much higher in summer than in winter

Excess precipitation gives excess run-off which increases the risk of flooding.

The flood hydrograph

The amount of water in a river channel at a given time is called the **discharge**. Discharge is measured in cumecs (cubic metres of water per second). Following an increase in rainfall, there will also be an increase in the level and the discharge of the river. The relationship between precipitation and the level of a river is illustrated by the **flood** (or storm) **hydrograph** (diagram **B**).

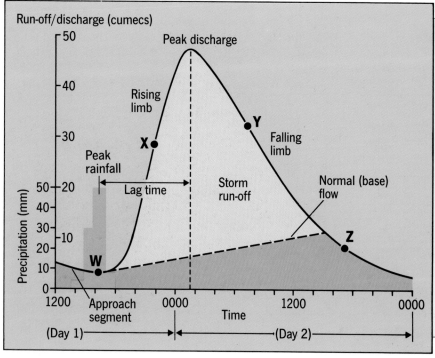

B

The **approach segment** shows the discharge of the river before it rains.

The **rising limb** results from a rapid increase in rainwater reaching the river.

Lag time is the difference between the time of the heaviest rainfall and the maximum level and/or discharge of the river.

The **falling limb** is when some rainwater is still reaching the river, but in decreasing amounts.

Points **W**, **X**, **Y** and **Z** are not usually shown on a flood hydrograph, but have been added here to help to explain its shape.

W – a very small amount of rain falls straight into the river channel.

X – water reaches the river rapidly by surface run-off.

Y – water reaches the river more slowly by throughflow.

Z – a limited amount of groundwater eventually reaches the river.

By showing the relationship between precipitation and run-off, the flood hydrograph indicates whether a particular river has a high or low flood risk. It therefore provides essential information for any river management scheme. The shorter the lag time and the steeper the rising limb, the greater is the flood risk. This is because much of the precipitation reaches the channel so quickly, mainly due to surface run-off, that the river has insufficient time to transport the excess water. In contrast, a river with a long lag time and a very gentle rising limb will have a very low flood risk. This is because rainwater reaches the channel slowly and over a longer period of time, allowing the river time to transport the excess water.

Activities

1 a) Using the information in table **C**, draw a graph to show the precipitation and run-off totals for a one-year period at a river recording site.
   b) In which season are the figures at their highest for:
      i) precipitation,
      ii) run-off?
   c) Why is there a bigger difference between the precipitation and run-off totals in summer than in winter?
   d) Suggest reasons why run-off was slightly higher than precipitation in March.

C

	J	F	M	A	M	J	J	A	S	O	N	D
Precipitation (mm)	116	164	71	103	83	75	74	79	86	81	130	148
Run-off (mm)	103	143	79	84	47	17	22	26	41	64	106	125

2 Diagram **D** shows the hydrograph for a British river for three days.
   a) i) How many hours did storm **1** last?
      ii) What was the time of peak rainfall in storm **1**?
      iii) How many hours was the lag time?
   b) i) Why is there lag time between peak rainfall and peak discharge?
      ii) Why is the rising limb much steeper than the falling limb?
      iii) Give two reasons why discharge was higher after storm **2** than after storm **1**.
   c) If the level of the river reached the top of its banks with a discharge of 70 cumecs, what must have happened after storm **2**?

D

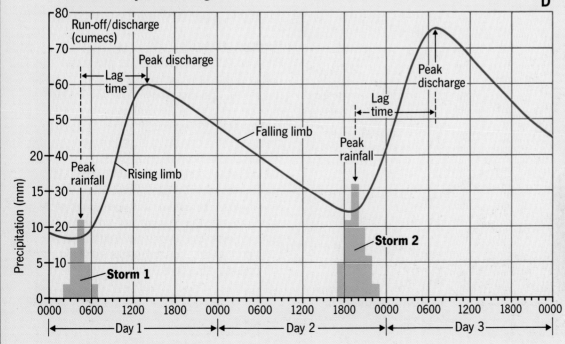

Summary

Precipitation and run-off are two variables. It is possible to identify a relationship between them showing that river run-off (discharge) depends upon the amount of precipitation. The flood hydrograph illustrates discharge and indicates the level of flood risk.

►*Why do some rivers flood?* ◄

Not every river has a high flood risk. However, those which do, may flood for a combination of reasons. Often the four most important reasons are the:

- type of precipitation,
- type of soil and underlying rock,
- land use of the river basin,
- human activity.

Type of precipitation

The most frequent cause of flooding is heavy rainfall which lasts over a period of several days. The ground will become saturated and infiltration will be replaced by surface run-off. The most severe cause of flooding usually follows short, but very intense thunderstorms. In Britain these storms are more likely to occur after a hot, dry spell in summer. The ground becomes too hard for the rain to infiltrate, and the surface run-off causes river levels to rise rapidly causing a **flash flood**.

Heavy snowfalls over several days mean that water is held in storage (photo **A**). When temperatures rise, there will be a release of water. The flood risk is greater if there is a large rise in temperature, if the rise in temperature is accompanied by a period of rain, and if the ground remains frozen preventing infiltration.

Types of soil and underlying rock

Rocks which allow water to pass through them, like chalk, limestone and sandstone, are said to be **permeable**. Rocks which do not let water pass through them, such as granite, are **impermeable**. It is the same with soil. Sandy soils are permeable and allow water to infiltrate, whereas clay soils are impermeable. Surface run-off, and the flood risk, is much greater in river basins where the soil and underlying rock is impermeable.

Land use

River basins which have little vegetation cover have a much higher flood risk than forested river basins. This is because trees intercept rainfall, delaying the time and reducing the amount of water reaching the river (diagram **B**).

Human activity

There is sufficient evidence to prove that the risk of flooding is increasing in many parts of the world. The increase in both the frequency and the severity of flooding is usually linked to human activity, especially when this activity changes the land use of a basin through either deforestation or urban growth. Bangladesh is one country where the already high flood risk has increased due to deforestation in the Himalayas. Elsewhere, as urban areas grow in size, impermeable tarmac and concrete surfaces replace fields and woodland. Infiltration and throughflow are reduced, while surface run-off is increased (diagram **C**).

A Water held in storage

B How trees help to reduce the flood risk

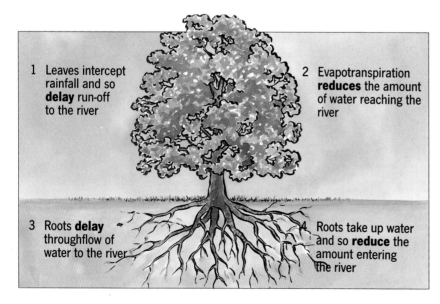

1 Leaves intercept rainfall and so **delay** run-off to the river

2 Evapotranspiration **reduces** the amount of water reaching the river

3 Roots **delay** throughflow of water to the river

4 Roots take up water and so **reduce** the amount entering the river

Drains and gutters are constructed to remove surface water. This might decrease the time take by rainwater to reach the river, but it increases the risk of a flash flood. Small streams are forced to travel along culverts (photo **D**) or underground pipes. Drains and underground pipes may not be large enough to cope with rainwater falling during thunderstorms.

C

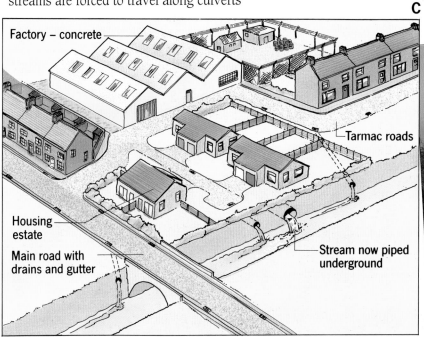

Factory – concrete
Tarmac roads
Housing estate
Main road with drains and gutter
Stream now piped underground

D

Activities

1 Explain why there is a high flood risk:
   a) after a long period of heavy rainfall;
   b) after a summer thunderstorm;
   c) when a heavy snowfall follows a few days when temperatures remained below freezing;
   d) in an area with an impermeable underlying rock;
   e) in a river basin which has just been deforested.

2 Copy and complete diagram **E** to show how the river basin system (diagram **C**, page 13) is changed by urban growth.

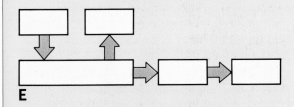

E

3 Diagram **F** shows flood hydrographs following a rainstorm for a stream in a wooded rural area and a stream in a nearby urban area.

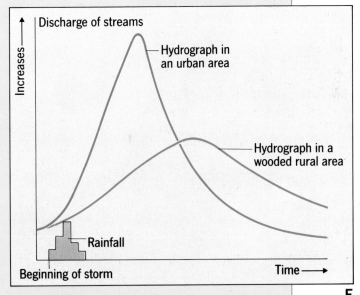

Discharge of streams
Increases
Hydrograph in an urban area
Hydrograph in a wooded rural area
Rainfall
Beginning of storm
Time

F

a) Give three differences between the shape of the two hydrographs.
b) Give reasons for the differences between the two hydrographs.

Summary The risk of a river flooding depends upon several factors including the type of precipitation, soil, underlying rock, and land use. Recently the risk has increased due to human activities which have led to deforestation, and urban growth.

17

▶ What were the causes and effects of the Mississippi flood? ◀

The Mississippi River is 3 800 km in length and flows through ten states. It receives over 100 major tributaries, including the Missouri which joins it at St Louis (map **A**). Its drainage basin covers one-third of the USA and a small part of Canada (diagram **F**, page 5).

Frequent flooding by the Mississippi has created a wide flood plain. The flood plain is 200 km at its widest point, and consists of fertile silt deposited by the river at times of flood. Even before the area was settled by Europeans, the river flowed above the level of its flood plain and between natural levees (page 10). Nineteenth century Americans considered the Mississippi to be 'untameable', and a major flood in 1927 caused 217 deaths. Since then over 300 dams and storage reservoirs have been built, and natural levees have been heightened and strengthened to protect major urban areas. The levee at St Louis is 18 km long and 16 metres high. Flooding continued throughout the 1950s and 1960s, but the last big flood was in 1973. The Americans believed that, due to large investments of money and modern technology, they had at last 'controlled' the river. Certainly, the danger to human life and damage to property had been considerably reduced. . . but that was before the events of summer 1993.

B The Mississippi and Missouri Rivers as they approach their confluence above St Louis. The bluish-purple colour shows the flooded area.

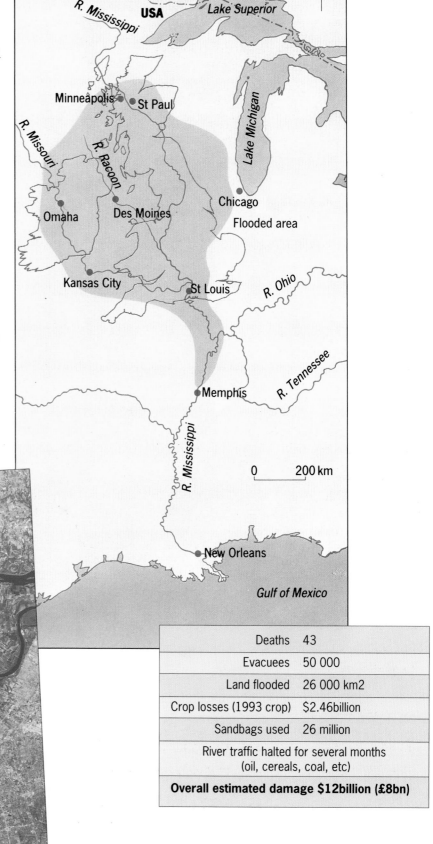

A

The Mississippi floods, 1993

N

Canada
USA

R. Mississippi

Lake Superior

Lake Michigan

Minneapolis • St Paul

R. Missouri

R. Racoon

Chicago

Omaha   Des Moines   Flooded area

Kansas City   St Louis   R. Ohio

R. Tennessee

• Memphis

R. Mississippi

0   200 km

• New Orleans

Gulf of Mexico

Deaths	43
Evacuees	50 000
Land flooded	26 000 km2
Crop losses (1993 crop)	$2.46billion
Sandbags used	26 million
River traffic halted for several months (oil, cereals, coal, etc)	
Overall estimated damage $12billion (£8bn)	

C

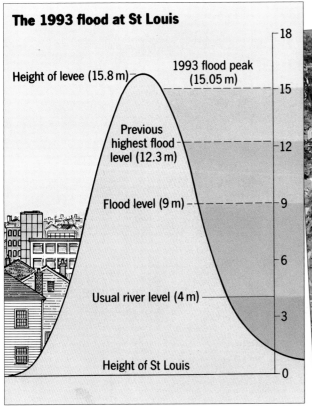

The 1993 flood at St Louis

Height of levee (15.8 m)

1993 flood peak (15.05 m)

Previous highest flood level (12.3 m)

Flood level (9 m)

Usual river level (4 m)

Height of St Louis

D
Mississippi river floods 1993

Heavy rain in April 1993 saturated the upper Mississippi basin. Thunderstorms throughout June caused rapid surface run-off and flash floods (page 16). During July the thunderstorms increased in severity with one giving 180 mms of rain in a few hours. By mid-July the level of the Mississippi had reached an all-time high (diagram **C**). Levees surrounding towns were put under tremendous pressure from the weight of water in the river, and in many places they collapsed (photo **B**). Away from towns the river spread across its flood plain up to a width of 25 km (photo **D**). An area, larger than the British Isles, was affected by flooding (map **A**). Only one road bridge, and no rail bridge, remained open for 400 km north of St Louis. River traffic on one of the world's busiest highways had long since been brought to a stop. The Mississippi proved it had not been tamed as it claimed lives and destroyed property (diagram **A**). Many Americans felt that the effects of the flood had been made worse unintentionally, because people had interfered with nature in trying to manage and control the river.

The effects of the flood did not end when the river levels began to fall. It took several months for the water to drain off the land. Although the land was covered in fertile, silt, the ground was too wet for planting crops. The contents of houses and factories, even if not the buildings themselves, were ruined. Cleaning-up operations took months. Where sewage had been washed into waterways, there was a threat of disease. Stagnant water attracted mosquitos and rats. Insurance claims were expected to be considerable.

Activities

1 a) Why is the Mississippi a high flood risk river?
   b) What caused the flood of 1993?
   c) What were the immediate effects of the flood?
   d) What might be some of the long-term effects of the flood?

2 Why had human activity unintentionally increased the flood risk?

Summary

When rivers flood they can put lives in danger, damage property and disrupt people's normal way of life. Sometimes attempts to reduce the flood risk can unintentionally make the effects of flooding worse.

► How might the flood risk be reduced? ◄

In 1718 the site for a town was chosen near to the mouth of the Mississippi River. To protect this town, the present day New Orleans, from the risk of flooding, a levee one metre high was built. For the next two hundred years the Mississippi flooded parts of its basin between St Louis and its mouth almost annually. The response was always the same… make the levees a little bit higher. The large flood of 1927 (page 18) made people realise that the main cause of flooding was not the Mississippi itself, but its main tributaries – the Missouri, Ohio and Tennessee, and that more drastic methods were needed if the flood risk was to be reduced. Some of these methods are described in diagram **A**.

A

1 Dams and reservoirs
The Missouri River Much of the Missouri, which is longer than the Mississippi, appears on a modern atlas map to be a series of long lakes. Six huge dams have created a 1600 km chain of 105 reservoirs which apart from preventing flooding, provide water supply and hydro-electricity. If these dams had not been built then much more water would have been added to the Mississippi, making the 1993 floods even worse.

2 Afforestation
The TVA has also been responsible for planting many trees. Trees (page 16) delay run-off and reduce the amount of water reaching the river.

5 Strengthening levees
Levees used to consist only of soil covered by bundles of willow and were vulnerable to erosion by the river. Now a specially designed barge backs away from the shore laying concrete mattresses, each mattress measuring 25 metres by 8 metres. The process is repeated until the bank is covered from the deepest point of the river to above the flood level.

4 Making the course straighter and shorter
This method was aimed at trying to get rid of flood water from the river basin as quickly as possible. It was achieved by cutting through the narrow necks of several large meanders (pages 8 and 9). Between 1934 and 1945 a 530 km stretch of river was shortened by almost 300 km. By shortening the distance, the gradient, and therefore the speed, of the river is increased.

Lake Superior

St Paul
Minneapolis

Lake Michigan

Chicago

R. Mississippi

R. Missouri

R. Ohio

St Louis

R. Tennessee

R. Arkansas

Memphis

R. Red

R. Mississippi

Lake Pontchartrain

Baton Rouge
New Orleans

Houston

Gulf of Mexico

New 'artificial' course

Original meandering course of the Mississippi River

New levees

Flood plain

3 Diversionary spillways
These are overflow channels which can take surplus water during times of flood. The Bonnet Carré Floodway begins 50 km north of New Orleans. In times of flood, it diverts excess water from the Mississippi along a 9 km spillway, through 350 small bays (reservoirs), into Lake Pontchartrain, and eventually into the Gulf of Mexico. This has greatly reduced the flood risk at New Orleans and Baton Rouge.

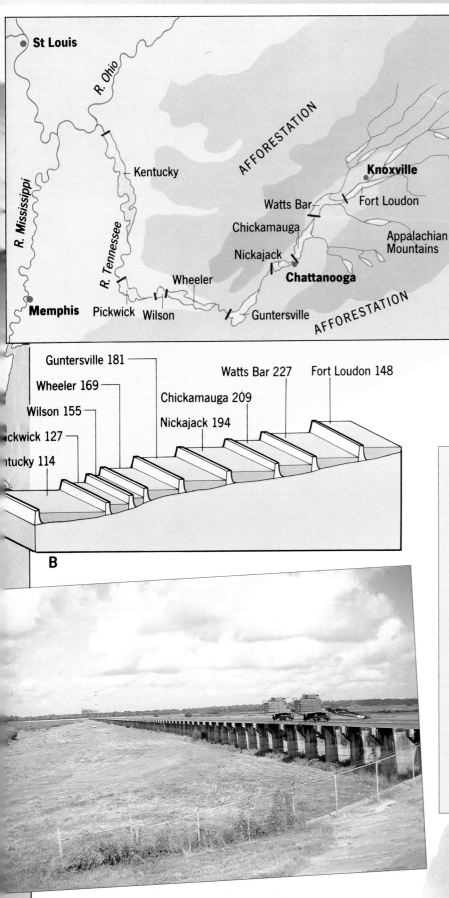

1 Dams and reservoirs
The Tennessee River The Tennessee Valley Authority (TVA) was set up in the 1930s. It had many functions (diagram **B**), one of which was to control the flooding of the river. Nine reservoirs were created on the main river and 10 on its tributaries. Dams hold back water during times of flood and release it when river levels are lower. One measure of success came in 1957. Instead of the river rising to a dangerous peak of 16.5 metres, the dams and reservoirs limited the level to a harmless 9.8 metres.

The TVA is a multipurpose scheme which:
- controls flooding;
- provides water supply;
- produces hydro-electricity;
- improves navigation;
- increases afforestation;
- reduces soil erosion;
- encourages industry;
- encourages tourism.

B

Guntersville 181
Wheeler 169
Wilson 155
Pickwick 127
Kentucky 114
Chickamauga 209
Nickajack 194
Watts Bar 227
Fort Loudon 148

Activities

1 What was the only method used to try to prevent the Mississippi River from flooding before 1927?

2 a) Describe four of the methods used since 1927 to try to reduce the flood risk on the Mississippi River.
   b) Which of the methods do you think will be
   i) the cheapest to use
   ii) the most expensive to use
   iii) the most successful in reducing the flood risk?

3 Why is it harder to reduce the flood risk in economically less developed countries than in economically more developed countries?

4 What attempts have been made to reduce the flood risk on a river near to where you live?

Summary

It often needs considerable amounts of capital and high levels of technology to reduce the flood risk. It is therefore the economically more developed countries which can make a positive response to the river flood hazard.

C Bonnet Carre Floodway. The sluices allow water out of the Mississippi

▶ How do waves wear away the land? ◀

Although waves may some times result from submarine earth movements (page 59), they are usually formed by the wind blowing over the sea. The size of a wave depends upon the:

- strength of the wind;
- length of time which the wind blows;
- distance of sea which the wind has to cross.

As the wave approaches shallow water near to the coast, its base is slowed down by friction against the sea-bed. The top of the wave will therefore move faster, increase in height and will eventually break ('tumble over') onto the beach.

Coastal erosion

There are four main processes by which the sea can erode the land. These are similar to those of a river (page 6).

- Hydraulic pressure is the sheer force of the waves, especially when they trap and compress air in cracks and holes in a cliff.
- Corrasion results from large waves hurling beach material against the cliff.
- Attrition is when waves cause rocks and pebbles on the beach to bump into each other and to break down in size.
- Corrosion is when certain types of cliff are slowly dissolved by acids in the sea-water.

There are three main groups of landforms which result from erosion by the sea.

Headlands and bays These form along coasts which have alternating resistant (harder) and less resistant (softer) rock. Where there is resistant rock the coast will be worn away less quickly leaving a **headland** which sticks out into the sea. Where there is softer rock, erosion will be more rapid and a **bay** will form (diagram **A** and pages 48 and 49). As the headland becomes more exposed to the full force of the wind and waves, it will become more vulnerable to erosion than the sheltered bay.

A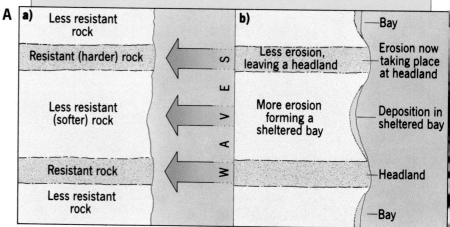

Cliffs and wave cut platforms Erosion is greatest when large waves actually break against the foot of a cliff. The foot of the cliff is undercut to form a **wave cut notch** (diagram **B**). As the notch gets larger, the cliff above it will become increasingly unsupported and in time will collapse. As this process is repeated the cliff will slowly retreat and, usually, increase in height. The gently sloping land left at the foot of the retreating cliff is called a **wave cut platform** (diagram **B**).

B

b) Wave cut platform

a) Wave cut notch

Caves, arches and stacks Although cliffs, especially where they form headlands, consist of resistant rock they are still likely to contain areas of weakness. Areas of weakness will be the first to be worn away by the sea. Diagram **C** shows a typical sequence in which a weakness is enlarged to form a **cave**, and later, an **arch** where the sea cuts right through the headland. The arch is widened by the sea undercutting at its base. As the rock above the arch becomes unsupported it collapses to form a **stack**. Further undercutting causes the stack to collapse leaving only a stump.

C

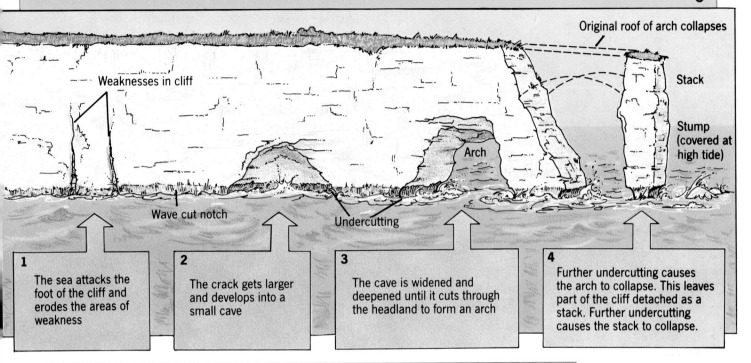

Original roof of arch collapses

Weaknesses in cliff

Stack

Arch

Stump (covered at high tide)

Wave cut notch

Undercutting

1 The sea attacks the foot of the cliff and erodes the areas of weakness

2 The crack gets larger and develops into a small cave

3 The cave is widened and deepened until it cuts through the headland to form an arch

4 Further undercutting causes the arch to collapse. This leaves part of the cliff detached as a stack. Further undercutting causes the stack to collapse.

D

Activities

1 Give three reasons why, on diagram **D**, the waves at **X** are likely to be higher and more powerful than the waves at **Y**.

2 Describe briefly four processes by which the sea can erode the land.

3 Photo **E** shows several coastal features.
   a) Make a landsketch of the photo and add the following labels: *corrasion by waves – wave cut notch – wave cut platform – cave – arch – stacks*
   b) Use broken lines to show the position of two collapsed arches.

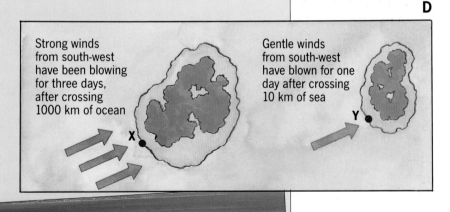

Strong winds from south-west have been blowing for three days, after crossing 1000 km of ocean

X

Gentle winds from south-west have blown for one day after crossing 10 km of sea

Y

E

Old Harry Rocks, Dorset

Summary

Waves are caused when the wind blows over the surface of the sea. There are four processes by which the sea can erode the land to produce such landforms as headlands, bays, cliffs, wave cut platforms and stacks.

23

► *How does the sea transport material?* ◄

Material can be moved both along and up and down a beach.

Transportation along a beach Waves rarely approach a beach at right angles. They usually approach at an angle that depends upon the direction of the wind (diagram **A**). The water which rushes up a beach after a wave breaks is called the swash. The swash, which picks up sand and shingle, travels up the beach in the same direction as the breaking wave. When this water returns down the beach to the sea it is called backwash. Due to gravity the backwash, and any material it is carrying, tends to be straight down the beach (diagram **A**). The result is that material is transported along the beach in a zig-zag movement. This movement of beach material is called **longshore drift**. Longshore drift is usually in one direction only, that of the prevailing wind. For example, the prevailing wind in Britain is from the south-west and so material is moved from west to east along the south coast of England.

A

Beach

Swash carries material up the beach following the angle of the waves

Position 2

Backwash takes material straight down the beach under gravity

Position 4

Position 6

Prevailing (usual) wind direction

Pebble

Position 1

Position 3

Position 5

Position 7

Waves approach the beach at an angle similar to that of the wind

Sea

Material carried along the beach by **longshore drift**

Longshore drift can affect human activities. In response, people sometimes erect wooden breakwater fences down the beach (photo **B** a) and b)). The fences, called groynes, act as obstacles. Apart from reducing the force of the waves, they cause sand to pile up on their windward side (the side facing the prevailing wind). This is an advantage to people living in a sea-side resort who do not wish to lose their sand and to sailors in a small port who do not want their harbour to become blocked.

B

a) Longshore drift

b) Groynes at a British coastal resort

Transportation up and down a beach
Under normal conditions waves will tend to move material up a beach. Photo **C** shows how shingle has been piled up at the foot of a cliff. The shingle will, in this case, protect the cliff from erosion. However, under storm conditions, larger waves often move material back down the beach.

How can human activities affect the rate of landform development?

We have already seen that the building of groynes can slow down the transport of material along the beach. Around many parts of our coastline sea walls have been constructed to try to reduce the force of the waves and to protect cliffs from erosion. Sometimes, however, human activity can unintentionally speed up the rate at which cliffs are eroded. During one year at the end of the last century, 660 000 tonnes of shingle were removed from the beach at Hallsands in Devon. It was used for the construction of the naval dockyard at Plymouth. The speed at which the shingle was removed was far greater than the rate at which nature could replace it. The cliff was exposed to erosion, and within a century it had retreated by almost 10 metres. Buildings in Hallsands became threatened as the cliff retreated and the village has now been left virtually abandoned and in ruins (photo **D**).

C Shingle at the foot of a cliff

D Deserted village of Hallsands, Devon

Activities

1 a) What name is given to the process by which material is moved along a stretch of coastline?
   b) How can waves transport sand from point **A** to point **X** on diagram **E**?
   c) Why might people in each of i) place **R** and ii) place **S** want to reduce the movement of material along the beach?
   d) How might they stop material from point **A** moving to point **X**?
   e) How might waves move material from point **A** to point **Y**?
   f) A building firm applied to the local council for permission to remove shingle from point **Y**. Why do you think that their application was turned down?

E

Small port

Seaside resort

S

Harbour

R

Y

X

A

Summary The movement of material along a beach is called longshore drift. Human activities can affect the rate at which coastal landforms develop.

How do landforms result from deposition by the sea?

Deposition occurs in sheltered areas where the build up of sand and shingle is greater than its removal. The most widespread coastal deposition feature is the beach. Although rocky beaches are formed by erosion (wave cut platforms, page 22), sand and shingle beaches result from deposition. Diagram **A** shows the differences in steepness between sand and shingle beaches, and how material of different sizes is distributed on those beaches.

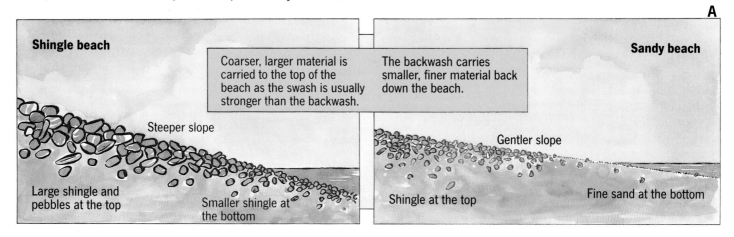

A

Shingle beach

Coarser, larger material is carried to the top of the beach as the swash is usually stronger than the backwash.

The backwash carries smaller, finer material back down the beach.

Sandy beach

Steeper slope

Gentler slope

Large shingle and pebbles at the top

Smaller shingle at the bottom

Shingle at the top

Fine sand at the bottom

Spits

A **spit** is an area of sand or shingle which either extends at a gentle angle out to sea or which grows across a river estuary (diagrams **B** and **C**). Many spits are characterised by a hooked, or curved, end. Spits only develop in places where:

- longshore drift moves large amounts of material along the beach;
- there is a sudden change in the direction of the coastline;
- the sea is relatively shallow and becomes progressively more sheltered.

Diagram **B** shows how a typical spit forms. The line **X** – **Y** marks the position of the original coastline. The prevailing wind, in this example, is from the south-west and so material is carried eastwards by longshore drift (**A**). Where the coastline changes direction (**B**), sand and shingle are deposited in water which is sheltered by the headland. This material builds upwards and outwards (**C**) forming a spit. Occasionally strong winds blow from a different direction, in this case the south-east. As waves will now also approach the land from the south-east, then some material will be pushed inland causing the end of the spit to curve (**D**). When the wind returns to its usual direction the spit will continue to grow eastwards (**E**), developing further hooked ends during times of changed wind direction (**F**). The spit cannot grow across the estuary (**G**) due to the speed of the river carrying material out to sea. Spits become permanent when the prevailing wind picks up sand from the beach and blows it inland to form sand dunes. Salt marsh develops in the sheltered water behind the spit (**B**).

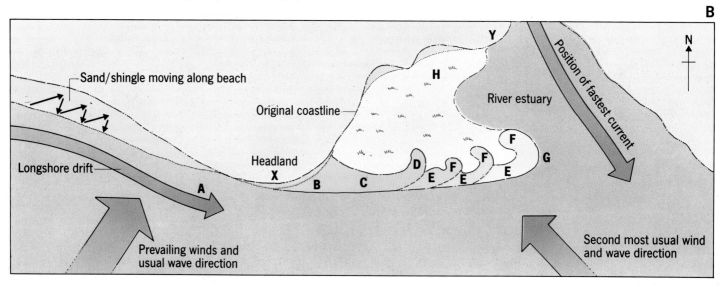

B

Sand/shingle moving along beach

Original coastline

Longshore drift

Headland

River estuary

Position of fastest current

N

Prevailing winds and usual wave direction

Second most usual wind and wave direction

C Exmouth

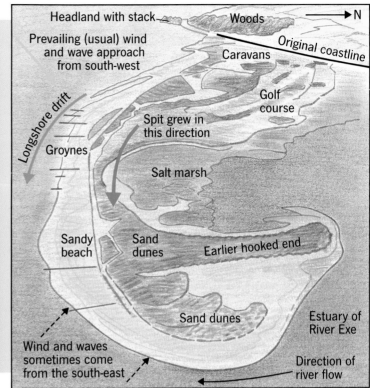

Headland with stack — Woods → N

Prevailing (usual) wind and wave approach from south-west

Original coastline

Caravans

Golf course

Longshore drift

Spit grew in this direction

Groynes

Salt marsh

Sandy beach

Sand dunes

Earlier hooked end

Sand dunes

Estuary of River Exe

Wind and waves sometimes come from the south-east

Direction of river flow

Bars

A **bar** is a barrier of sand stretching across a sheltered bay. It is only able to extend across the bay due to the absence of any large river (diagram **D**). Bars may form in several ways. One way is when a spit is able to grow right across a bay. A second is when a sand bank develops some distance off the shore, but parallel to it. Waves slowly move the sand bank towards the coast until it joins with the mainland. In both cases a lagoon is usually found to the landward side of the bar.

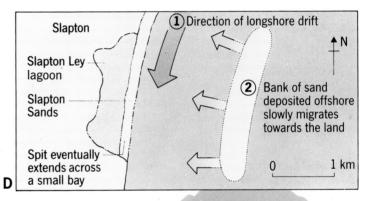

Slapton

Slapton Ley lagoon

Slapton Sands

Spit eventually extends across a small bay

① Direction of longshore drift

N

② Bank of sand deposited offshore slowly migrates towards the land

0   1 km

D

Activities

1 How does the appearance of a sandy beach differ from that of a shingle beach?

2 The following sketches show several stages in the formation of a spit. Unfortunately they are not in the correct order.
   a) Redraw the sketches putting the stages into the correct order
   b) Describe how each stage developed.

E

Summary

Sand and shingle are deposited where the sea is calm and gentle. Beaches, spits and bars are examples of landforms which result from deposition.

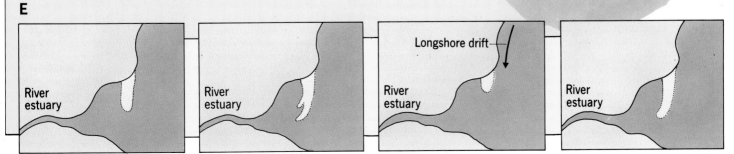

River estuary

River estuary

Longshore drift

River estuary

River estuary

► Coastal flooding in Britain ◄

The worst coastal flood in recent years in Britain occurred during the night of 31 January/1 February 1953. The worst affected area was between the estuaries of the Humber and the Thames.

Causes

Most of the area between the Humber and the Thames is low-lying. Indeed, some parts surrounding The Wash are actually below sea-level. These areas were protected by small sea walls and embankments many of which were in a state of disrepair due to a lack of attention during and after the Second World War. Although people realised that there was a high flood risk, they were totally unprepared for that night in 1953. Four main factors combined to cause a **storm** (or **tidal**) **surge**. A storm surge is when the level of the sea rises rapidly to a height well above that which was predicted.

1 An area of low atmospheric pressure, called a depression, moved southwards into the North Sea. Air rises in a depression. As the air rose it exerted less pressure, or weight, upon the sea. The reduction in pressure was enough to allow the surface of the sea to rise by half a metre.
2 The severe northerly gale created huge six-metre high waves. These waves 'pushed' sea-water southwards down the North Sea to where it gets shallower and narrower, as shown on map **A**. As the extra water 'surged' southwards, it was unable to escape fast enough through the Straits of Dover. The result was a further two metre rise in sea-level, especially in river estuaries.
3 It was a time of spring tides. These occur every month and are when tides reach their highest level.
4 Rivers flowing into the North Sea were in flood but could not discharge their water due to the high sea-levels.

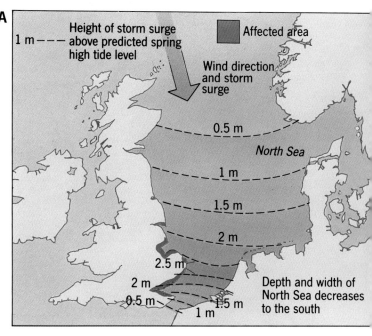

A

Consequences

The flood caused the deaths of 264 people and damage to 25 000 homes (map **B** and photos **C** and **D**). Sea-water covered over 1000m² of land in Lincolnshire, East Anglia and the Thames Estuary. Thousands of farm animals were drowned. The high death rate among humans and animals was partly due to the flood being unexpected and no advance warnings being given. The greatest loss of human life was in places where people were asleep in bungalows. Even when the flood subsided, sea water was still able to penetrate gaps in sea defences, and farmland remained contaminated by salt water. The disaster was even worse across the North Sea where, in the Netherlands, over 1800 people died.

B

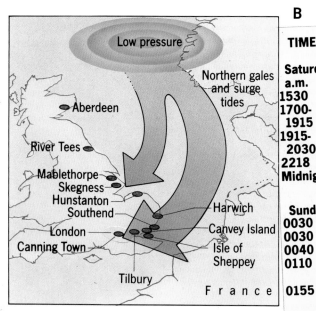

TIMETABLE

Saturday 31 January 1953:

a.m.	Aberdeen	Gales with gusts of 130 km/hr (80 mph)
1530	River Tees	Water overflows banks
1700–1915	Lincolnshire	Flooding along coast, 16 die and 1600 evacuated at Mablethorpe. 20 die as Skegness floods
1915–2030	Norfolk	Train forced back to Hunstanton as waves break through sand dunes, engulfing the village and killing 65
2218	Southend	Tanker *Kosmos V* runs aground.
Midnight,	Isle of Sheppey	Much of island, including the Naval dockyard, flooded

Sunday 1 February:

0030	Harwich:	1200 homes flooded, eight die
0030	Southend	600 homes engulfed, two killed
0040	Tilbury	Thames overflows killing one and making 6102 homeless
0110	Canvey Island	Sea bursts through defences flooding entire island. 11 000 homeless, 58 dead
0155	Canning Town	Sea breaks in making 150 homeless and killing one

C

D

E

Responses

- The first response was to build stronger sea defences and higher embankments. At first concrete was used to 'bounce' storm waves back out to sea. However, it was realised that the power of storm waves limited the life span of a concrete defence to under 30 years. Modern sea defences use either cages filled with stones or sloping wooden fences (photo **E**). The idea is to reduce the power of the waves by allowing some of the water to pass through the structures.
- Sand and shingle is now dumped offshore to reduce the power and the height of the waves.
- A storm tide early warning system gives at least 12 hours notice of extra high tides.
- The building of the Thames Barrier to reduce the flood risk in London (photo **F**).

F The Thames Barrier at Woolwich

G

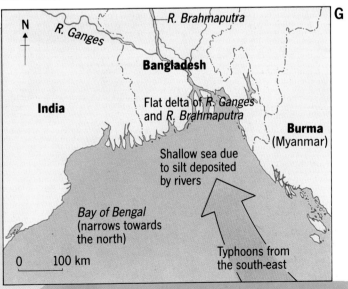

Activities

1 Those parts of India and Bangladesh which border the Bay of Bengal have a high risk of coastal flooding resulting from storm surges (map **G**).
   a) What is a storm surge?
   b) Give three reasons why the Bay of Bengal experiences storm surges.
   c) What were the consequences of the storm surge which affected the east coast of England in 1953?
   d) What has been done to try to reduce the effect of future storm surges in eastern England?
   e) Why do you think similar precautions have not been taken in those areas around the Bay of Bengal?

Summary Storm surges are a major cause of coastal flooding. They can cause serious disruption to human activity and prevention schemes are expensive to implement.

► *How do changes in sea-level affect landforms?* ◄

Sea-level has rarely stayed constant for a lengthy period of time. It has risen and fallen, usually due to earth movements or changes in climate. Changes in sea-level can either create new or submerge existing landforms.

At the beginning of the ice-age large amounts of water were held in storage as ice and snow (page 12). With no water being returned to the oceans, sea-level fell. At the end of the ice-age, the melting of glaciers led to a release of water and a rise in sea-level. Many coastal areas were drowned and new landforms, such as **fjords** and **rias**, were formed (diagram **A**).

A

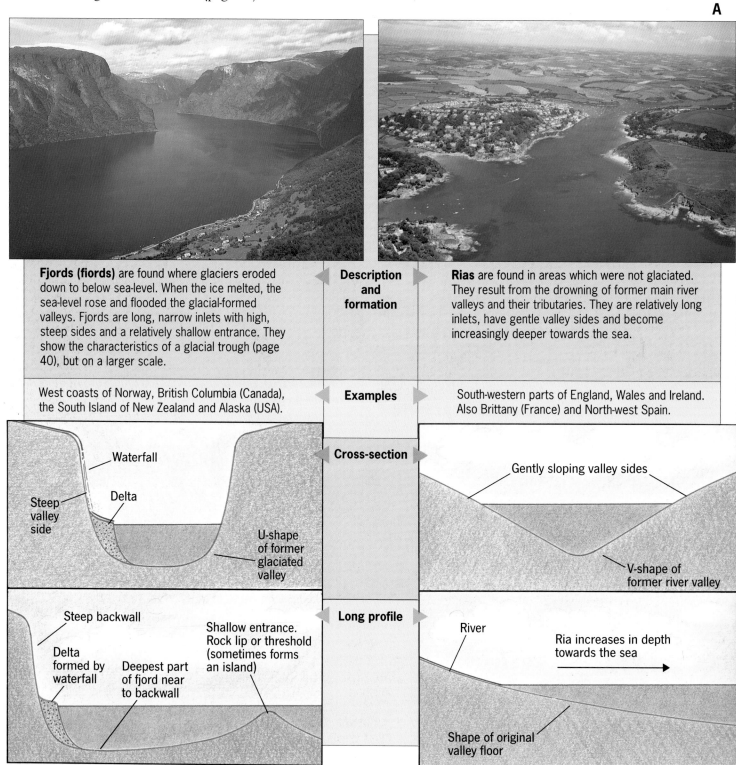

Fjords (fiords) are found where glaciers eroded down to below sea-level. When the ice melted, the sea-level rose and flooded the glacial-formed valleys. Fjords are long, narrow inlets with high, steep sides and a relatively shallow entrance. They show the characteristics of a glacial trough (page 40), but on a larger scale.	► Description and formation ►	Rias are found in areas which were not glaciated. They result from the drowning of former main river valleys and their tributaries. They are relatively long inlets, have gentle valley sides and become increasingly deeper towards the sea.
West coasts of Norway, British Columbia (Canada), the South Island of New Zealand and Alaska (USA).	► Examples ►	South-western parts of England, Wales and Ireland. Also Brittany (France) and North-west Spain.
	► Cross-section ►	
	► Long profile ►	

Waterfall

Steep valley side

Delta

U-shape of former glaciated valley

Steep backwall

Delta formed by waterfall

Deepest part of fjord near to backwall

Shallow entrance. Rock lip or threshold (sometimes forms an island)

Gently sloping valley sides

V-shape of former river valley

River

Ria increases in depth towards the sea

Shape of original valley floor

How might global warming affect coasts?

During this century, average world temperatures have risen by 0.5 °C. Many scientists predict that the earth's temperature will continue to increase, rising by between 1.5 °C and 4.5 °C by the year 2030. One consequence of this **global warming** will be a melting of some of the polar ice-cap. Melting ice will increase the flow of water into the sea, causing levels to rise by anything up to 3 metres. Although this rise in sea-level will be small in comparison to that at the end of the Ice Age, it will still flood many low-lying coastal areas. Map **B** shows the world's most vulnerable areas. Worst hit will be some Pacific Islands, which will be totally submerged, and large river deltas. In Egypt (map **C**) a rise in sea-level of 0.5 metres would swamp the main ports of Alexandria and Port Said and ruin the fishing industry in the coastal lagoons. A rise of 1 metre would flood 30 per cent of Egypt's arable land and displace 8 million people (remember the 1953 coastal surge in eastern England was 2.5 metres).

Map **D** shows places in Britain which are vulnerable to a rise in sea-level. The compilers of this map assume that sea-levels will increase by 0.5 to 1.5 metres within the next century. The effect of such a rise would include a loss of beaches, an increase in coastal erosion, a loss of wetland and other wildlife habitats, and the drowning of cities and low-lying farmland. A United Nations-backed agency estimates the cost to Britain of combating rising sea-levels will be over £6.5 billion (bn) next century. Of this, £2.6 bn will be needed to protect coastal cities from inundation, £0.7 bn to safeguard harbours and ports, £2 bn to defend low-lying coastal land, and £1.2 bn to rescue beaches.

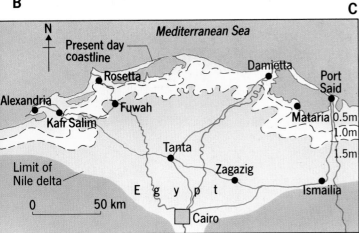

Areas of the world vulnerable to a rising sea level

B

C

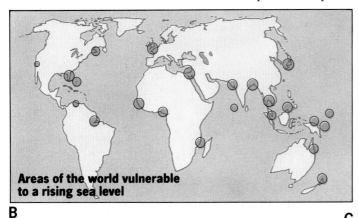

Mediterranean Sea

Present day coastline
Rosetta
Damietta
Port Said
Alexandria
Fuwah
Mataria 0.5m
Kafr Salim
1.0m
Tanta
1.5m
Zagazig
Limit of Nile delta
Ismailia
E g y p t
0   50 km
Cairo

D

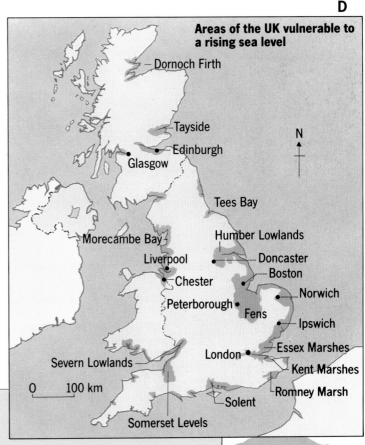

Areas of the UK vulnerable to a rising sea level

Dornoch Firth
Tayside
Edinburgh
Glasgow
Tees Bay
Morecambe Bay
Humber Lowlands
Liverpool
Doncaster
Chester
Boston
Norwich
Peterborough
Fens
Ipswich
Severn Lowlands
Essex Marshes
London
Kent Marshes
Romney Marsh
Solent
Somerset Levels
N
0   100 km

Activities

1 a) Why did sea-levels rise after the ice-age?
   b) Describe the main differences between fjords and rias under the headings below.
      ● Formation   ● Appearance
      ● Cross-section shape   ● Long profile

2 Global warming is likely to cause a rise in the world's sea-level.
   a) Which parts of the world are at greatest risk from flooding by the sea?
   b) What effect will a rise in sea-level have upon Egypt?

   c) Many parts of Britain are also at risk from a rise in sea-level.
   i) Which parts of Britain have the highest risk from coastal flooding?
   ii) How will a rise in sea level affect human activities in these parts of Britain?
   iii) Why might Britain have to spend £6.5 billion to combat a rise in sea-level?

Summary

Changes in sea-level affect coasts. The large rise in sea-level after the ice-age created new landforms. A small rise due to global warming is expected to drown many low-lying areas.

3 Water pollution

▶ What causes water pollution? ◀

In England and Wales in 1990, 89 per cent of rivers and canals were of good or fair water quality (graph **A**). However, since 1980 there had been a slight decline in water quality. In 1991 there were almost 30 000 reported pollution incidents, more than in previous years. This figure did not include the increasing occurrences of algal blooms, which are excessive growths of algae caused by nitrate pollution (diagram **D**, page 127). Graph **B** shows the major types of reported pollution incidents.

Sewage disposal Most sewage is sent to treatment works where waste products are removed to leave sewage sludge (page 34). The resultant effluent, which should be 95 per cent waste water, is discharged into rivers. However, there is still about one-quarter of the population not served by sewage treatment works. It is from this source that untreated sewage may reach rivers.

Agricultural run-off Farm waste and silage effluent are normally spread on farmland, but accidents, careless use, and periods of heavy rain can lead to them reaching a river and causing serious pollution. Undiluted farm slurry (animal waste) is 100 times more polluting than raw sewage, and silage effluent (from grass fermenting in storage) is 200 times more polluting. Bacteria in rivers use up large amounts of oxygen to break down the slurry and silage. This leaves the river short of oxygen causing damage to fish and other water life. Fertiliser, including nitrate, is added to crops to encourage growth. If the nitrate reaches a river, it will cause excessive plant growth (including algal blooms) which also results in deoxygenation.

Industrial discharge Some industrial waste is discharged directly into the river. Some of this waste, especially that containing chemicals, can be extremely harmful to river life, can discolour the water, and may give off an odious smell.

Power stations Many power stations extract water for cooling purposes before returning it, at a much higher temperature, to the river (page 132). Although the warm water does not actually pollute the river, it can harm river life as it contains less oxygen.

Landfill sites Pollutants, from waste landfill sites, can leach slowly into rivers. Diagram **C** shows how these various types of pollution can reach the river and, eventually, the sea.

A

River and canal quality by region, 1990
England and Wales

Anglian
Northumbria
North West
Severn Trent
Southern
South West
Thames
Welsh
Wessex
Yorkshire

0   20   40   60   80   100%

☐ **Good quality (class 1)**
High quality – suitable for drinking water. High quality fishing. High recreation value.

☐ **Fair quality (class 2)**
Suitable for drinking water after extensive treatment. Good fishing. Moderate recreation value.

☐ **Poor quality (class 3)**
Polluted. Fish either absent or only sporadically present. Unsuitable for drinking purposes. Low grade industrial abstract. Low recreation value.

☐ **Bad quality (class 4)**
Heavily polluted. Likely to cause health and environmental problems.

Water pollution incidents, by source of pollution, 1991
England and Wales

B

Industrial 12%
Farm 13%
Other 23%
Oil 24%
Sewage 28%

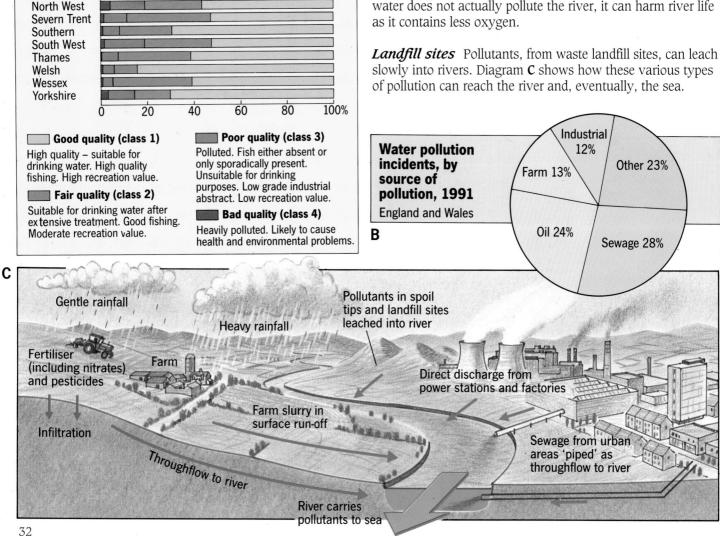

C

Gentle rainfall

Heavy rainfall

Pollutants in spoil tips and landfill sites leached into river

Fertiliser (including nitrates) and pesticides

Farm

Farm slurry in surface run-off

Direct discharge from power stations and factories

Infiltration

Throughflow to river

Sewage from urban areas 'piped' as throughflow to river

River carries pollutants to sea

The Ganges, in India, is a sacred river to the Hindus. It is also severely polluted, as described in diagram **D**.

D

The Ganges is one of the earth's longest and most polluted rivers. It descends from the Himalayas and flows some 2500 km across India before it fans into the Bay of Bengal.

It poses a unique dilemma for environmentalists. Every year, Hindus dump more than 45 000 bodies in the Ganges, first inserting a red-hot coal into the mouth of each corpse before casting it adrift. No sane ecologist would ever dare to prevent this. Hindus believe that the Ganges can free the dying from the cycle of rebirth, so in many river cities, such as Varanasi, Calcutta and Allahabad, ashes from the cremation pyres are sprinkled into the river. Dead babies, lepers, suicides, people killed by snakebites and sages are also given a river burial. Sometimes in Varanasi the body-burners scrimp on wood for the pyre and simply toss the half-charred remains into the river, just upstream from where thousands of Hindus bathe every day.

The main pollutants, however, are not dead bodies but the waste spewed into the Ganges from hundreds of factories, tanneries, petro-chemical plants, paper mills and sugar refineries along its banks. The Ganges provides water for more than 250 million people living in the flat, hot Gangetic plains. It irrigates their crops and quenches their spiritual thirst. At its source, in the Himalayan glaciers above Gangotri, it is a fast

shining-white stream. By the time it reaches Patna, the Ganges has widened to six miles and begins to divide itself into a delta before reaching the ocean. At one time there were freshwater dolphins, giant 6-metre crocodiles, turtles and more than 265 species of fish living in the Ganges. Six years ago environmentalists calculated that 1000 million litres of waste water a day were pouring into the Ganges. If left unchecked, the sacred river would die.

Adapted from The Independent on Sunday, *9 August 1992*

Activities

1　a) Which region in England and Wales has the highest percentage of good and fair quality water?
　　b) Which two regions have the highest percentage of poor and bad quality water?
　　c) For each region you named in b) suggest a reason why it has a higher than average amount of poor and bad quality water.

2　Table **E** lists the major types of river pollution.
　　a) For each of the first four types, explain how it can cause pollution in rivers.
　　b) Complete the table by listing the major causes of pollution in the three named areas.
　　c) Why do you think it is difficult to reduce river pollution in the
　　　i) Rhine　ii) Ganges?

F

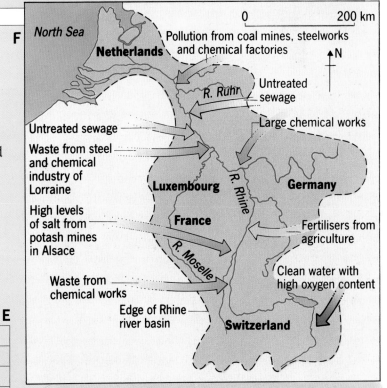

E

	English river	The Ganges	The Rhine
Sewage disposal			
Oil			
Agricultural run-off			
Industrial discharge			
Others (names)			

Summary　Rivers throughout the world are vulnerable to pollution resulting from sewage disposal, agricultural run-off and industrial discharge.

33

▶ *What are the causes of sea pollution?* ◀

In the past, it was believed that the seas were so large and deep that they could not be harmed by human activity. The North Sea has, for centuries, absorbed the waste of North-west Europe. The waste either settled harmlessly on the sea-bed, or was cleansed naturally by the sea. This attitude of 'disperse and dilute' assumed that everything would mix with enough water to become harmless eventually. However, there are increasing signs that the health of seas, such as the North Sea, is suffering badly from the twin problems of pollution and overfishing. There are limits to the amount of waste that can be put into the sea and to the number of fish that can be taken out. The North Sea is in danger of becoming an empty sea.

Causes of pollution in the North Sea

About 85 per cent of sea pollution comes from land-based activities and 90 per cent of this stays in water near to the coast. The Rhine is responsible for 45 per cent of the river pollutants which enter the North Sea. It collects these as it flows through Switzerland, France, Germany and the Netherlands. Britain is the largest single polluter. Its rivers, mainly the Thames, Tees, Humber and Forth, are responsible for 20 per cent of the total pollutants. The main causes of North Sea pollution are given in diagram **A**. Table **D** shows some of the effects of marine pollution.

A

North Sea

Rivers Pollutants reaching a river (page 32) will eventually end up in the sea. This problem is magnified as many rivers flow into the North Sea.
A Agricultural run-off includes fertiliser (nitrate and phosphate) and pesticides.
B Industrial waste includes toxic chemicals and heavy metals. Heavy metals include mercury, zinc, lead and copper. These cannot be broken down by the sea and so they remain on the sea-bed or may be taken into the food chain by marine life.

Sewage
A Untreated (raw) sewage, including excrement, condoms and sanitary items, is piped out to sea but often returns to beaches. Britain alone discharges 300 million gallons a day.
B Sludge dumped at sea, unlike that discharged into rivers (page 32), only needs to be 50 per cent waste water. Sewage sludge contains nitrate and metals.

Oil Oil can come from ships illegally washing (cleaning) their tanks at sea, direct dumping or from accidents (*Braer*, page 131).

Incineration Some toxic waste was burned on specially designed incinerator ships. This ended in 1991.

Atmospheric pollution Many air pollutants eventually fall directly into the sea (e.g. as acid rain).

Direct dumping There are many large settlements next to the coast. People often dump rubbish (glass, plastic, polythene and aluminium containers, as well as litter) into the sea or leave it on beaches. This includes chemical containers accidentally washed overboard.

B *Left*: Water pollution along the shoreline in northern England

C Cleaning oil pollution from the Alaskan coast

D Consequences of pollution in the North Sea

Causes of sea pollution	Effects
Agricutural run-off	Nitrates and phosphate fertiliser cause a build-up of algae. Algae uses up oxygen, leaving insufficient for fish and marine life. Pesticides reaching thè sea can kill small marine life.
Industrial discharge	Could be a cause for decline in number of mammals (whales and dolphins), and for deformed fish found off British estuaries. Includes metals, e.g. mercury affects the nervous system and lead causes kidney damage.
Untreated sewage	Visual pollution on beaches. Health risk. Bathers can get stomach upsets, eye infections, skin rashes. In the short term there is a risk of typhoid and salmonella and a risk of hepatitis and polio in the long term.
Sewage sludge (to end by 1998)	Includes nitrates (Agricultural run-off) and metals (Industrial discharge). Long term effects are not known, but it breaks down the sea-bed ecosystem.
Oil	Spoils beaches, kills birds (oil on feathers), fish (oil in gills), shellfish (suffocation) and plankton (cannot photosynthesize).
Incineration (ended 1991)	Produced smells, fumes and smoke.
Atmospheric pollution	Includes radio-active fallout and acid in rainwater.

Activities

Sketch **E** below shows a stretch of coastline bordering the North Sea. It is affected by most of the types of sea pollution described in diagrams **A** and **D**.

a) What type of sea pollution is most likely to occur at each of the places numbered **1** to **6** on the sketch?

b) What might the effects of sea pollution be on
  i)   the beach at Thorneyhurst,
  ii) the Bushell Bird Sanctuary and Nature Reserve,
  iii) fish and sea mammals in Stanley Bay?

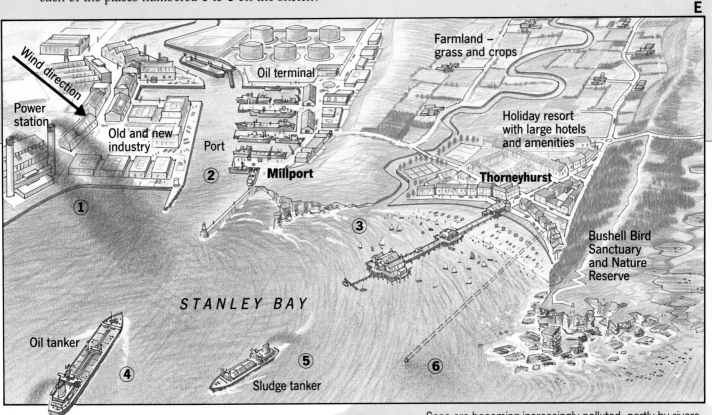

E

Summary Seas are becoming increasingly polluted, partly by rivers which flow into them and partly because they are still considered to be dumping grounds for waste material.

▶ Why does North Sea management need international co-operation? ◀

Scientists and environmentalists first warned of the increasingly high levels of pollution in the North Sea in 1967. Governments have, however, paid little attention to the warning. So, how badly polluted is the North Sea? The simple answer is that 'nobody knows because of insufficient scientific information'. Instead there are extremely diverse opinions as shown in diagram **A**.

A

EC and British government officials
The 1987 North Sea conference (diagram **C**) agreed that 'marine water quality in the North Sea is generally good and the environmental problems are confined to specific areas (i.e. off the Dutch and German coasts). There are, however, many gaps in information'. In 1990 '90 per cent of water in British estuaries was of good and fair quality' and 'the increase in herring in the North Sea was the reason for the return of sea mammals like dolphins and whales'.

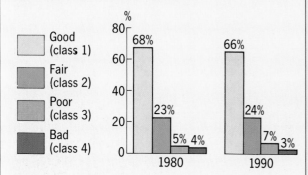

- Good (class 1)
- Fair (class 2)
- Poor (class 3)
- Bad (class 4)

%
80

1980: 68%, 23%, 5%, 4%
1990: 66%, 24%, 7%, 3%

Greenpeace
Following a campaign highlighting the dumping of toxic waste by Britain in the North Sea, Greenpeace Report No 11 (November 1992) claimed that, 'the right to use its seas as a free conduit for industrial wastes has been the cornerstone of Britain's antiquated approach to industrial effluent management. Such policies have been responsible for [the] catastrophic decline in the environmental quality of these areas over the past two decades'. Oceans may be nearing a breaking point due in part to 'toxins entering the seas from industrial sources. Huge numbers of seals and dolphins have died, there have been outbreaks of cancer in fish, and dramatic declines in some populations of sea-birds'.

The North Sea does not belong to one country; it does not even belong to the eight countries which border it. It is an international sea and therefore no country sees the North Sea as being its own problem. Britain blames those countries through which the River Rhine flows as being the major pollutants. Those countries blame Britain which they call the 'Dirty Man of Europe'. Casting blame does little to solve the problem. Map **B** shows surface currents in the North Sea, and how they cross international boundaries. Notice how any pollution caused by Britain is carried towards the Netherlands and Germany, and how pollution from the Rhine affects the largely non-polluting countries of Denmark and Norway. North Sea pollution affects all the countries which border it. It needs, therefore, international agreement and co-operation if pollution is to be reduced. Some of the agreements made so far are listed in diagram **C**.

B

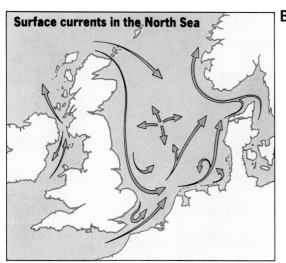

Surface currents in the North Sea

C

Belgium, Denmark, France, (West) Germany, Netherlands, Norway, Sweden and the UK

1972 London Dumping Agreement – guidelines laid down.

1983 Bonn Agreement – covered the spillage of oil, bulk chemicals and packaging of dangerous goods.

1987 Second North Sea Conference. Report claimed quality of North Sea water was good apart from off the coasts of Germany and the Netherlands.
Release of dangerous substances (e.g. mercury) into rivers to be reduced by 50%.

1987 Blue Flag Beach Campaign (diagram **C**).

1988 Illegal to dump plastics and synthetics.

1990 Third North Sea Conference. Some countries had already banned the dumping of industrial waste and untreated sewage. UK agreed to meet these two requirements by 1993 and 1998 respectively. Agreement to reduce by half the levels of 37 dangerous chemicals.

Blue Flag beaches

The EC directive is concerned only with water quality. A much more comprehensive quality assessment of beaches, called the Blue Flag campaign, was launched in 1987 by the Foundation for Environmental Education in Europe. The scheme aims to improve the standard of beaches and marinas used by large numbers of holidaymakers. It is sponsored by the EC Commission and by a number of public and private bodies throughout the EC.

Blue Flags are awarded annually by a jury at the beginning of the bathing season and can be withdrawn in the course of the season if the bathing ceases to meet the required standards. To be eligible for a Blue Flag award, the water must comply with some of the microbiological standards specified in the EC Bathing Water Directive and in addition the beach has to satisfy a broad range of other criteria, including good management and safety, provision of basic facilities and environmental information to beach users.

In 1992 17 UK beaches were awarded the Blue Flag. They are shown in map **C**.

Source: UK Environment, HMSO

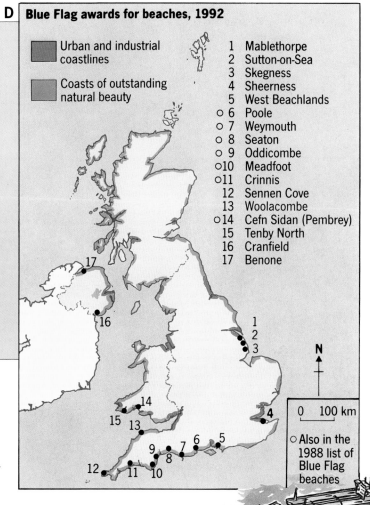

D

Blue Flag awards for beaches, 1992

- Urban and industrial coastlines
- Coasts of outstanding natural beauty

1	Mablethorpe
2	Sutton-on-Sea
3	Skegness
4	Sheerness
5	West Beachlands
○ 6	Poole
○ 7	Weymouth
○ 8	Seaton
○ 9	Oddicombe
○10	Meadfoot
○11	Crinnis
12	Sennen Cove
13	Woolacombe
○14	Cefn Sidan (Pembrey)
15	Tenby North
16	Cranfield
17	Benone

N

0   100 km

○ Also in the 1988 list of Blue Flag beaches

Problems in implementing international agreements

- Conflict of interest. The more industrial countries are concerned that the cost of reducing pollution will lower their profits and increase unemployment. As the main polluters they are expected to pay the most in any 'clean-up' scheme. Less industrialised countries expect to pay less on improving the environment.
- Schemes to reduce pollution are expensive and can take several years to implement, e.g. sewage treatment plants to reduce the discharge of untreated sewage, finding safe storage places for toxic waste. Such schemes get shelved during times of economic recession.
- Even when agreements are made between countries, who then enforces them?

What of the future?

'Although pollution of the North Sea continues, there is much more public concern than there used to be. It now seems likely that industry and governments will be forced to do something, particularly to reduce the extent of dumping. It will, however, take several years before restrictions lead to improved water quality'

Source: 'North Sea Pollution', *GeoActive*, Summer 1991

E

Activities

1 a) Which eight countries border the North Sea?
   b) Why is it important for all eight countries to agree and to co-operate if pollution in the North Sea is to be reduced?
   c) Why is it often difficult to get international co-operation?
   d) Why do you think Britain is often the last to sign agreements aimed at reducing pollution in the North Sea?

2 As a class, discuss the attitudes of the two groups of people named in diagram **A**.
   - Are governments and industrialists too complacent, and too concerned with earning money than saving the environment?
   - Are the views of Greenpeace too emotional and exaggerated, and does their concern for the environment come at the expense of jobs?
   - Is there a compromise between the two opposing viewpoints.

Summary

The North Sea is an important resource. While there is uncertainty as to its level of pollution, there is agreement that pollution gets carried across political boundaries by sea-currents. This creates problems which can only be solved by international co-operation and environmental management.

► How does ice shape the land? ◄

A

B

| Water fills a crack in a rock | The water freezes and the crack is made wider | The rock breaks into several pieces |

C

Photo **A** shows a glacier in Greenland. It is hard to imagine that only a few thousand years ago, very recently in the life history of the earth, all of northern Britain looked like this. Glaciers form when there is an interruption in the hydrological cycle (page 12). The climate becomes cold enough for precipitation to fall as snow, and water is held in storage in the system. The weight of new snowfalls turns the underlying snow into ice. When ice moves downhill under the force of gravity it is called a glacier, and glaciers replace rivers in valleys. Like rivers, ice picks up and transports large amounts of material. As the material moves downhill it erodes the land, forming extremely scenic landforms in highland areas. Later material will be deposited in valleys and across lowlands.

Much of the material carried by a glacier results from a process called **freeze-thaw** weathering (or frost shattering). Freeze-thaw weathering occurs when temperatures are often around freezing point. Water gets into cracks in rocks and freezes (diagram **B**). As the water turns to ice it expands, putting pressure on the surrounding rock. When the ice melts back into water the pressure is released. Repeated freezing and thawing widens the cracks and causes jagged pieces of rock to break off. Photo **C** shows how material resulting from freeze-thaw has fallen onto a glacier. This material, called **moraine**, is then transported by the glacier either on its surface, within it (if covered by later snowfalls or avalanches), or dragged along under it. Moraine is able to erode the sides and floor of the valley just as a river erodes its banks and bed.

Glacial erosion

Glaciers erode much faster than rivers. The two main processes of glacial erosion are **abrasion** and **plucking**. Abrasion is when the material carried by a glacier acts like sandpaper on a giant scale, rubbing against and wearing away, the sides and floor of a valley. It is a similar process, therefore, to corrasion by rivers and waves. Plucking is when ice freezes and sticks to rock. When the ice moves, large pieces of rock are pulled away with it. These two processes are perhaps better understood when explaining the formation of one typical landform of a glaciated highland area, the **corrie** (diagram **D**).

Landforms of glacial erosion – corries

Corries are also known as cirques or cwms. They are deep, rounded hollows with a steep backwall and a rock basin (photo **F**). Some corries contain a deep, rounded lake, or tarn. Corries develop when snow collects in pre-glacial hollows. As more snow accumulates, it turns to ice, and begins to move downhill. Freeze-thaw and plucking cut into the backwall of the hollow, making it steeper (diagram **D**).

Abrasion, underneath the glacier, deepens the floor to give a basin shape. A rock lip marks the place where there was less erosion and, sometimes, where moraine was deposited. After the ice melts, water may be trapped by the rock lip creating a small lake, or tarn (diagram **E**). An example of a corrie in Snowdonia is Llyn (lake) Glaslyn (grid square 6154, page 43).

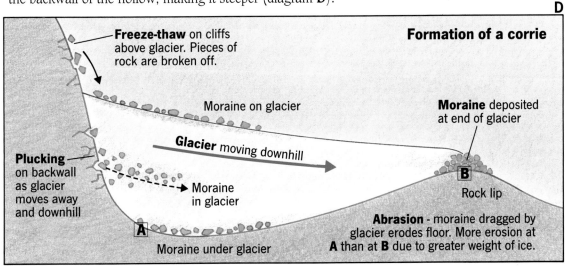

D

Formation of a corrie

Freeze-thaw on cliffs above glacier. Pieces of rock are broken off.

Moraine on glacier

Glacier moving downhill

Moraine deposited at end of glacier

B

Rock lip

Plucking on backwall as glacier moves away and downhill

→ Moraine in glacier

A

Moraine under glacier

Abrasion - moraine dragged by glacier erodes floor. More erosion at **A** than at **B** due to greater weight of ice.

E

Corrie shape today

Jagged summit

Steep backwall due to freeze-thaw and plucking

Corrie lake (tarn) – deep and rounded

Moraine marking end of glacier

Deep rock basin due to abrasion

Rock lip where erosion was less

F

Summary

Erosion, transport and deposition by glaciers produces a distinctive group of highland landforms. Freeze-thaw weathering and erosion by plucking and abrasion, are three of the most significant glacial processes.

Activities

1 a) How does snow eventually become a glacier?
   b) What causes a glacier to move downhill?

2 a) What is the name given to material transported by a glacier?
   b) Why is this material sometimes transported
      i)   on the surface of,
      ii) inside,
      iii) underneath a glacier?

3 a) Name the glacial process likely to be found at each of **A**, **B** and **C** on diagram **G**.

   b) Describe each of the three processes.
   c) Describe, using a labelled sketch only, the shape and appearance of a corrie.

G

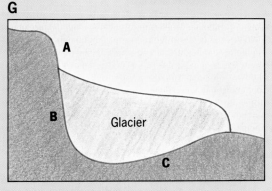

A

B   Glacier

C

39

▶ *What landforms result from glacial erosion?* ◀

Arêtes and pyramidal peaks

Corries are rarely found in isolation. Several usually form within the same mountainous area. Corries sometimes form in adjacent river valleys. In this case erosion of the sidewalls between them creates a narrow knife-edged ridge. At other times they may form back-to-back in valleys on either side of a watershed. On this occasion erosion of the backwalls narrows the distance between them until, again, a narrow knife-edged ridge is formed (diagram **A**). This narrow knife-edged ridge is called an **arête** (photo **B**). Crib Goch is one of several arêtes on Snowdon (grid square 6255, page 43).

When three or more corries cut back into the same mountain, a **pyramidal peak** is formed. The most famous, and scenic, is the Matterhorn in Switzerland (photo **C**). Arêtes radiate from pyramidal peaks (diagram **D**).

Glacial troughs, truncated spurs and hanging valleys

Glaciers tend to follow the easiest route when moving downhill which, in most cases, is along an existing river valley. As glaciers move downwards, they erode both the floor and the sides of the valley to form a **glacial trough**. The characteristic V-shape of a river valley (page 7) is turned into the typical U-shape of a glaciated valley. A glacial trough is deep, and has a wide, flat valley floor and steep valley sides (photo **E**). The Glaslyn Valley (Afon Glaslyn) is an example of a glacial trough in Snowdonia (grid square 6553, page 43).

A

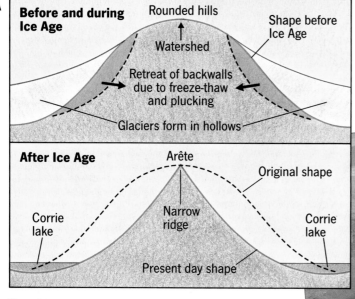

Before and during Ice Age

Rounded hills

Shape before Ice Age

Watershed

Retreat of backwalls due to freeze-thaw and plucking

Glaciers form in hollows

After Ice Age

Arête

Original shape

Corrie lake

Narrow ridge

Corrie lake

Present day shape

B Crib Goch

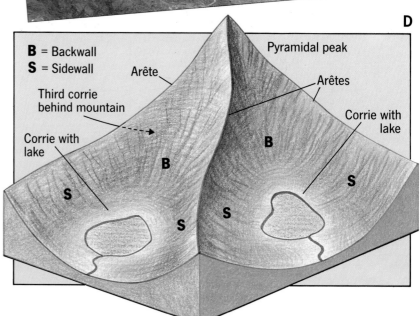

C The Matterhorn

D

B = Backwall
S = Sidewall

Pyramidal peak

Arête

Arêtes

Third corrie behind mountain

Corrie with lake

Corrie with lake

B

B

S

S

S

S

The valley is usually straightened by the glacier moving down it. The ends of interlocking spurs (page 7) are removed by abrasion to leave cliff-like features called **truncated spurs**. **Hanging valleys** result from differences in the rate of erosion between glaciers in the main and in a tributary valley (photo **F**). The floor of the smaller tributary valley is deepened more slowly than the floor of the main valley. When the ice melts, the tributary valley is left 'hanging' above the main valley, and its river has to descend by a single waterfall, or by a series of falls (grid square 6251, page 43).

E Nant Ffrancon, Snowdonia

F Jotunheim Mountains, Norway

Activities

1 Landsketch **G** shows a typical highland area which has been glaciated. The numbers refer to one glacial process (freeze-thaw) and six glacial landforms (corries, arêtes, pyramidal peaks, a glacial trough, truncated spurs and hanging valleys). Match up the numbers with the correct process or landform.

2 Explain how glaciation turns the:
   a) V-shape of a river valley into a U-shape;
   b) interlocking spurs of a river valley into truncated spurs;
   c) rounded watersheds of a river basin into jagged pyramidal peaks and arêtes.

G

Summary   Glacial erosion turns a gently rounded landscape formed by water into one which has steep and jagged landforms.

41

▶ *What landforms result from glacial deposition?* ◀

We have already seen that glaciers erode and transport large amounts of material. This material will be deposited either on the floor of glacial troughs in highland areas or across lowlands at the foot of highland areas. Deposition occurs when a rise in temperature causes ice to melt and the glacier is no longer able to carry as much material. A group of deposition landforms develop, mainly at the snout (end) of the melting glacier.

Erratics

Erratics are rocks and boulders picked up and transported many kilometres by the glacier, and deposited in an area of different rock (photo **A**). Rocks from Norway have been found in coastal cliffs in East Anglia, and granite from the Lake District on Anglesey in Wales.

Terminal and recessional moraines

Moraine is material which is transported and later deposited by a glacier. **Terminal moraine** marks the furthest, or maximum, point that a glacier reached (photo **B**). It is deposited at the end, or snout, of the glacier. If the glacier remains in the same position for a long time, terminal moraine can build up into a sizeable ridge which will extend across a valley (diagram **C**). The moraine is a mass of unsorted rocks, clays and sands. At the end of the ice age, glaciers began to melt and to retreat. This retreat was, however, rarely even but took place in several stages. At times the ice would stop melting and the glacier would remain in one position long enough for moraine to once again build up across the valley. This is a **recessional moraine** (diagram **C**). Some valleys may have several recessional moraines behind, and parallel to, the terminal moraine. Both terminal and recessional moraines can block valleys, acting as a dam to meltwater and to present day rivers. Long, narrow **ribbon lakes** have formed on the floors of many glacial troughs in highland Britain. One example of a ribbon lake in Snowdonia is Llyn Gwynant (grid square 6451, page 43).

Following the retreat of the ice, various post-glacial

A

B

processes continue to shape and alter the landscape. The main process results from meltwater which is released in enormous quantities as ice higher up in the mountains continues to melt. Meltwater can pick up angular, unsorted material originally left by the ice. The water rounds and sorts the material depositing the largest particles first and the smallest last.

C

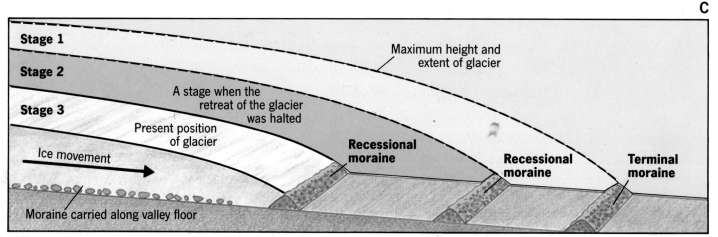

Stage 1

Stage 2

Maximum height and extent of glacier

Stage 3

A stage when the retreat of the glacier was halted

Present position of glacier

Ice movement

Recessional moraine

Recessional moraine

Terminal moraine

Moraine carried along valley floor

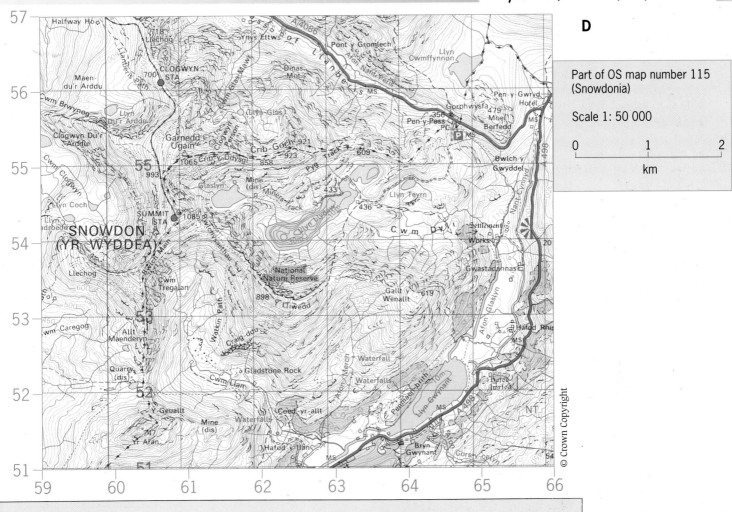

D

Part of OS map number 115
(Snowdonia)

Scale 1: 50 000

0   1   2
km

© Crown Copyright

Activities

1 a) Under what conditions will a glacier deposit the materials which it is carrying?

b) What are erratics?

c) What is the difference between a terminal moraine and a recessional moraine?

2 The OS map (map **D**) shows a glaciated highland area around Snowdon in North Wales.

a) Locate the following glacial landforms on the OS map, and then copy and complete table **E** by adding the landforms to it.

- Afon Glaslyn (6553)
- Crib-Goch (6255)
- Waterfalls (6251)
- Llyn Glaslyn (6154)
- Llyn Gwynant (6451)
- The summit of Snowdon (6054)
- Waterfalls (6352)
- Cliffs along the side of Llanberis (6356)
- Pass of Llanberis (6356)
- Bwlch Main (6053)
- Llyn Du'r Arddu (6055)

b) What glacial feature might you find at the exit to Llyn Gwynant (637514)? Give a reason for your answer.

3 Which of the two cross valley profiles in diagram **F** do you think represents Afon Glaslyn (6553)? Give two reasons for your answer.

E

Landform	Example
Corrie (cirque, cwm)	
Arête	
Pyramidal peak	
Glacial trough	
Truncated spur	
Hanging valley	
Ribbon lake	

F

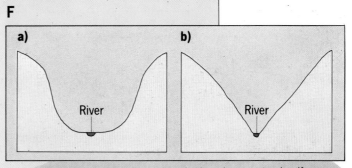

a)   b)

River   River

Summary Deposition by ice also creates landforms, although these are far less spectacular than those formed by glacial erosion.

▶ Why do limestone areas have their own special type of scenery? ◀

Limestone is a rock consisting mainly of calcium carbonate. Calcium carbonate comes from the remains of sea shells and coral. This means that limestone was formed on the sea bed. There are several types of limestone (map **A**). Each type produces its own special type of scenery, with **karst** landforms developing in areas of Carboniferous limestone (photo **B**).

A Location of limestone in England and Wales

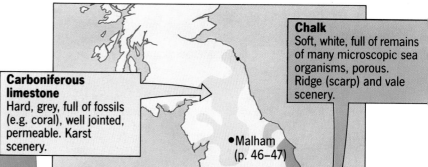

Chalk
Soft, white, full of remains of many microscopic sea organisms, porous. Ridge (scarp) and vale scenery.

Carboniferous limestone
Hard, grey, full of fossils (e.g. coral), well jointed, permeable. Karst scenery.

●Malham (p. 46–47)

Jurassic limestone
(Age of dinosaurs) Soft, yellowish, many fossils, porous. Ridge (scarp) and vale scenery.

Isle of Purbeck (p. 48–49)

B Guilin, China

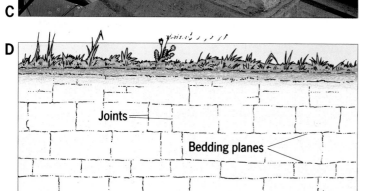

C

D

Joints

Bedding planes

There are three basic reasons why Carboniferous limestone produces distinctive landforms.

1 Chemical weathering Rainwater contains carbon dioxide in solution (carbonic acid). Although it is a weak acid, it reacts with rocks which include calcium carbonate, like limestone. The limestone is slowly dissolved and is removed in solution by running water (page 6). This process of **chemical weathering** allows rocks to decompose where they are located. It is different to the actions of water, waves, ice and the sea as these include the transport of material. The effects of chemical weathering can be seen on tombstones, statues and buildings made from limestone (photo **C**).

2 Rock structure Limestone is a sedimentary rock which means it was laid down in layers. Each layer is separated by a bedding plane (diagram **D**). At right angles to bedding planes are joints. Bedding planes and joints are areas of weakness which are dissolved and widened by chemical weathering.

3 Permeability Carboniferous limestone is pervious, unlike chalk which is porous. A porous rock consists of many small pores which allow water to pass through it. A pervious rock restricts water to flowing along bedding planes and down joints.

Carboniferous limestone (karst) landforms

Rivers flow over the ground's surface across impermeable rocks until they reach an area of limestone. When a river reaches limestone, it begins to dissolve joints and bedding planes. In time it will 'disappear' down a **swallow hole**, or sink (diagram **E** and photo **A**, page 46). Sometimes solution is so active that **underground caves** form. Where a series of caves develop, they are linked by narrow passages - ideal for potholers. Water drips constantly from the roof of these caves. As the water drips, some of it will slowly evaporate and calcium carbonate is deposited. In time a **stalactite** will form. A stalactite is an icicle shaped feature which hangs downwards from the roof. Stalactites, in Yorkshire caves (photo **F**), grow by only 7 mm a year. As the water drips to the floor, further deposition of calcium carbonate forms **stalagmites**, features that grow up from the cave floor.

Meanwhile, the underground river will be constantly looking for new routes through the limestone. It will seek lower levels until eventually it meets an underlying layer of impermeable rock. It will then flow over the impermeable rock until it reaches the surface. The place where it reappears it called a **resurgence** (photo **D**, page 46).

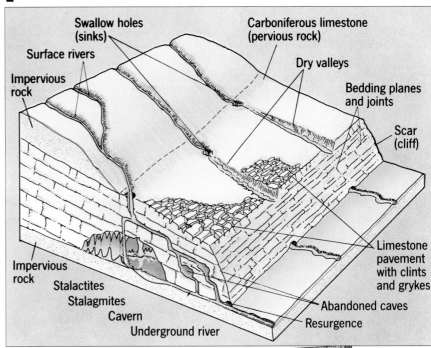

E

Swallow holes (sinks)
Surface rivers
Impervious rock
Carboniferous limestone (pervious rock)
Dry valleys
Bedding planes and joints
Scar (cliff)
Impervious rock
Stalactites
Stalagmites
Cavern
Underground river
Limestone pavement with clints and grykes
Abandoned caves
Resurgence

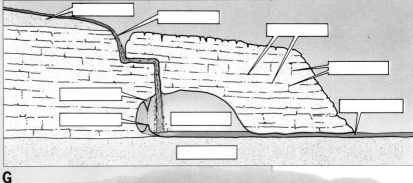

F

G

Activities

1 a) What evidence is there that limestone was formed on the sea bed?
   b) Name three different types of limestone found in Britain.
   c) What other name is given to landforms developed on Carboniferous limestone?
   d) How do the following affect the development of landforms on Carboniferous limestone?
      i)   Chemical weathering
      ii) Rock structure
      iii) Pervious rock

2 a) Rivers in Carboniferous limestone areas usually flow underground. Copy sketch **G**, and complete it by adding appropriate labels to the empty boxes.
   b) What is the difference between:
      i)   a bedding plane and a joint,
      ii) a stalactite and a stalagmite,
      iii) a swallow hole and a resurgence?

Summary

A distinctive group of landforms develops on Carboniferous limestone. These landforms occur because limestone is vulnerable to chemical weathering, has a structure composed of bedding planes and joints, and is pervious.

▶ What does a Carboniferous limestone area look like? ◀

Landforms of Carboniferous limestone areas are often very scenic, and attract many visitors. The area around Malham Cove (map **A**, page 44), in the Yorkshire Dales National Park, is a honeypot (page 154). A walk, or a transect across the OS map (map **E**), between Malham Tarn (8966) and Malham Village (9063) illustrates most surface limestone features.

Malham Tarn lies on impermeable rock. A small stream flows southwards from the tarn. After several hundred metres it comes to limestone and 'sinks' underground through a swallow hole (photo **A**, 895654). Another stream, with its source at 871663, also sinks underground on reaching the limestone (882659). The confluence of the streams used to be at 893650. South of here is the steep sided Watlowes **dry valley** (photo **B**). This valley indicates that a river once flowed on the surface, perhaps during the ice-age when meltwater could not infiltrate into the frozen ground.

The Watlowes valley widens onto a **limestone pavement**, a flat area of exposed rock (photo **C**, 896642). A limestone pavement appears flat as it corresponds to the surface of a bedding plane. In reality it is very uneven. Rainwater has dissolved the joints in the rock to form **grykes**, leaving detached blocks of limestone called **clints**. The limestone pavement ends abruptly at the top of Malham Cove where, in the distant past, the surface river dropped as a 90 metre waterfall. The foot of the cove marks the junction of limestone and impermeable rock, and the resurgence of the river (photo **D**, 897641) which disappeared at 882659.

The stream from Malham Tarn resurfaces further south at Aire Head 909622. At nearby Gordale (9164) the roof of an underground cavern is believed to have collapsed leaving a steep sided gorge.

B Watlowes dry valley (between 893650 and 897641)

A Water sinks (895654)

C Limestone pavement with clints and grykes above Malham Cove (896642)

D Resurgence at the foot of Malham Cove (897641)

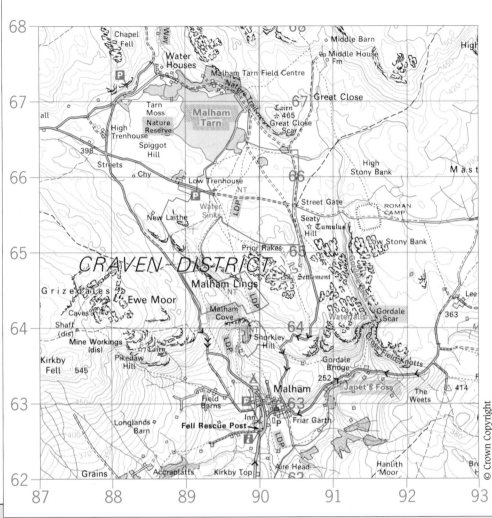

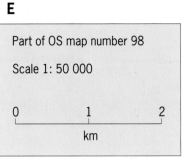

Part of OS map number 98

Scale 1 : 50 000

0   1   2
km

© Crown Copyright

Activities

1 Make an enlarged copy of grid **F** opposite which covers the same area as the OS map (figure **E**).

a) Mark on in blue and name: *Malham Tarn – two streams before they disappear underground – the river which flows through Malham village – Gordale Beck.*

b) Add the following labels in their correct places: *source – two swallow holes – dry valley – limestone pavement with clints and grykes – Malham Cove – resurgence – collapsed underground cavern.*

c) Colour, in yellow, the part of the map where there is carboniferous limestone.

2 Refer to the OS map above.

a) Give names and map references of other pieces of evidence (to those asked for in Activity **1**) to suggest that much of the area is limestone.

b) List some limestone landforms which are not found on this particular OS map.

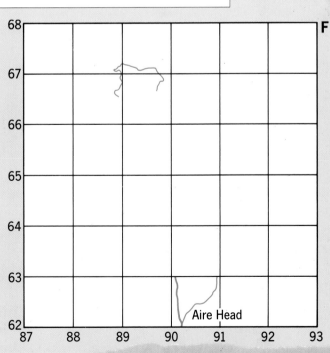

Summary

Carboniferous limestone areas have distinctive landforms which make them attractive to visitors.

How do different rock types affect landforms?

The Isle of Purbeck is not an island. It is a small peninsula located on the south coast of England (map **A**, page 44). It consists of four main types of rock – limestone, clays, chalk and sands. Chalk and limestone were formed on the sea-bed (page 44) and later uplifted and tilted by earth movements. Compared with the clays and sands, chalk and limestone are

- much harder and more resistant to erosion,
- permeable rocks.

All four rock types cross the Isle of Purbeck in bands that are more or less parallel to each other. They reach the east coast of the peninsula, at Swanage Bay, at right angles (diagram **B**).

Since the formation of the rocks and the uplift of the land, the area has been affected by different types of erosion. The sea has mainly been responsible for erosion on the coast, and rain and running water (rivers) for erosion on places inland. The result has been the formation of greatly contrasting types of landform. The resistant chalk and limestone rocks have been eroded less quickly leaving ridges inland and headlands on the coast. The less resistant clays and sands have been eroded more quickly to form vales (valleys) inland and bays on the coast (diagram **B** and cross-section **D**). A summary of the major landforms found on the different rock types is given in table **C**.

A Satellite photo of the Isle of Purbeck

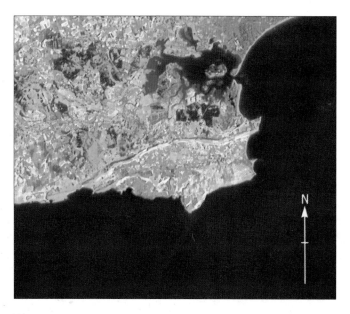

B

Limestone — Ridge — 124 — 79 — Tilly Whin caves — Headland, high cliffs, caves — Durlston Head

Clays — Vale — 25 — Swanage — Small headland — Peveril Point — Sandy bay, longshore drift

Chalk — Ridge — 160 — 67 — 116 — High cliffs — Ballard Point

Sands and clays — Vale — 15 — Studland — Sandy bay with longshore drift — 23 — Old Harry Rocks — Headland with stacks — The Foreland

Looking west — Poole Harbour — Sand dunes

Key
● 23 Height above sea level

C

Rock type	Rock strength/ resistance to erosion	Coastal landforms	Inland landforms
Limestone	Hard, resistant, pervious	Cliffs, headlands, caves	Ridge; no rivers
Clay	Soft, weak, impermeable	Bay	Low-lying vale with rivers
Chalk	Soft, resistant, porous	Cliffs, headlands, stacks (photo **E**, page 23)	Ridge (escarpment) with no rivers
Clays and sands	Soft, weak, mainly impermeable	Bay	Low-lying vale with rivers

Ridge and vale landscape

Ridges and vales form a common landscape in many parts of south and east England. They occur when mainly resistant and permeable rocks alternate with mainly impermeable and less resistant rock. Softer limestones, such as chalk and Jurassic limestone, are porous (page 44). As water passes easily through them, they are resistant to erosion and so are left as rounded hills or as **ridges** where the rock has been tilted. The impermeable clays, on the other hand, are worn away more easily by rivers and become **vales** (diagram **D**).

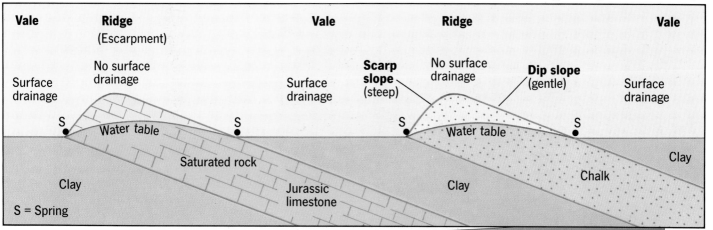

D Cross-section of a typical ridge and vale landscape

Chalk ridges are often called escarpments. Escarpments have a steep scarp slope and a gentle dip slope (photo **E**). Rivers and streams are usually absent on the ridges, but springs occur at the junction of the permeable and impermeable rocks. The springs and impermeable clay account for the surface drainage in the vales.

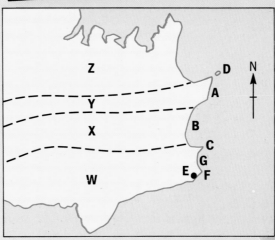

E

Activities

1 Sketch **F** shows the east coast of the Isle of Purbeck. Using photo **A** and landsketch **B**:
   a) name the coastal landforms found at places **A** to **G**;
   b) name the type of rock found at places **W** to **Z**.

2 a) Why should chalk and limestones:
   i) form cliffs where they reach the coast;
   ii) form ridges (escarpments) and hills in inland areas;
   iii) have very little surface drainage?
   b) Why should clays:
   i) form bays where they reach the coast;
   ii) form vales in inland areas;
   iii) have much surface drainage?

3 a) Draw a simple sketch of photo **E**. On it label: *chalk ridge – scarp slope – dip slope – clay vale*.

F

   b) What differences does the photo show in land use between the chalk ridge and the clay vale ? Suggest reasons for these differences.

Summary

The landforms of an area are often the consequence of the varying resistance and structure of the different types of rock found within that area, and of processes operating over long periods of time.

► *What are the effects of earth movements?* ◄

A

B

Earth movements usually result from a release of pressure. Over a period of time pressure can build up within the earth. Often it is released so slowly that it is hardly noticed by people living on the surface. Sometimes the release of pressure can be very sudden. This can cause a violent movement on the earth's surface, and can result in considerable damage, and even loss of life. Pressure can be released through **earthquakes** and **volcanoes**.

Earthquakes

It is estimated that there are over 150 000 earth movements every year. However, most of these are so gentle that they can only be detected by highly sensitive instruments called seismometers. The 10 000 or so earth movements per year which are strong enough to be felt are called tremors. (Of these 1000 occur in Japan – an average of three per day!) Earthquakes are violent earth movements where the ground actually shakes. Each year there are something like 20 to 50 earthquakes which are violent enough to cause serious damage and loss of life (photo **A**). The strength of an earthquake is measured on the Richter Scale (diagram **B**). At first glance the scale is misleading as each point is actually ten times greater than the one below it. That means an earthquake which registers 6 on the scale is ten times greater than one measuring 5, and one hundred times greater than one measuring 4.

Richter Scale		Effects
Down to 0		
3		Only detected by instruments (seismometers)
	3.4	Noticed only by very sensitive people
	3.5	
		Felt by most people sitting down, like the rumble of traffic
4	4.2	
		Felt by walkers; windows and doors rattle
	4.4	Suspended objects swing; sleeping people are wakened
	4.8	
5		Furniture moves, objects fall, plaster begins to crack
	5.4	
		Chimneys fall, walls crack, difficult to stand up
6	6.0	
		Severe structural damage to houses
	6.7	
		Some houses collapse; underground pipes crack
7	6.9	Many houses collapse; landslides; cracks in the ground
	7.3	
		Most buildings collapse; bridges destroyed; large gaps appear in ground
8	8.1	
		Total destruction; ground actually rises and falls
9	8.9	8.9 Lisbon earthquake (max)
Up to 12		

Volcanoes

Pressure under the earth's crust keeps the rock there in a semi-solid state. If pressure is released, the rock turns to liquid and rises. Volcanoes form where the liquid rock, or lava, escapes onto the earth's surface. Lava can escape by either a gentle or a violent movement. If the lava is very 'runny' it will find its way through cracks in the crust and spread out slowly across the surrounding countryside (photo **C**). The result is either a **lava flow** or a low, gentle-sided volcano (diagram **D**). Where there are no natural cracks, lava can only escape if there is a violent explosion, or eruption (photo **E**). Materials, such as lava, ash and rock, shoot out into the air from a single opening called a **crater**. Most of the material falls back around the crater building up into a high, steep-sided volcanic **cone** (diagram **F**).

C

E

D

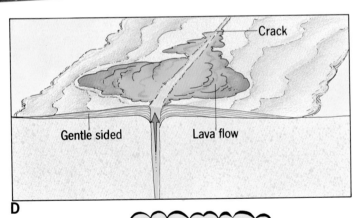

Crack

Gentle sided — Lava flow

F

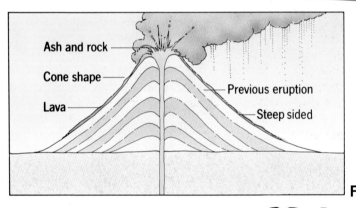

Ash and rock

Cone shape

Lava

Previous eruption

Steep sided

Activities

I come from San Francisco. In 1989 we had an earthquake which recorded 6.9 on the Richter scale.

In Tokyo we get many earthquakes. The one we had this morning was 4.9.

G

I live in Mexico City. We had an earthquake in 1985 which measured 7.8.

1 a) These three schoolchildren have all experienced earthquakes. Describe their experiences.

   b) How many times greater is an earthquake registering 6.9 than one measuring 4.9?

   c) What is the highest ever recorded earthquake reading?

2 a) Why do gentle eruptions of lava produce gentle-sided volcanoes?

   b) Why do violent eruptions form steep-sided volcanoes?

Summary

Earth movements occur frequently. The most violent movements involve earthquakes and volcanic eruptions, both of which can cause severe damage and loss of life.

Where do earthquakes and volcanoes occur?

One task undertaken by geographers is to plot distributions on maps, and then to see if the maps show any recognisable patterns. Map **A** shows the distribution of world earthquakes and map **B** the distribution of volcanoes. In both cases there are some very obvious patterns.

A

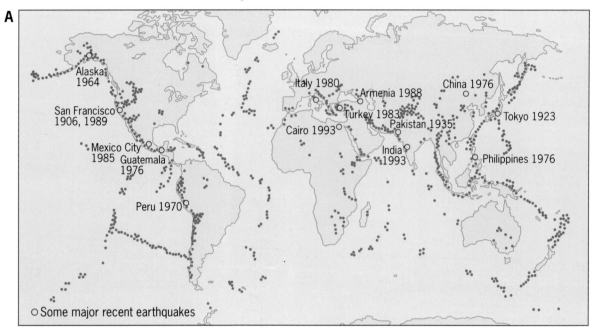

○ Some major recent earthquakes

Earthquakes

Earthquakes occur in long narrow belts. The largest belt is the one which goes around the entire Pacific Ocean. The second most obvious is the one which runs through the middle of the Atlantic Ocean for its entire length. A third belt stretches across the continents of Europe and Asia from the Atlantic to the Pacific. There are other shorter belts, including one going westwards from the west coast of South America.

Volcanoes

Volcanoes also appear in long narrow belts. The largest belt is the one which goes around the entire Pacific Ocean, the so-called 'Pacific Ring of Fire'. The second most obvious is the one which runs through the middle of the Atlantic Ocean for its entire length. Three other notable locations are in Southern Europe, the centre of the Pacific Ocean, and eastern Africa.

B

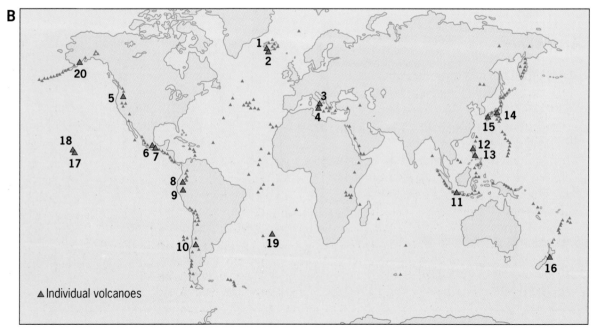

▲ Individual volcanoes

Geographers noticed that when the two maps were laid side by side or, better still, when one was laid on top of the other, that earthquakes and volcanoes both seemed to occur in narrow belts and in the same places. These narrow belts are referred to as zones of activity. Having discovered both a pattern and a relationship between the two maps, the geographer then has to ask the question, 'Why?' In this case, why are earthquakes and volcanoes found within the same narrow belts?

Diagram **C** is a cross-section through the earth. It shows the crust to be the very thin surface layer of cooled rock. It also shows that the crust is not one single piece but is broken into several slabs of varying sizes, called **plates**. Plates float, like rafts, on the molten (semi-solid) mantle. There are two types of crust, and it is important to accept three main differences between them.

- Continental crust is lighter, it cannot sink, and it is permanent (i.e. it is neither renewed nor destroyed).
- Oceanic crust is heavier (denser), it can sink, and it is continually being renewed and destroyed.

Heat from the centre of the earth sets up convection currents in the mantle (diagram **D**). Where these currents reach the surface they cause the plates above them to move. Most plates only move a few millimetres a year. In some places two plates move towards each other. In others plates may either move apart or pass sideways to each other. A **plate boundary** is where two plates meet. It is at plate boundaries that most of the world's

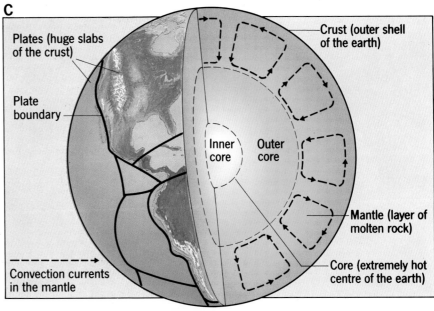

C

Plates (huge slabs of the crust)

Plate boundary

Crust (outer shell of the earth)

Inner core

Outer core

Mantle (layer of molten rock)

Core (extremely hot centre of the earth)

Convection currents in the mantle

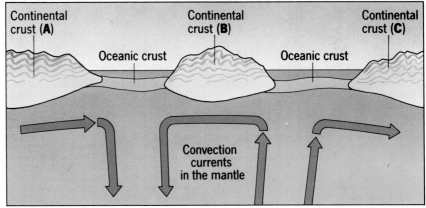

Continental crust (**A**)

Oceanic crust

Continental crust (**B**)

Oceanic crust

Continental crust (**C**)

Convection currents in the mantle

D

earthquakes occur and volcanoes are found (maps **A** and **B**). Pages 54 and 55 explain why there are so many earthquakes and volcanic eruptions, and why some are gentle and others violent, at plate boundaries.

Activities

1 Earthquakes and volcanoes seem to occur in long narrow belts.
   a) Name two belts (areas) where both earthquakes and volcanic eruptions occur.
   b) Name an area in Europe where both earthquakes and volcanic eruptions occur.

2 The following 20 volcanoes have been numbered but not named on map **B**:
   Aconcagua – Chimborazo – Cotopaxi – Etna – Fuji – Heimaey – Katmai – Kilauea – Krakatoa – Mauna Loa – Mayon – Paricutin – Pinatubo – Popocatepetl – Mount St Helens – Ngauruhoe – Surtsey – Tristan da Cunha – Unzen – Vesuvius.

   a) Name the volcanoes numbered **1** to **20**.
   b) Copy and complete table **E** by giving their locations.

3 a) Give three differences between continental and oceanic crust.
   b) i) What are plates?
      ii) Why do they move?
      iii) What happens at plate boundaries?
   c) On diagram **D**, what do you think will happen between:
      i) continents **A** and **B**;
      ii) continents **B** and **C**?

Pacific Ring of Fire	Middle of oceans	Others
	1 = Heimaey	

E

Summary

The earth's crust is broken into several plates. Convection currents cause these plates to move about slowly. Earthquakes and volcanic eruptions occur at plate boundaries.

▶ *What happens at plate boundaries?* ◀

Map **A** shows the major plates and their boundaries (margins). The map key indicates that there are four types of plate boundary – destructive, collision, constructive and conservative. Earthquakes occur at all four types of boundary, but are more violent at some than others. Volcanic eruptions tend to occur at only two types of plate boundary, being violent at one and more gentle at the other.

A

Direction of plate movement

Destructive margin – one plate sinks under another (subduction)

Constructive margin – two plates move away from each other

Conservative margin – two plates move past each other

Collision margin – two continental plates move together

Uncertain plate boundary

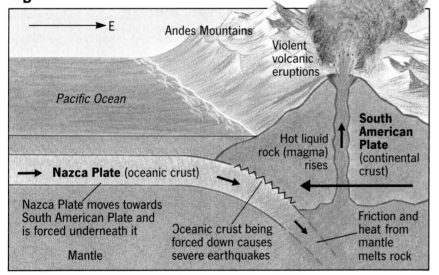

Simplified map showing major plates and plate boundaries

Eurasian Plate

Juan de Fuca Plate

North American Plate

Philippines Plate

Caribbean Plate

Cocos Plate

African Plate

Indo-Australian Plate

Nazca Plate

Pacific Plate

South American Plate

Antarctic Plate

B

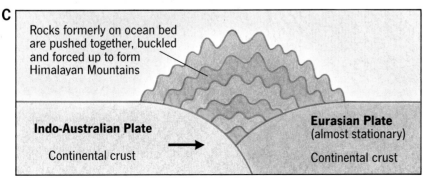

E

Andes Mountains

Violent volcanic eruptions

Pacific Ocean

South American Plate (continental crust)

Hot liquid rock (magma) rises

Nazca Plate (oceanic crust)

Nazca Plate moves towards South American Plate and is forced underneath it

Oceanic crust being forced down causes severe earthquakes

Friction and heat from mantle melts rock

Mantle

C

Rocks formerly on ocean bed are pushed together, buckled and forced up to form Himalayan Mountains

Indo-Australian Plate

Continental crust

Eurasian Plate (almost stationary)

Continental crust

Destructive margins

A destructive margin is when oceanic crust moves towards continental crust, for example the Nazca Plate moving towards the South American Plate (diagram **B**). As the oceanic crust is heavier it is forced downwards. As it is forced downwards pressure increases which can trigger extremely violent earthquakes. At the same time the heat produced by friction turns the descending crust back into liquid rock called magma. The hot magma tries to rise to the surface. Where it succeeds there will be violent volcanic eruptions. Notice that most of the Pacific Ocean is bounded by destructive margins where oceanic crust is being destroyed.

Collision margins

Collision margins occur when the two plates moving together are both continental crust (diagram **C**). As continental crust cannot sink or be destroyed, then the land between them is buckled and pushed upwards to form high 'fold' mountains, such as the Himalayas. Although pressure created by the plates moving together can cause severe earthquakes, there are no volcanic eruptions at collision margins.

Constructive margins

A constructive margin is where two plates move apart, for example the North American Plate moving away from the Eurasian Plate (diagram **D**). As a 'gap' appears between the two plates, then lava can easily escape either in the form of a relatively gentle eruption or as a lava flow. The lava creates new oceanic crust and forms a mid-ocean ridge. While not all earthquakes and volcanic eruptions on Iceland are 'gentle', they are compared to those at other plate margins.

Conservative margins

At conservative margins two plates try to slide slowly past each other, as in the case of the North American and Pacific Plates (diagram **E**). When the two plates stick, as they often do along the notorious San Andreas fault in California, pressure builds up. When it is finally released, it creates a severe earthquake. As crust is neither created nor destroyed at conservative margins, then there are no volcanic eruptions.

D — Volcanic islands, e.g. Iceland; Mid-Atlantic Ridge; North American Plate; Eurasian Plate; Atlantic Ocean; Magma from mantle

E — San Francisco; Pacific Plate moving faster than North American Plate; San Andreas Fault; North American Plate moving slower than, and towards, Pacific Plate; Los Angeles; Pacific Ocean; N

Activities

1. a) Describe the differences between destructive, collision, constructive and conservative plate margins?

   b) What type of plate margin can be found between the plates listed below?

   - Nazca and South American
   - North American and Eurasian
   - Nazca and Pacific
   - Indo-Australian and Eurasian
   - North American and Pacific
   - African and Eurasian
   - Pacific and Eurasian

2. Make a copy of diagram **F**. Add the correct letters to the empty boxes.

3. Copy and complete table **G** by putting one tick in the earthquake column and one tick in the volcanic eruption column for each of the four types of plate boundary.

C – continental crust
O – oceanic crust
X – where new crust is being formed
Y – where crust is being destroyed
V – violent volcanic eruptions
G – less violent volcanic eruptions
E – severe earthquakes
F – fold mountains
M – a mid-ocean ridge

F

Plate margin	Earthquakes			Volcanic eruptions		
	Violent	Less violent	Rare	Violent	Fairly gentle	None
Destructive						
Collision						
Constructive						
Passive						

G

Summary   Plates can either move towards, away from or sideways past other plates. The resultant earth movements can cause earthquakes and volcanic eruptions of differing severity.

▶ *How are people affected by a volcanic eruption?* ◀

In 1990 the US Geological Survey claimed that there were 540 active volcanoes in the world. Three-quarters of those were in the Pacific Ring of Fire. The list did not include a little known volcano in the Philippines which had not erupted since 1380. On 9 June 1991, Mount Pinatubo hit the headlines. It became one of the three largest eruptions in the world this century (photo **A**).

The Philippines lie on a destructive plate margin. The Philippines Plate, composed of oceanic crust, moves north-westwards towards the Eurasian Plate, which is continental crust. Where they meet, the Philippines Plate is forced to dip steeply down under the Eurasian Plate (map **B**). The oceanic crust is turned into magma, rises, and erupts on the surface. The Philippines owe their existence to the almost constant ejection of lava over a period of several million years. Even before Pinatubo erupted, there were over 30 active volcanoes spread across the country's many islands.

A

B

China
0   2000 km
Japan
N
Eurasian Plate
(continental crust)
Pacific Plate
(oceanic crust)
Philippines Plate
(oceanic crust)
Philippines
Indonesia
Indo-Australian Plate
(continental crust)
Australia

Luzon
N
Mt Pinatubo
Manila
Pacific Ocean
South China Sea
Philippines
0   400 km

What were the immediate effects?

Fortunately there were several advance warnings of a possible eruption. On 7 June the Americans evacuated all 15 000 personnel from their nearby airbase. From 9 June there were many eruptions, but none matched that of 12 June. An explosion sent a cloud of steam and ash 30 km into the sky. As the ash fell back to earth, it turned day into night. Up to 50 cms of ash fell on nearby farmland, villages and towns. Over 10 cms fell within a 600 km radius, and some even reached as far away as Australia. The eruptions continued for several days. They were accompanied by earthquakes and torrential rain – except that the rain fell as thick mud. The weight of the ash caused buildings to collapse, including 200 000 homes, a local hospital, most of the schools and many factories. Power supplies were cut off for three weeks and water supplies were contaminated. Roads became unusable and bridges were destroyed making relief operations even more difficult.

What were the longer term effects?

The area surrounding Mount Pinatubo was excellent for rice growing. The thick fall of ash, however, ruined the harvest in 1991, and made planting for 1992 impossible. Over one million farm animals died, either through starvation (no grass to eat) or from drinking contaminated water. Hundreds of farmers and their families were forced to move to cities to seek shelter and food. Huge shanty-type refugee camps were set up. Disease spread rapidly, especially malaria, chicken-pox and diarrhoea. Within a few days the monsoon rains started. Normally these rains are welcomed as they bring water for the rice crop. In 1991, and again in 1993, they were

so heavy that they caused flooding and lahars (mud flows). Lahars form when heavy rain flows over, and picks up, large amounts of volcanic ash. Lahars and landslides covered many low-lying areas in thick mud (photo **C**). Finally, ash ejected into the atmosphere encircled the earth within a few days. It blocked out some of the sun's heat for several months, and lowered world temperatures. Scientists believe the eruption may delay global warming by several years. The eruption and after effects caused the deaths of about 700 people. Only six died as a direct result of the initial eruption. Over 600 died later through disease, and another 70 were suffocated by lahars.

C

Activities

1 Make a copy of diagram **D**. On it label: *Philippines Plate – Eurasian Plate – Mount Pinatubo – continental crust – oceanic crust – magma – earthquakes – cloud of steam and ash.*

2 a) Why were so many people living on the slopes of Mount Pinatubo in June 1991?
  b) What caused the eruption of Mount Pinatubo?
  c) List the
   i) immediate effects
   ii) long term effects
   of the eruption of Mount Pinatubo.

D

Summary The most violent volcanic eruptions occur at destructive plate margins. Eruptions can be a considerable hazard to human activity and, sometimes, to human life.

► How are people affected by an earthquake? ◄

Tokyo lies in the Kanto region of Japan. In 1923 most of Tokyo, and nearby Yokohama, were destroyed as the result of an earthquake which measured 8.2 on the Richter Scale. Today many scientists are predicting that another earthquake of similar size will occur in the near future. It is now realised that Tokyo lies on the edge of **two** destructive plate margins (map **A**). The 1923 earthquake was caused, like the 1991 Mount Pinatubo eruption, by the Philippines Plate dipping under the Eurasian Plate. Further north in Japan it is the Pacific Plate dipping under the Eurasian Plate which causes frequent earthquakes (resulting in nearly 200 deaths in Hokkaido in 1993). However, the situation is complicated offshore from Tokyo where the Pacific Plate dips under the Philippines Plate, which in turn dips under the Eurasian Plate. This gives a double earthquake threat.

The earthquake of 1 September 1923 occurred at 11.58 a.m. Its focus (centre) was 30 km beneath the sea-bed, and 80 km south of Tokyo (diagram **B**). The seismic waves first hit the port of Yokohama. Buildings collapsed, many more caught fire and places near to the harbour were swamped by a 5 metre high tsunami (diagram **E**). Forty-four seconds later, the shockwaves hit Tokyo. The time of 11.58 and the fact that it was windy were to prove critical. As it was almost noon, thousands of families were beginning to heat their charcoal-burning braziers or to light cooking stoves in their small wooden homes in preparation for the midday meal. In office blocks and factories, workers were also preparing for their lunch break.

The first shockwaves destroyed most large buildings in the city centre killing, perhaps, 5000 people. The real disaster, though, resulted from the shockwaves upsetting thousands of blazing braziers and setting fire to the wooden houses. Broken gas mains and fallen power cables caused many local fires. Soon individual fires, fanned by the strong wind, merged into a single wall of flames. People rushed towards a roadbridge over the 200 metre wide Sumida River. The bridge had been destroyed except for one iron beam, wide enough for only one person to crawl over at a time. In the crush behind, many were trampled and suffocated to death. Others either jumped, or were pushed, into the river. Many of these were later to die when the water, heated by the fires, began to boil. Yet the major tragedy was to occur nearby.

Tokyo residents had grown up with the advice that they should seek open space in the event of a large fire. One such place was an 8 hectare site of a derelict army clothing depot. By mid-afternoon estimates suggest that up to 40 000 people had gathered there. Separate fires tend to be drawn towards each other. This is because air above the fires heats up and rises, creating a vacuum on the ground. Replacement air and flames rush into the vacuum at an ever increasing pace, incinerating everything in their path.

N

0   500km

Eurasian Plate (continental crust)

1958
1969
1973
1952
1993
1983
1935   1968
1931   Pacific Plate
1964   1936
1948
Tokyo   1938
Yokohama
1923
Izu Peninsula
1944   1953
1946
Philippines Plate (oceanic crust)   1952
Pacific Plate (oceanic crust)

A

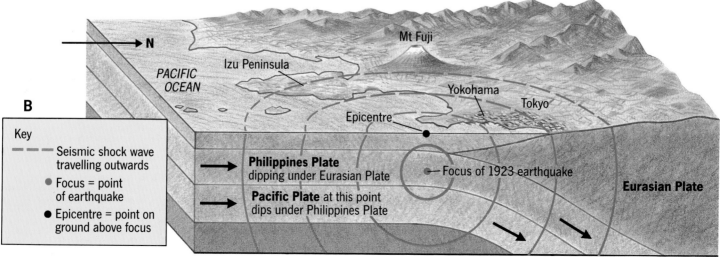

N

PACIFIC OCEAN

Izu Peninsula

Mt Fuji

Yokohama
Tokyo

Epicentre

Philippines Plate dipping under Eurasian Plate

Focus of 1923 earthquake

Pacific Plate at this point dips under Philippines Plate

Eurasian Plate

B

Key

- - - Seismic shock wave travelling outwards
● Focus = point of earthquake
● Epicentre = point on ground above focus

On this occasion spirals of flame sucked people out of the crowd and then dropped them as fireballs. Only a few hundred people escaped a holocaust which was far more devastating than the fire which swept through parts of San Francisco after the 1906 earthquake. Elsewhere in Tokyo people died from inhaling smoke, and some were trapped as their feet stuck in melting tarmac when they tried to escape. The fires raged for two whole days, and only died down when there was nothing left to burn.

About 140 000 people died in the Kanto earthquake – 100 000 in Tokyo and 40 000 in Yokohama. Of these only 5 per cent died as buildings collapsed, with most of the remainder being burnt to death. Two-thirds of Tokyo was destroyed, including 700 000 homes and 9000 factories (photos **C** and **D**).

In many earthquakes affecting coastal areas, the most common cause of death is tsunamis (diagram **E**). When Krakatoa erupted in 1883, 50 000 of the 86 000 deaths were due to tsunamis which were large enough to travel several times around the world.

C Tokyo in the aftermath of the great earthquake of 1923

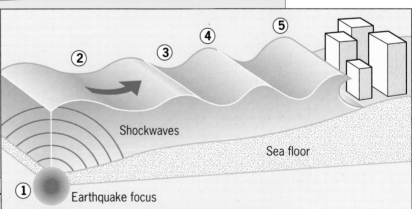

D Wrecked tramways in a Tokyo street after the great earthquake of 1923

1 Tsunamis are tidal waves triggered off by large underwater earthquakes.
2 They can travel across oceans at speeds of up to 800 km/hour.
3 They usually occur at 15 minutes (200 km) intervals.
4 As the waves approach shallower coastal water, they slow down in speed but rise up rapidly in height; some are up to 15 metres high.
5 When they break they cause much destruction and loss of life.

Shockwaves

Sea floor

① Earthquake focus

E

Activities

1 a) Why are earthquakes so frequent in the area surrounding Tokyo?
  b) Give an eye-witness account of the main effects of the 1923 Kanto (Tokyo) earthquake.
  c) If another Kanto earthquake occurs, as is predicted, why might damage and loss of life be even greater than in 1923?

2 a) What are tsunamis?
  b) Why do most tsunamis occur in the Pacific Ocean? (Page 54 may help you with this.)

Summary Earthquakes are a major natural hazard as they are difficult to predict and usually occur without giving any advance warning. They can cause considerable damage and loss of life.

▶ *How do people respond to the hazards?* ◀

It is impossible to prevent earthquakes and volcanic eruptions. Earthquakes usually occur with no advance warning, often in areas where large numbers of people live (e.g. San Francisco, Tokyo). Volcanic eruptions, which may give some warning signs, usually occur in less populated parts of the world.

In either case all people can do is to try to

- **prepare** for the event by attempting to reduce the damage likely to be caused and to have emergency services available;
- **predict** where and when the event will happen. At present there is hope that volcanic eruptions may be predicted with considerable accuracy within twenty years, but there is less optimism over earthquake prediction.

A

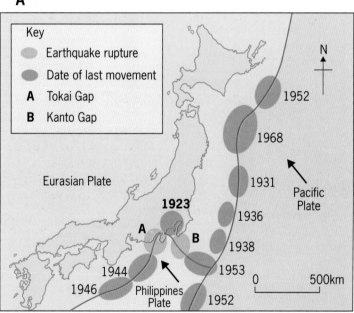

Key
- Earthquake rupture
- Date of last movement
- **A** Tokai Gap
- **B** Kanto Gap

Eurasian Plate

1923

A

B

N

1952
1968
1931
1936
1938
1953
1952

Pacific Plate

1944
1946 Philippines Plate

0   500km

B

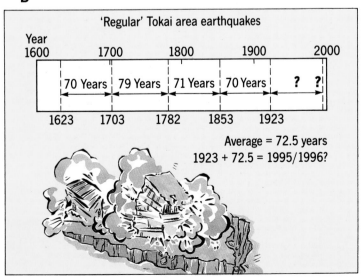

'Regular' Tokai area earthquakes

Year
1600   1700   1800   1900   2000

| 70 Years | 79 Years | 71 Years | 70 Years | ? | ? |

1623   1703   1782   1853   1923

Average = 72.5 years
1923 + 72.5 = 1995/1996?

How might it be possible to predict future earthquakes?

- Sensitive instruments can be used to measure possible earth movements and to check for a build up of pressure. Tokyo is surrounded by 64 observation points measuring crustal pressure, seismic waves and tidal fluctuations.
- Observing unusual animal and fish behaviour is less scientific, and is dismissed by most developed countries, but it saved thousands of lives during the 1975 China earthquake. Unusual behaviour included horses rearing, pandas moaning, mice fleeing houses, dogs howling and fish jumping. Unfortunately no warning was given the following year when tens of thousands died in a second China earthquake.
- By mapping centres of previous earthquakes along a plate boundary. Map **A** shows two places near to Tokyo which have not experienced earthquakes for many years. It is these two places where scientists believe pressure will be building up, and where Japan's next two major earthquakes will occur. An earthquake at Tokai would cause considerable damage in western parts of Tokyo. A Kanto earthquake would probably destroy Tokyo and could kill several million people. In 1923 an earthquake in the Tokai region is believed to have triggered off the Kanto earthquake (page 58).
- The regularity of earthquakes can be plotted. Diagram **B** shows that earthquakes in the Tokai area have occurred every 72.5 years, suggesting that the next one could be due in 1995–96. Using similar data, the next Kanto earthquake will not be until 2020.

How can people plan for earthquakes?

- Residents in Japan's danger zone celebrate Disaster Day every 1 September. It is a public holiday to 'prepare' for the next earthquake. In reality it becomes a carnival. Public information posters tell people what to do if an earthquake happens. They show happy people running around with buckets of water to throw on fires, ensuring furniture in the home or office does not fall upon them, switching off gas stoves, and telling everybody there is no need to panic. While most people accept the likelihood of an earthquake, they do not believe it will actually happen.
- New buildings in San Francisco and Tokyo are being built to withstand earthquakes. Modern skyscrapers are considered to be extremely safe as they have steel frames and have been designed to 'sway' as the earth moves. Bricks are never used, but fire resistant materials are. The Transamerica building in San Francisco (photo **C**) is a specially designed earthquake-proof building. The Shirahige-Higashi apartment complex (photo **D**) is a line of interlocking buildings containing 2300 flats, stretching along the Sumida River in Tokyo. It is meant to act as a firebreak should the mass of crowded, wooden houses.

C The Transamerica building, San Francisco

D

The Shirahige-Higashi apartment complex, Tokyo

behind it catch fire. Between the complex and the river there is a large area of open space - room to hold 60 000 evacuees, with enough food, water and medical supplies to last for a week.

- Avoid building on clay. During earthquakes water rises to the surface turning clay into mud, a process called liquefaction. Buildings literally sink into the 'quicksand' and collapse. This was why over 250 major buildings collapsed in Mexico City in 1985. The only buildings to collapse during the 1989 San Francisco earthquake were in the Marina district, built on reclaimed land. Vast areas of Tokyo are built either on river deltas (mud) or on land reclaimed from the sea. The foundations of numerous modern buildings being constructed on new land in Tokyo Bay reach down 40 metres to underlying rock.

How will earth movements cause landforms to change in the future?

The processes which cause crustal plates to move, and earthquakes and volcanic eruptions to occur, will obviously continue in the future. If plates go on moving in the same direction and at the same speed as at present, it is predicted that in 50 million years time the earth will look like map **E**. Such predictions are now done by computers and should, over time, become more accurate. It also means that new land will be created in some parts of the world (constructive margins) and lost elsewhere (destructive margins).

E Tomorrow's world – 50 million years from now

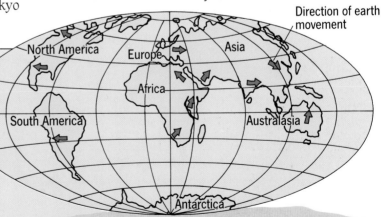

Direction of earth movement

Activities

1 a) Why is Tokyo in the worst possible site for a large modern city?
   b) What is being done to try to give the people of Tokyo (or San Francisco) advance warning of a future earthquake?
   c) What has been done to try to limit the effects of a large earthquake in Tokyo (or San Francisco)?

2 Map **E** shows how scientists predict the world will look in 50 million years time.
   a) Compared to today, list five changes in the shape and position of the continents.
   b) Give one reason for each of the five changes.

Summary

People can only try to predict when earth movements might occur, and to plan so that the effects of such hazards as earthquakes and volcanic eruptions are minimised. Processes, causing the movement of plates, will alter the shape and position of the continents as we know them today.

▶ *Where do most people in Britain live?* ◀

Map **A** shows the **population distribution** of Britain; it shows where most people in Britain live. It is obvious that people are not distributed evenly across the country. Some places are very crowded while others have very few inhabitants. The map uses **population density** to show how crowded different places are. Population density is the number of people living in a given area and is usually given as the number of people per square kilometre. Population density is found by dividing the total population of an area by the size of the area where they live. For example:

Population of the UK	57 237 000	= 234 per square kilometre
Area of the UK (sq km)	244 880	

Places that are crowded are described as **densely populated** and have a high population density. Places that have few people living there are described as **sparsely populated** and have a low population density.

When looking at population maps which show either distributions or densities, a geographer has to try to observe any notable patterns. Map **A** shows two patterns:

1 Areas with the highest densities appear to be in the south and east while those places with the lowest densities are more to the north and west.

2 The highest densities are in large **urban** areas (photo **B**) and the lowest densities are in **rural** areas (photo **C**).

Population density maps are simplified to show general patterns. As a result they cannot show local variations.

- In urban areas, population density tends to be higher in older inner city areas, rather than towards the edge of cities.
- In rural areas population density tends to be higher in larger market towns rather than places with dispersed farms.

A Population distribution of Britain

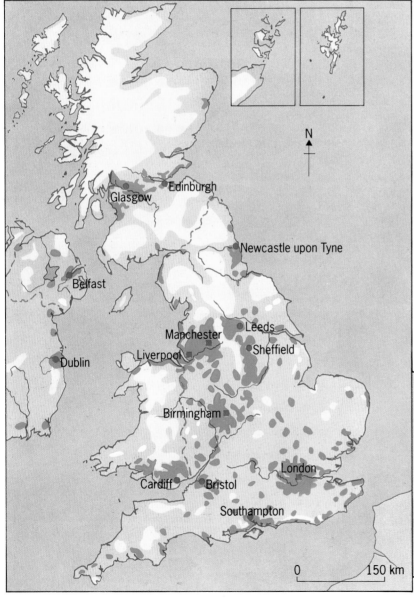

City	Population ('000s)	City	Population ('000s)
Glasgow	730	London	6378
Edinburgh	404	Bristol	367
Newcastle upon Tyne	617	Cardiff	273
Leeds	432	Southampton	192
Manchester	1669	Belfast	281
Liverpool	1060	Dublin	921
Birmingham	1400	Sheffield	445

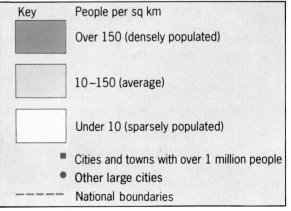

Key	People per sq km
	Over 150 (densely populated)
	10–150 (average)
	Under 10 (sparsely populated)
■	Cities and towns with over 1 million people
●	Other large cities
– – – – –	National boundaries

C The Roman Wall in the Northumberland National Park

B A street in London

Activities

1 What is the difference between population distribution and population density?

2 Give the population densities of the countries listed in table **D**.

3 Look at photos **B** and **C**. Try to give five reasons why the place in:
   a) Photo **B** is very crowded
   b) Photo **C** is sparsely populated.

4 Find a map of your home region or of the area around your school. Try to find possible patterns showing the distribution of population.
   a) Which places have most people living there? Give reasons for your answer.
   b) Which places have least people living there? Give reasons for your answer.
   c) Attempt to draw a simple sketch map to show the location of places which have:
      • a high population density
      • an average population density
      • a low population density.

D

Country	Population (thousands)	Area (thousand sq km)	Density
Brazil	150638	8511	
CIS	288595	22402	
France	56138	551	
India	853094	3512	
Japan	123460	378	
Kenya	24031	580	
USA	249224	9372	

Summary

The distribution of population is not even throughout Britain. Population densities are highest in the south and east and in urban areas, and lowest in the north and west and in rural areas.

▶ *Why are people distributed unevenly?* ◀

Map **A** is made up from many photos taken from satellites which orbit the earth. The frozen polar regions and snow covered mountain ranges stand out white. Forests are green, grasslands a browny-green and deserts a light brown. Red dots have been added to this map to show the distribution of population over the earth's surface. Although over 5000 million people live in the world, their distribution is very uneven. Most of them are crowded into a third of the land surface, leaving large areas almost uninhabited (graph **B**).

A

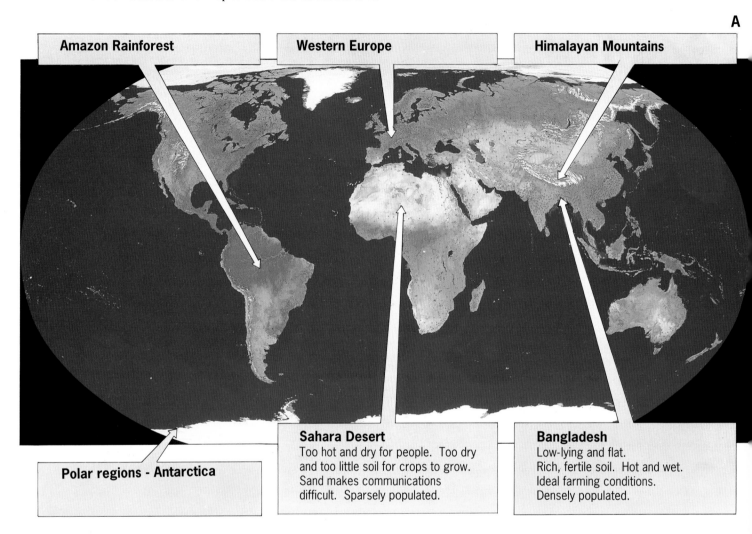

Amazon Rainforest

Western Europe

Himalayan Mountains

Polar regions - Antarctica

Sahara Desert
Too hot and dry for people. Too dry and too little soil for crops to grow. Sand makes communications difficult. Sparsely populated.

Bangladesh
Low-lying and flat.
Rich, fertile soil. Hot and wet.
Ideal farming conditions.
Densely populated.

There are many reasons for the different population patterns shown on map **A**. Some of these reasons discourage people from living in an area. These are **negative factors** and result in low population densities. Other reasons encourage people to live in an area. These are **positive factors** and create high population densities. Both the negative and positive factors can be sub-divided into **environmental** (physical) factors and **human** factors.

Negative factors causing low population densities
Environmental factors People are not naturally attracted to areas which have extremes of climate and which are either very cold, very hot, very dry or very wet. Relief discourages settlement especially in areas which have high, steep-sided mountains or are liable to experience volcanic eruptions and earthquakes. The dense coniferous and tropical rain forests have relatively few permanent inhabitants. There are also few people living in places where soils are too thin and lack sufficient humus for cultivation or which are experiencing increased erosion caused by deforestation and overgrazing. Areas which lack natural resources such as minerals or energy supplies are less likely to develop industries or to create many jobs. Settlements are less likely to grow in areas which lack a permanent water supply or are troubled by disease and pests.

Human factors Areas which are isolated or where it is difficult to construct and to maintain transport systems are more likely to be sparsely populated. This is also true of places which are a long way inland and away from coasts. Economic reasons for low population densities include a lack of wealth and insufficient technology to overcome the environmental factors listed above.

Political decisions by governments may also affect the distribution of population if there is a failure to invest money or to create new settlements with jobs and services.

Positive factors causing high population densities

These factors, mainly a reverse of the negative factors described above, have been summarised in diagram **C**.

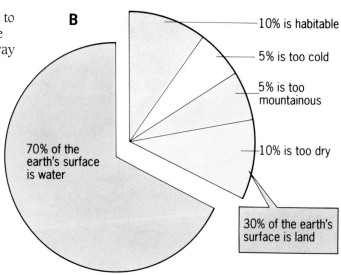

B

- 10% is habitable
- 5% is too cold
- 5% is too mountainous
- 10% is too dry
- 70% of the earth's surface is water
- 30% of the earth's surface is land

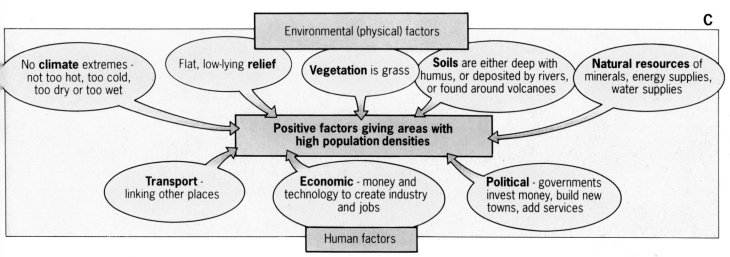

C

Environmental (physical) factors

- No **climate** extremes - not too hot, too cold, too dry or too wet
- Flat, low-lying **relief**
- **Vegetation** is grass
- **Soils** are either deep with humus, or deposited by rivers, or found around volcanoes
- **Natural resources** of minerals, energy supplies, water supplies

Positive factors giving areas with high population densities

- **Transport** - linking other places
- **Economic** - money and technology to create industry and jobs
- **Political** - governments invest money, build new towns, add services

Human factors

Activities

1 Map **A** names six parts of the world which have either a high or a low population density. Two of these areas have been described on the map. For each of the remaining four regions:
   a) state whether its population density is high or low;
   b) give as many reasons as possible why its population density is high or low.

2 Choose one area in the world with a high population density and one with a low population density. Choose **different** places to those named on map **A**. Copy and complete diagram **D** by adding information from your chosen areas.

3 What negative factors and what positive factors have affected the density of population in your home region?

D

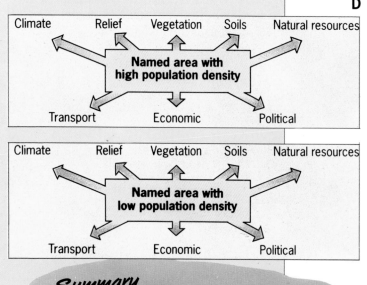

Climate Relief Vegetation Soils Natural resources

Named area with high population density

Transport Economic Political

Climate Relief Vegetation Soils Natural resources

Named area with low population density

Transport Economic Political

Summary

People are not spread evenly throughout the world. Negative factors discourage settlement giving low population densities, while positive factors encourage settlement, creating high population densities.

▶ *How do birth and death rates affect population growth?* ◀

The world's population is growing very rapidly. This is because the number of babies born each year is greatly exceeding the number of people who are dying. In 1992 the United Nations estimated that the total world's population of 1988 was likely to double by 2025 (graph **A**). During *each* year in that time, the population will rise by 97 million – the combined population of Britain and Spain in 1993. This rapid growth has been called 'a population explosion'. However, this explosion is not evenly distributed, as 97 per cent of the increase will take place in the three developing continents of Africa, Asia and Latin America.

The major reason for population changes, whether in a particular country or for the whole world, is the change in **birth rates** and **death rates**. The birth rate is the number of live babies born in a year for every 1000 people in the total population. The death rate is the number of people in every 1000 who die each year. The **natural increase** is the difference between the birth rate and the death rate. If the birth rate is higher then the total population will increase (diagram **B**). If the death rate is higher then the total population will decrease.

Birth rates and death rates for all countries change over periods of time. Through the study of many countries a **model** can be made to show population changes. This model is called the **demographic transition model**. A model is used to simplify difficult real world situations to make them easier to understand. The demographic transition model suggests that

population changes for all countries go through four stages. Diagram **C** shows these stages and gives some of the reasons why many of the less economically developed countries are in Stage 2, while the more economically developed countries have reached Stage 4. Recently several Western European countries appear to have reached a new and fifth stage where death rates are exceeding birth rates.

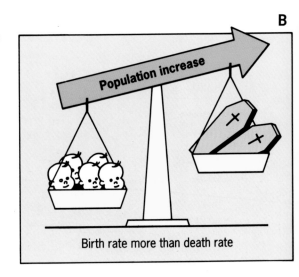

B

Birth rate more than death rate

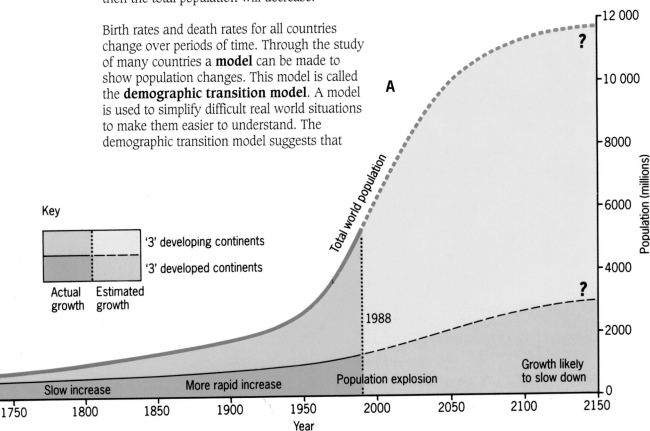

Key

'3' developing continents

'3' developed continents

Actual growth | Estimated growth

A

Total world population

1988

Population (millions)

Slow increase   More rapid increase   Population explosion   Growth likely to slow down

1750   1800   1850   1900   1950   2000   2050   2100   2150

Year

C

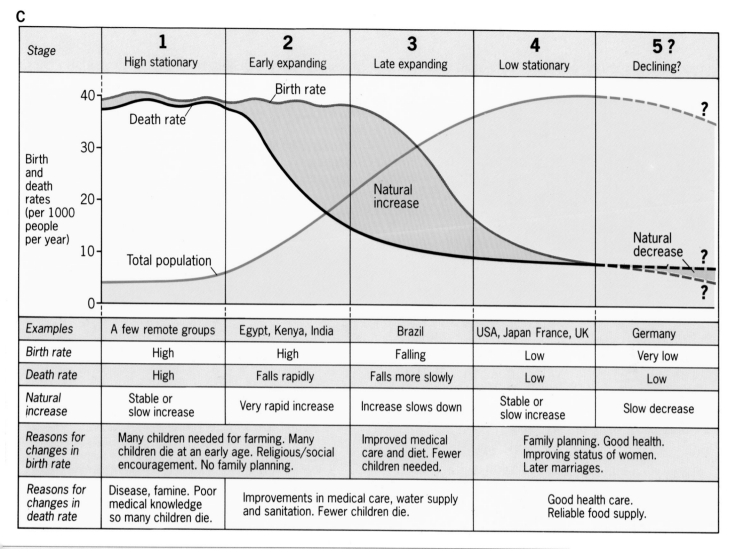

Stage	**1** High stationary	**2** Early expanding	**3** Late expanding	**4** Low stationary	**5 ?** Declining?
Examples	A few remote groups	Egypt, Kenya, India	Brazil	USA, Japan France, UK	Germany
Birth rate	High	High	Falling	Low	Very low
Death rate	High	Falls rapidly	Falls more slowly	Low	Low
Natural increase	Stable or slow increase	Very rapid increase	Increase slows down	Stable or slow increase	Slow decrease
Reasons for changes in birth rate	Many children needed for farming. Many children die at an early age. Religious/social encouragement. No family planning.		Improved medical care and diet. Fewer children needed.	Family planning. Good health. Improving status of women. Later marriages.	
Reasons for changes in death rate	Disease, famine. Poor medical knowledge so many children die.	Improvements in medical care, water supply and sanitation. Fewer children die.		Good health care. Reliable food supply.	

Activities

1 a) What was the world's population when you were born?
   b) What will it be on your 18th and 60th birthdays?
   c) What was the world's population in 1988?
   d) How many years will it take for that population to double?
   e) Complete diagram **D** to show how rapidly the world's population is increasing.

2 What is meant by each of the following terms:
   • birth rate
   • death rate
   • natural increase?

3 a) Name a developing country which you have studied.
   b) Why does it have a high birth rate?
   c) Why is its death rate still high but beginning to fall?
   d) Name a developed country which you have studied.
   e) Why does it have a low birth rate and a low death rate?
   f) In which stage of the demographic transition model are each of your chosen countries?

D

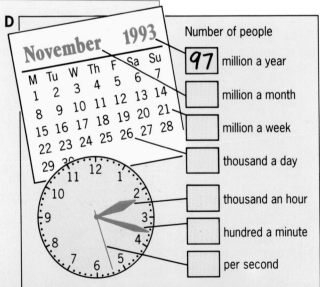

Number of people	
97	million a year
	million a month
	million a week
	thousand a day
	thousand an hour
	hundred a minute
	per second

Summary

Population growth depends upon changes in birth and death rates. Changes in a country's population seem to pass through several stages known as the demographic transition.

▶ *Why do birth and death rates differ?* ◀

It has already been suggested that birth rates, death rates and natural increases differ between developed and developing countries. Likewise, there are differences between **infant mortality rates** and **life expectancy**. Infant mortality is the number of children out of every 1000 born alive who die before they reach the age of one year. Life expectancy is the average number of years a person born in a country can expect to live. As table **A** shows, developing countries have high birth rates, high infant mortality rates, rapid population growth and a relatively short life expectancy. Due to high birth rates in developing countries most people in every 1000 are younger than 15 and there are relatively few elderly people. Death rates are high but appear to be low compared to the huge numbers living. As countries develop economically and become more wealthy this pattern is reversed.

A

Country (1992)	Birth rate	Death rate	Natural increase	Infant mortality rate	Life expectancy
Kenya	47	10	37	64	61
Bangladesh	41	14	27	108	53
India	31	10	21	88	62
Egypt	31	9	22	57	62
Brazil	26	8	18	57	66

Country (1992)	Birth rate	Death rate	Natural increase	Infant mortality rate	Life expectancy
USA	14	9	5	8	76
UK	14	12	2	8	76
France	13	10	3	7	77
Japan	12	8	4	5	79
Germany	11	12	-1	8	75

Differences in birth and death rates

Developing countries, e.g. India
Birth rates are high often because people want and need large families. The relatively short life expectancy is more likely to result from a lack of wealth.

Developed countries, e.g. UK
Birth rates are low often because people do not need many children and prefer small families. The longer life expectancy results from the greater amount of wealth which is available.

Why a high birth rate?   **Why a short life expectancy?**

We need many children:
• to help us work on the land and to carry wood and water,
• to care for us when we are ill or old and cannot work,
• because so many die from disease. Four of my eight children died before their first birthday.

Both my parents died when they were quite young. My mother died during a famine. My father caught cholera from dirty water. There was no hospital near and we could not afford medical care.

One child might get a job in the city and send us money

My religion forbids birth control

Having a big family increases my importance in the village.

Why a long life expectancy?   **Why a low birth rate?**

Both my parents are still alive. They live near to a doctor and a hospital. Their home has central heating. They are very comfortable.

Family planning controls the size of our family.

We only wanted two children and we are sure they will live a long life, free from disease.

We can afford to spend more money on our car, holidays and entertainment .

We have pensions for when we are old.

I wanted to return to my career and not stay at home.

B

C

How can birth rates be reduced?

The demographic transition model on page 67 shows death rates falling before birth rates. This suggests that birth rates are the harder of the two to lower. Yet it is essential that poorer countries, like India, do lower their birth rates (extract **D**). However, many of them seem a long way from imitating some of the methods which have proved to be successful in the better-off developed countries.

The United Nations state that there are two basic needs which must be accepted if birth rates are to be controlled:

1 To improve the status of women and to realise that they have the right (not accepted in many countries) to make the decision between having more children or birth control.

2 To provide further education, especially for women, on family planning.

A lesser, but still important, need is to try to reduce poverty. It was previously believed that high birth rates were a result of poverty. However, in those parts of the world where the status of women has been raised, there has been a decline in the birth rate even though there has been no obvious reduction in poverty (extract **D**).

D

Birth control in India

In the minute of time that a motorist has to wait for a red traffic light to change colour in Calcutta or Bombay, another 35 babies will have been born in India. In London the motorist might miss the green light waiting for a birth in Britain. Unless India can reduce its birth rate its population will exceed 2 billion, and that of China's, by 2035. India's population control efforts so far have failed. The aim was to have two children per family by the year 2000, but the figures so far are double that.

Social workers have found the best contraceptive not to be condoms, the Pill, or sterilisation, but female literacy. Couples living in high literacy states, especially those where girls have also had an education, tend to have only two children. In the more populous states where fewer people can read, families still have more than five children.

E

Summary

Developing countries have higher birth and infant mortality rates than developed countries. Birth rates may only fall when the status of women and the standard of education improves.

How do population structures differ?

The **population structure** shows the number of males and females within different age groups in the population. Information, ideally collected through a census, is plotted as a graph. Because of the traditional shape of the graph, and the information shown, it is commonly referred to as either an **age-sex** or **population pyramid**.

Population pyramids show:

- the total population divided into five-year age groups.
- the percentage of people in each of those age groups.
- the percentage of males and females in each age group.

- trends in the birth rate, death rate, infant mortality rate and life expectancy.
- the proportion of elderly and young people who are dependant upon those of working age – the economically active.
- the results of people migrating into or out of the region or country.

The pyramid is useful when trying to predict both short and long term population changes. Graph **A** shows how to interpret the population pyramid for the United Kingdom.

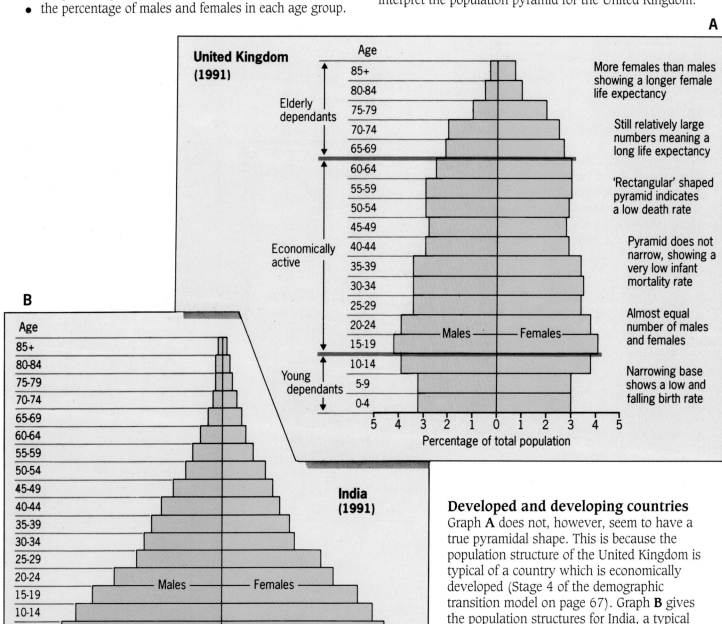

A

United Kingdom (1991)

More females than males showing a longer female life expectancy

Still relatively large numbers meaning a long life expectancy

'Rectangular' shaped pyramid indicates a low death rate

Pyramid does not narrow, showing a very low infant mortality rate

Almost equal number of males and females

Narrowing base shows a low and falling birth rate

B

India (1991)

Developed and developing countries

Graph **A** does not, however, seem to have a true pyramidal shape. This is because the population structure of the United Kingdom is typical of a country which is economically developed (Stage 4 of the demographic transition model on page 67). Graph **B** gives the population structures for India, a typical economically less developed country (Stage 2 of the demographic transition model).

Most Indian families are large. The wide base to the graph indicates a high birth rate and a rapidly growing population. The pyramid narrows rapidly, initially as a result of a high infant mortality rate and later due to a relatively short life expectancy. The shape of this graph is much closer to that of a true pyramid. India's population structure is typical of a developing country as it is 'bottom heavy' in contrast to the 'top heavy' population structure of a more developed country such as the UK.

C

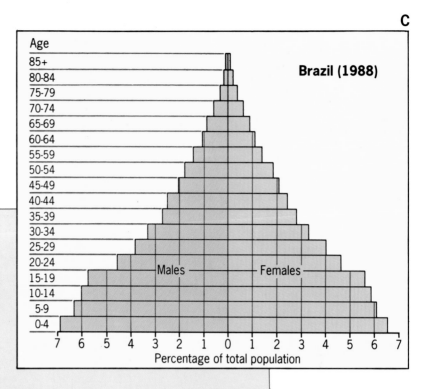

Brazil (1988)

Activities

1 Copy out table **E** and complete it by using information from graphs **C** and **D**.
   a) The answers in part **X** all need a percentage figure.
   b) For part **Y** put a tick in the correct column.

2 What would happen to the shape of Brazil's pyramid if there was a rapid decline in its:
   a) birth rate;
   b) death rate?

D

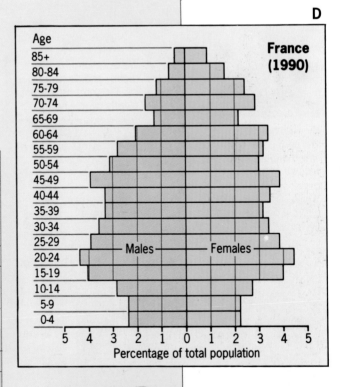

France (1990)

E

	France	Brazil
Part X		
% males aged 0–4	2.3	6.8
% females aged 0–4		
Total % aged 0–4		
Total % aged 0–14		
Total % aged 15–64		
Total % aged 65 and over		
Part Y		
Highest birth rate		
Fastest growing population (natural increase)		
Highest infant mortality rate		
Highest % living to middle age		
Lowest life expectancy		
Most people living over 65 years		
More economically developed country		

Summary

Population structures divide males and females into different age groups. Population pyramids show considerable differences in population structures between developed and developing countries.

▶ How can population structures differ within a country? ◀

Population structures vary between regions and towns within a country as well as differing between countries. These variations can have important effects upon local demands for particular services and facilities. It is therefore important to understand the present population structure of a place and to predict future changes if sufficient services and facilities are to be provided.

Look again at graph **A** on page 70. It refers to the **economically active** and to the **elderly and young dependants**. The economically active are those people in the 15 to 64 year age group. It is this group of people who usually earn most of the wealth for a town, region or country. Those people outside of this age group are referred to as the dependant population. The actual age limits are not particularly accurate as people aged 15 should still be at

school in the UK, women can retire before 65 and some people continue to work after they are 65. For planning purposes, however, it is assumed that people outside of the 15 to 64 year age group are dependent upon those within it. Problems arise in places where there is a large and growing number of either elderly or young dependants.

Places with many elderly dependants in the UK
Retired people form a high proportion of the population of counties and holiday resorts along the south coast of England. They settle here perhaps because the weather keeps them more healthy, it is relatively quiet for most of the year, or they remember the place from visits made when they were younger. However, their large numbers can create problems and needs. Some of these are illustrated in diagram **A**.

Places with many young dependants in the UK

Although, as we already have seen, Britain has a low birth rate, there are still places with a higher than average proportion of young families. These places are usually those with new industries which provide jobs, new houses and services. As such they attract young couples who will have young children. Areas with large numbers of young children will also have problems, although their needs will be different to those places which have an elderly population (diagram **B**).

B

We need more youth clubs to keep us out of trouble

Health Centre

The local primary school is very overcrowded, so teaching standards are falling

This is a main road with heavy traffic so there should be safe crossing places

We had to queue for ages before we saw the doctor

Midwives are rushed off their feet here

If I go back to my full-time job who will look after the children?

Newtown NURSERY

SORRY, NO VACANCIES

There are no safe play areas for small children

After school I go to my friend's house until my Mum gets home from work

Activities

1 Who are the:
   a) economically active,
   b) elderly dependants,
   c) young dependants?

2 Using diagram **A**, describe some of the problems facing places with a high proportion of elderly residents.

3 Using diagram **B**, describe some of the problems facing places with a high proportion of young families.

4 Look at graphs **C** and **D** showing population structures for two places in England.
   a) Give three differences between the two graphs.
   b) Which graph is for a holiday resort with many retired residents?
   c) Which graph is for a new town with many young families?

Summary

Population structures vary within a country. Some places have a high proportion of elderly residents while others have a high proportion of young families. Each place will have problems in providing adequate services and facilities.

C   **D**

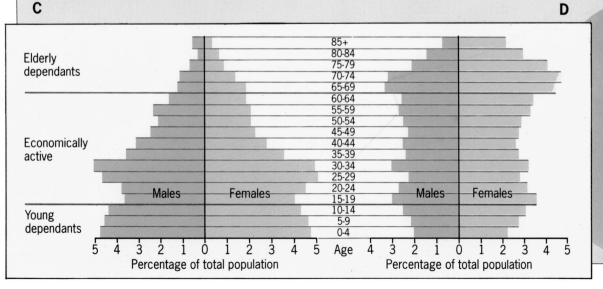

Elderly dependants

Economically active

Young dependants

| Males | Females | Age | Males | Females |

85+, 80-84, 75-79, 70-74, 65-69, 60-64, 55-59, 50-54, 45-49, 40-44, 35-39, 30-34, 25-29, 20-24, 15-19, 10-14, 5-9, 0-4

5 4 3 2 1 0 1 2 3 4 5 Age 4 3 2 1 0 1 2 3 4 5
Percentage of total population   Percentage of total population

▶ *Why are some places overpopulated?* ◀

People rely upon natural resources which are present in the environment in order to live. Natural resources include soils, plants, minerals, and supplies of energy and water. However, like people, their distribution is not evenly spread over the earth's surface. Places where the number of people living there outweigh the availability of resources are said to be **overpopulated**. Overpopulation can result from either:

- an increase in population, perhaps due to a high birth rate or large numbers of people moving into the area;
- a decrease in resources, perhaps resulting from soil erosion or the using up of a mineral such as iron ore.

Overpopulation is not always confined to, or found in, places which have a high population density. Hong Kong, and parts of Japan and the UK have over 1000 people per square kilometre yet are not considered to be overpopulated. In comparison, countries like Sudan and Somalia with fewer than 15 people per square kilometre are overpopulated. Overpopulation is, however, more likely to occur in developing rather than in developed countries.

The following fact files (**A**, **B** and **C**) illustrate why three very different environments all suffer from overpopulation. The problem with people does not lie in their total numbers but in the amount of resources which they use.

Fact file A: Sudan, Somalia and Ethiopia

- High birth rates - more people to feed.
- Soils originally good, but have been over-used to try to produce more crops. Soil is then eroded by rain and wind.
- Trees have been cut down to be used as fuel and to allow more room for crops. Overgrazing by animals. Both have caused an increase in desertification.
- Less rain in last 20 years. Drought has led to disease, malnutrition and famine.
- No minerals and few energy supplies.
- Lack of money to develop or buy resources.
- Civil wars have destroyed resources and increased the number of refugees.

As the birth rate and total population increase then the few natural resources are rapidly being used up.

Refugee camp on the Somalia/Ethiopia border

Fact file B: cities in developing countries

As the birth rate and total population increase and the few natural resources in rural areas are used up, then people have to move to large cities. Within these cities there will be:
- a decrease in food supplies;
- a shortage of houses and jobs;
- inadequate supplies of fresh water and electricity and methods of disposing of sewage and rubbish;
- improvements in health care, but the numbers of people arriving in the cities outpace the building of hospitals and schools;
- congested and inadequate transport.

There is neither the money nor the resources to keep pace with the increase in population.

Calcutta, India

Fact file C: Tokyo Bay region of Japan

It is misleading to think that overpopulation only occurs in developing countries.

- Japan is the richest country, and Tokyo the richest city in the world. There is plenty of money to buy and use natural resources.
- 25 million people live around Tokyo Bay. Central Tokyo has the highest population density in the world - over 20 000 people per square kilometre. There is a huge demand for resources such as timber, minerals, energy supplies and fish.
- Tokyo has enough jobs, food and services but not enough space. Houses are very small in size and are packed closely together. There are few areas of open space.
- The city is growing outwards, using up land once used for farming and recreation.

The Japanese are trying to conserve their own natural resources but are rapidly using up resources from other countries.

Ginza area of Tokyo

Key
Developing countries
Developed countries

Percentage graph with categories: World's population, Use of world's resources, Use of energy, Food consumed, Waste produced

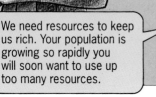

We need to use more resources if we are to develop and get richer. At present it is you in the developed countries who are using up all our resources.

We need resources to keep us rich. Your population is growing so rapidly you will soon want to use up too many resources.

D

Activities

1 What is meant by the term 'overpopulation'?

2 Choose two areas of the world which are overpopulated. One should have a low population density, the other a high population density. For each one draw a star diagram to show why it is overpopulated.

3 Refer to diagram **D** and answer these questions.
   a) Why are developing countries more likely to experience overpopulation than developed countries?
   b) Is it a rapid growth in population or a rapid use of resources which leads to overpopulation?

Summary

Overpopulation is when there are too many people for the resources available. It can occur in countries which either have a rapid population growth or which have economies that use up many resources.

75

▶ *What are the causes and effects of migration?* ◀

Migration is the movement of people from one place to another to live or to work. Sometimes this movement may only be to the next town or only for a short period of time. Sometimes the movement may be to a different country and the move can be permanent. Migration can either be **voluntary** or it can be **forced**. Voluntary migration is when people choose to move. This is usually because of the 'pull' or attraction of a better quality of life elsewhere, or of a higher standard of living or greater personal freedom. Forced migration is when people have no choice and are made to move. They can be 'pushed' out of a place because of natural disasters or to avoid religious and political persecutions.

Migration of Jews into Israel

Jews and Palestinians lived in this part of the world long before the arrival of the Ancient Greeks and Romans. By Ancient Greek times many Jews had become involved in trade and commerce, and chose to migrate to other places surrounding the Mediterranean Sea. During Roman times the Jews were forced to move out of their capital of Jerusalem and were dispersed all over the then known world.

Following their persecution in Europe in the 1880s, several thousand Jews returned to a land settled by Palestinian Arabs. In 1947 the United Nations voted, despite opposition from Arab countries, to divide Palestine into Arab and Jewish states. Since the creation of Israel in 1948, many Jews have returned (figures **A** and **B**).

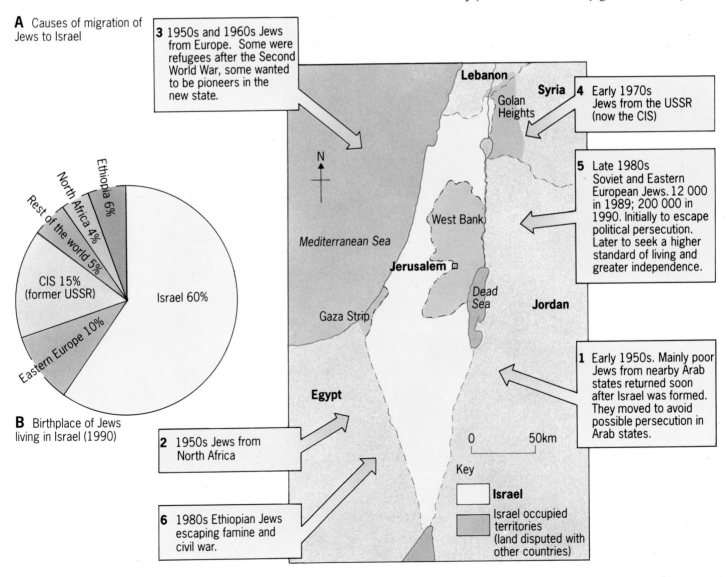

A Causes of migration of Jews to Israel

3 1950s and 1960s Jews from Europe. Some were refugees after the Second World War, some wanted to be pioneers in the new state.

4 Early 1970s Jews from the USSR (now the CIS)

5 Late 1980s Soviet and Eastern European Jews. 12 000 in 1989; 200 000 in 1990. Initially to escape political persecution. Later to seek a higher standard of living and greater independence.

1 Early 1950s. Mainly poor Jews from nearby Arab states returned soon after Israel was formed. They moved to avoid possible persecution in Arab states.

2 1950s Jews from North Africa

6 1980s Ethiopian Jews escaping famine and civil war.

Lebanon
Syria
Golan Heights
West Bank
Mediterranean Sea
Jerusalem
Dead Sea
Jordan
Gaza Strip
Egypt

0   50km

N

Key

Israel

Israel occupied territories (land disputed with other countries)

Ethiopia 6%
North Africa 4%
Rest of the world 5%
CIS 15% (former USSR)
Israel 60%
Eastern Europe 10%

B Birthplace of Jews living in Israel (1990)

How has this migration affected the Jews?

We have got our own country but:
- We have been attacked several times by our Arab neighbours. We have to spend a lot of money defending ourselves.
- The large number of immigrants means a big demand for new settlements. We have had to build some of these in the occupied territories (map **A**).
- As our population increases so too does the need for schools, hospitals and other services. This increases our cost of living and causes high inflation.
- Many recent Jewish immigrants are from Ethiopia. They have large families, do not speak much Hebrew and have limited skills.
- With so many migrants it is becoming harder for people to find jobs.

C

How has this migration affected the Palestinian Arabs?

- We have lived in this area as long as the Jews. It is our home.
- Over 1.75 million of us lost our homes. We have become refugees in places like the Gaza Strip and the West Bank. Many of us were born and have lived all our lives in camps.
- The Israelis are building new settlements in areas where we were meant to live.
- The land they were given was the best for farming. Where we live there are very few job opportunities. Our settlements do not have many services.

D

Activities

1. a) What is migration?
   b) What is the difference between voluntary and forced migration?
   c) Complete table **E** by giving four examples of voluntary migration and four examples of forced migration.

E

	Voluntary migration	Forced migration
1		
2		
3		
4		

2. a) Using diagram **A** give three reasons why many Jews have migrated back to Israel.
   b) Using diagrams **C** and **D** give three effects of this movement upon:
      i) Jews already living in Israel,
      ii) Palestinian Arabs living in the occupied territories.

3. People are always moving. Which groups of people have moved into and out of your home town or region in the last few years? Why have these groups moved?

Summary

Migration is the movement of people. It can be voluntary or forced. One large recent migration has been the voluntary return of Jews into the state of Israel and the forced movement of Palestinians out of Israel.

▶ *Why do ethnic groups live together?* ◀

Ethnic means a group of people who have similar characteristics. These characteristics may include language, colour, religion and nationality. Usually ethnic groups will have migrated into a place where they may form a minority within the total population. Nearly all the world's countries and cities have several ethnic groups and minorities. These groups are rarely, if ever, spread out evenly. They tend to concentrate in certain parts of a country or areas within a city. Although in most places these concentrations are voluntary, in the case of South Africa they were forced due to the government policy of **apartheid**.

Ethnic groupings in South Africa

Under apartheid all South Africans were classified as belonging to one of four ethnic groups (table **A**).

The South African Government's Group Areas Act of 1950 (repealed in 1990) 'allowed' white, coloured and Asian communities to live in cities, but each group was given different parts of the city in which they had to live. Buffer zones, at least 100 metres wide, were then created to try to prevent contact between the various ethnic groups. The whites were given the best residential areas which were usually near to centres of commerce and

A

Ethnic group	Total population	Came mainly from	Language
Black	25 million (74%)	Southern Africa	Bantu
White	5 million (14%)	Netherlands (3 million) Britain (2 million)	Afrikaans, English
Coloured	3 million (9%)	Black and white mixed marriages	English
Asian	1 million (3%)	India	English

industry (map **C** and photo **D**). Black people were treated differently. Those without jobs were forced to move out of cities and resettled, often over 100 kilometres away, on one of ten tribal 'homelands' (map **B**). These homelands take up only 13 per cent of South Africa's land yet they hold 75 per cent of its total population. The homelands offer very limited opportunity for work as they lack natural resources.

Black people who had been born in cities or had worked for the same employer for more than ten years were moved to 'townships' on

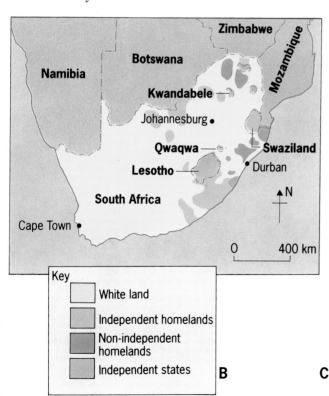

Key

- White land
- Independent homelands
- Non-independent homelands
- Independent states

B

C

5km	Distance from CBD
⤙	Main roads
▨	Commerce and industry
▨	High land
☐	Whites
▨	Shanty areas
☐	Improved black
☐	Coloured
☐	Asian

the edges of urban areas. These townships are often little more than **shanty** settlements (photo **E**). Some shanty settlements, such as parts of Crossroads (map **C**), have been bulldozed by the government and then partly replaced by rows of identical bungalows. The bungalows may have four rooms and a toilet, but they lack many other basic amenities. Other flattened areas await the building of new houses and here the inhabitants have only tents in which to live. As the townships are located far away from white residential districts and jobs, thousands of black people have to commute long distances each day to reach their places of work. Map **C** shows the main housing areas for the different groups in Cape Town.

Apartheid ended officially in 1993, but it will take time for peoples' attitudes and South African society to fully reflect this change.

D White residential area in Cape Town

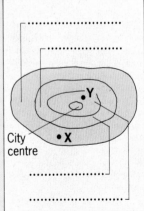

E Khayelitsha township in Cape Town

Activities

1 What is meant by the terms:
   a) ethnic group,
   b) apartheid?

2 The graphs in diagram **F** show the numbers within each ethnic group in South Africa's three largest cities.
   a) Why do you think there are most
      i) Black people in Johannesburg;
      ii) White and coloured people in Cape Town;
      iii) Asians in Durban?
   b) Is a shanty settlement more likely to be found at **X** or **Y** on diagram **G**?

3 Make a copy of diagram **G**. On it label the places where you would expect to find each of the following:
   White residents – Black townships – Asian and coloured residents – Commerce and industry

4 Photos **D** and **E** show two residential areas in Cape Town.
   a) List four differences between the two places.
   b) What do these photos suggest about the quality of life in the two places?

F

South Africa: 3%, 8%, 14%, 75%

Johannesburg: 2%, 5%, 32%, 61%

Cape Town: 1%, 12%, 53%, 34%

Durban: 12%, 33%, 6%, 49%

Key
Black	Coloured
White	Asian

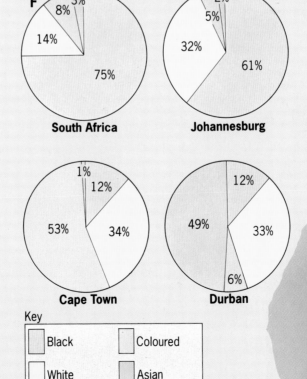

G

City centre • Y • X

Summary

Ethnic means a group of people sharing a common language, colour of skin, religion or nationality. In South Africa different groups of people were forced to live away from other groups although this is now changing.

Can you remember map skills?

A settlement is a place where people live. It can be as small as an isolated farm or a hamlet, or as large as a city or conurbation. Carlisle is the main settlement on the Ordnance Survey (OS) map used on pages 82 and 83. It is surrounded by many smaller settlements. This OS map will be referred to several times in this and in later units ... so first of all, 'Can you remember your map skills ?'

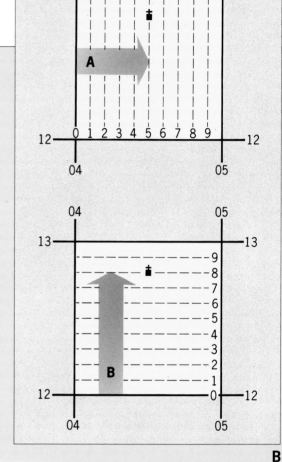

B

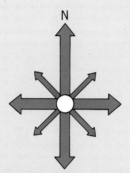

Eight point compass

A

Activities

1 Directions
a) Make a copy of diagram **A**. Complete it by adding the missing seven compass directions.
b) In which direction would you be going if you left the centre of Carlisle travelling along these roads?
   i)   A7
   ii) A69
   iii) A6
   iv) A595(T).

2 Grid (map) references and map symbols
a) Name the ten map symbols used in grid square 3650.
b) What is found at each of the following grid references?
   i)   467547
   ii) 329591
   iii) 417583
   iv) 388580
c) What is the six-figure grid reference for each of the following places?
   i)   Carlisle railway station
   ii) Junction 42 of the M6
   iii) The public house in Thursby.
d) Complete table **C** by choosing the occupation (job) from the following list to match the correct map reference: teacher, factory worker, farmer, doctor, forestry worker, chef.

3 Distance
How far is it:
a) From the western edge of the map to the eastern edge
b) Along the A595(T) road from the Cardewlees road junction to Newby Cross
c) By railway from Carlisle mainline station to the northern edge of the map?
d) Along the whole length of the B6263 from the A69 to the M6?

Map reference	Occupation
355532	
432538	
406563	
461587	
365520	
387537	

C

Activities

4 Following and describing a route

a) Follow the route described opposite. Choose the correct answer from the choice given in brackets. Start at Carlisle College (404560).

b) The Cumbria Cycle Way joins the map at 300593 (near Dykesfield) and leaves it at 480599. It is named **four** times as it crosses the map. Describe carefully the route followed by the cycle way. Your description should include:
distances - directions - grid references - important physical features seen or crossed - important buildings seen.

5 Relief

Relief can either be the shape of the land surface or the height of the land surface above sea-level.

a) i) Is the land higher in grid square 4650 or in 4556?
   ii) Is the slope of the land steeper in grid square 4753 or 4458?

b) Copy out and complete table **D** by matching the following relief descriptions with the correct grid reference:
60 metres contour small hill - flat - spot height of 34 metres - steep - triangulation point of 78 metres.

c) Diagram **E** shows three methods of showing height one of which, layer colouring, is not used on OS. maps. What is layer colouring?

6 Settlement patterns

Diagram **F** shows three settlement patterns which you should already have studied. Using the OS map, say which of the three patterns is shown by the following places:
i)   Carlisle
ii) Great Orton (3254)
iii) Thursby (3250)
iv) Woodlands (3155)
v)   Scotby (4454)
vi) Rockcliffe (3561)
vii) Burthwaite Hill (4150)

'Travel east along the (A6/A69). Cross over a (river/railway line). After (3/5)kms from the College turn left at the big roundabout which is junction (43/44) of the (M1/M6). Continue (north/south) crossing over a (railway/river) and going under (3/5) (rail/road) bridges. At motorway junction (43/44), which is at map reference (395599/599395), turn (north/south) towards Carlisle. Travel along the (A6/A7). After (3/5 km) a (main/'B') class road joins from the (south-west/north-east). Cross over the River (Eden/Thames) and visit the Leisure Centre.'

Map reference	Relief description	**D**
4458		
4753		
4652		
3254		
3552		
4161		

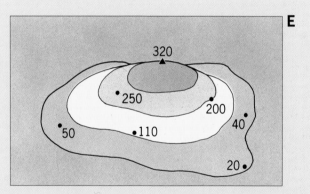

E

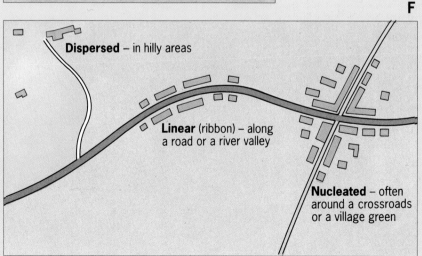

F

Dispersed – in hilly areas

Linear (ribbon) – along a road or a river valley

Nucleated – often around a crossroads or a village green

Parts of the OS maps numbers 85 and 86

Scale 1:50 000

0   1   2 km

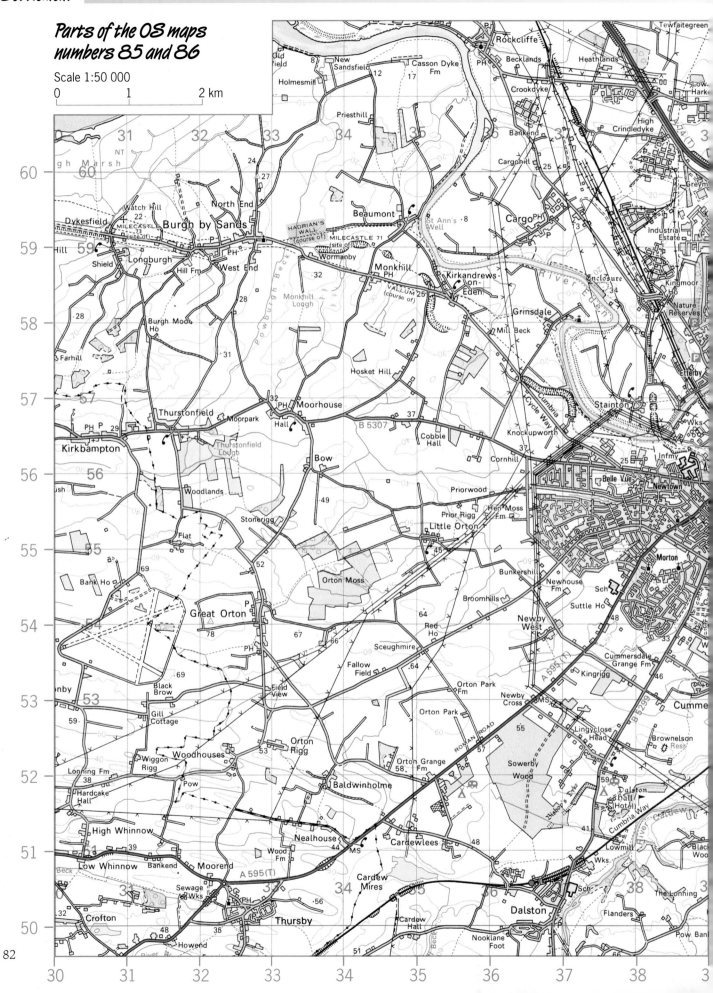

How were locations for early settlements chosen?

The location and growth of an individual settlement depended upon its **site** and **situation**. The site was the actual place where people decided to locate their settlement. The growth of that settlement then depended upon its situation in relation to natural resources (physical features) and other settlements (human features).

What did early settlers consider to be important when choosing a site? They needed to:
- be near a reliable supply of water
- be away from marshy areas or places which flooded
- be able to defend themselves in case of attack
- be near to materials for building their homes
- be able to feed themselves
- have access to other places
- have shelter from bad weather
- have a supply of fuel for cooking and heating.

Although the ideal site needed more than one of these **location factors**, it was unlikely to have them all. For example, while a hilltop site may have been excellent for defence, it probably would not have had a supply of water nor would it have been sheltered from strong winds. Diagram **A** shows several factors that influence the choice of site for a settlement.

A

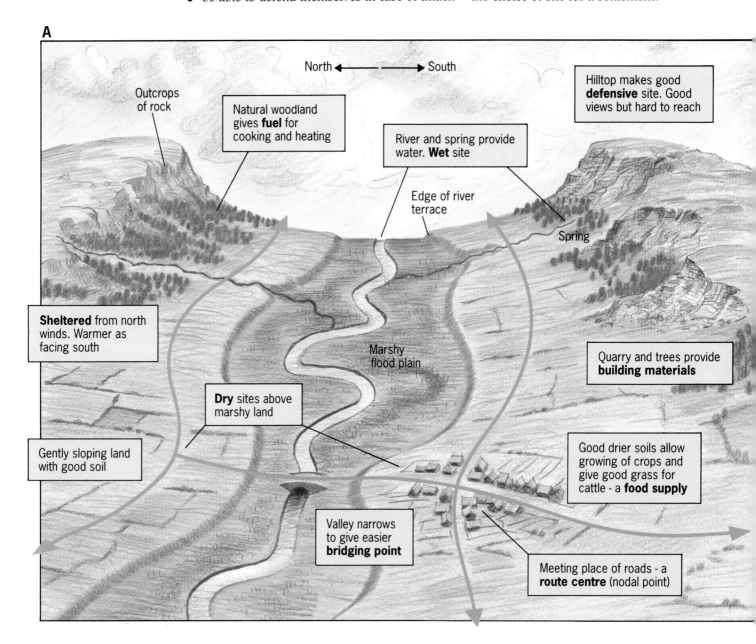

North ← → South

Outcrops of rock

Natural woodland gives **fuel** for cooking and heating

River and spring provide water. **Wet** site

Hilltop makes good **defensive** site. Good views but hard to reach

Edge of river terrace

Spring

Sheltered from north winds. Warmer as facing south

Marshy flood plain

Quarry and trees provide **building materials**

Dry sites above marshy land

Gently sloping land with good soil

Good drier soils allow growing of crops and give good grass for cattle - a **food supply**

Valley narrows to give easier **bridging point**

Meeting place of roads - a **route centre** (nodal point)

In the years since the settlement was founded it is likely to have grown in size and developed into a different shape. Several of the early factors are less important today, for example water is brought to our homes by pipe and marshy land can be drained. Even so, several of the original location factors may still bevisible not only when visiting a place but also when studying an OS map. Diagram **B** is an **annotated** or labelled sketch map showing how the site and location of a town is related to physical and human features. The sketch map, which is for Carlisle, has been taken from the 1:50 000 OS map on pages 82 and 83.

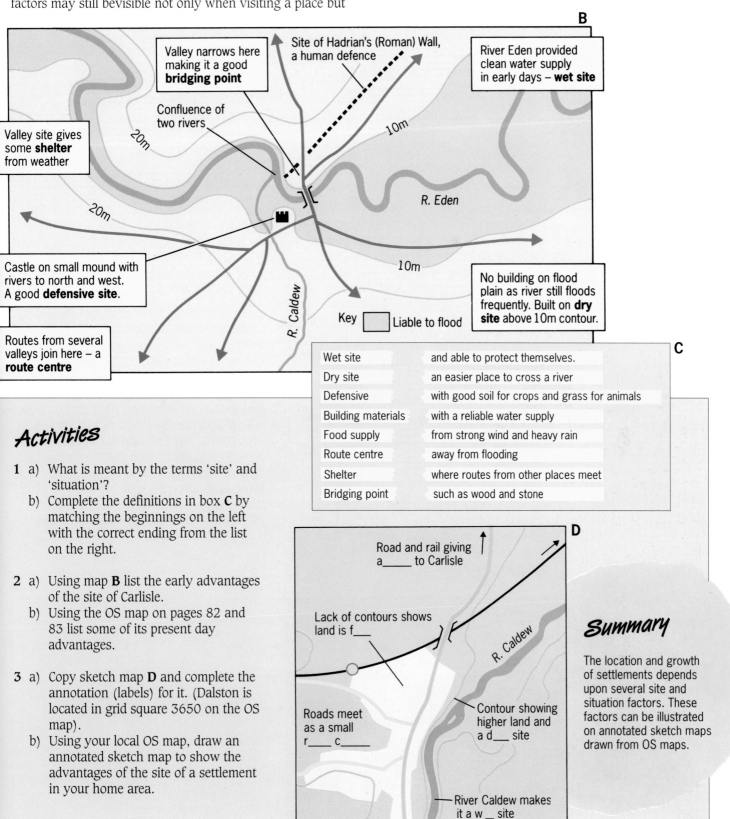

B

Valley narrows here making it a good **bridging point**

Site of Hadrian's (Roman) Wall, a human defence

River Eden provided clean water supply in early days – **wet site**

Confluence of two rivers

Valley site gives some **shelter** from weather

20m

10m

R. Eden

20m

R. Caldew

Castle on small mound with rivers to north and west. A good **defensive site**.

10m

No building on flood plain as river still floods frequently. Built on **dry site** above 10m contour.

Routes from several valleys join here – a **route centre**

Key ▢ Liable to flood

C

Wet site	and able to protect themselves.
Dry site	an easier place to cross a river
Defensive	with good soil for crops and grass for animals
Building materials	with a reliable water supply
Food supply	from strong wind and heavy rain
Route centre	away from flooding
Shelter	where routes from other places meet
Bridging point	such as wood and stone

Activities

1 a) What is meant by the terms 'site' and 'situation'?
   b) Complete the definitions in box **C** by matching the beginnings on the left with the correct ending from the list on the right.

2 a) Using map **B** list the early advantages of the site of Carlisle.
   b) Using the OS map on pages 82 and 83 list some of its present day advantages.

3 a) Copy sketch map **D** and complete the annotation (labels) for it. (Dalston is located in grid square 3650 on the OS map).
   b) Using your local OS map, draw an annotated sketch map to show the advantages of the site of a settlement in your home area.

D

Road and rail giving a_____ to Carlisle

Lack of contours shows land is f___

R. Caldew

Roads meet as a small r____ c____

Contour showing higher land and a d___ site

River Caldew makes it a w _ site

Summary

The location and growth of settlements depends upon several site and situation factors. These factors can be illustrated on annotated sketch maps drawn from OS maps.

85

What are the effects of urban growth in Britain?

A

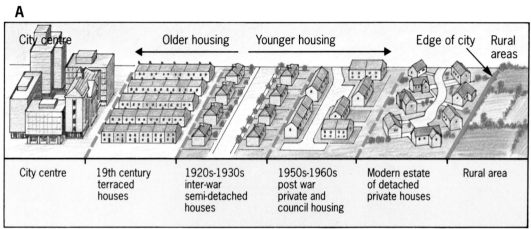

| City centre | 19th century terraced houses | 1920s-1930s inter-war semi-detached houses | 1950s-1960s post war private and council housing | Modern estate of detached private houses | Rural area |

B

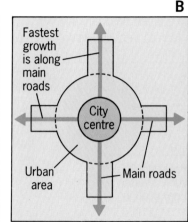

The sites of most towns in England and Wales were chosen by the Romans. By the beginning of the nineteenth century some 20 per cent of Britain's population lived in towns and cities. Since then, beginning with the Industrial Revolution in the early nineteenth century, people have moved to towns in increasing numbers. Today, 93 per cent of Britain's residents are urban dwellers.

This urban growth has had four important effects:

1 As towns have grown outwards this means that the oldest houses and buildings are near to the city centre and the newest properties are near to the urban boundary (diagram **A**).

2 Urban growth has been most rapid along main roads leading out of the city (diagram **B**). This process began with the development of public transport (horse-drawn buses and tram cars), and accelerated as people have turned increasingly to using their own private transport.

3 The ideal commercial sites are those in the city centre. This initially led to competition for these prime city centre sites which in turn pushed up the price of land (diagram **C**). Land values decrease rapidly with distance from the city centre.

4 As the cost of land decreases and the quality of the environment improves with distance from the city centre then many new commercial enterprises and housing developments are taking place on sites on the edge of the city (diagram **D**). This means that towns and cities are continuing to grow outwards, a process called **urban sprawl**. This growth has had, and is still having, a considerable effect upon the surrounding rural areas. Not only is good agricultural land being built upon and lost, but nearby villages are increasing in size and changing in character as they become **suburbanised**.

C

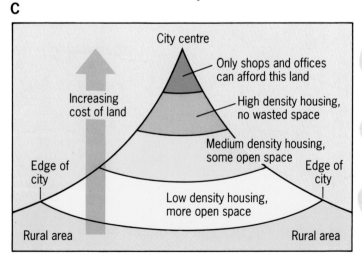

D

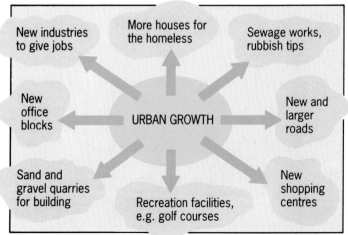

Suburbanised villages near Carlisle

Turn again to the OS map on pages 82 and 83. Until recently Scotby (4454), Wetheral (4654), Rockcliffe (3561), Dalston (3650) and Thursby (3250) were all quiet villages. Like many other similar settlements surrounding large urban areas in Britain, each village had its own church and shop (photos **E** and **F**). They were self-contained with most of the inhabitants having jobs in or near to the village. Recently places such as Scotby have attracted wealthy urban workers and retired people who see the village as providing a quieter environment and an improved quality of life. Large new expensive housing estates have been built (photo **G**). Although some services have been improved (e.g. Wetheral has had its railway station reopened and Rockcliffe has had its village shop enlarged), the rural appearance of the villages has changed. Not only do they look more like an extension of the suburbs of towns, they increasingly become **commuter villages**. A commuter village is a place where people who work in nearby towns live. The local community is swamped by newcomers and quite often is split into two groups. It is difficult to accommodate the greater number of vehicles both of residents and tourists on local narrow roads.

E

F

G

Activities

1 Complete diagram **H** by putting the following labels in the correct places:
oldest housing – newest housing – rapid growth along main roads – highest land values – cheaper land values – urban sprawl – suburbanised village.

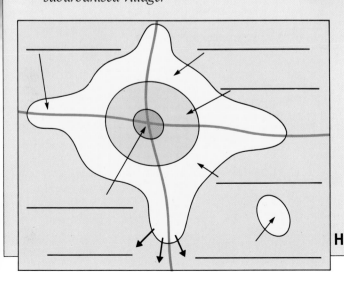

H

2 a) What is 'urban sprawl' and a 'suburbanised village'?
b) Why does urban sprawl occur?
c) Make a list of differences in a village and its inhabitants **before** and **after** it became suburbanised.

Summary

There is a pattern to the growth of towns. Urban growth affects nearby agricultural land use and rural communities.

What is a settlement hierarchy?

A **settlement hierarchy** is when settlements are put into order based upon their size or the services which they provide for people. A settlement hierarchy can be produced using three different methods:

1 Population size – the larger the settlement the fewer there will be of them.

2 Distance apart – the larger the settlement the further it will be from other large settlements.

3 Range and number of services – the larger the settlement the more services it will provide.

These methods, and the settlement hierarchy, have been summarised on diagram **A**. Note that the figures quoted are given for comparisons to be made and are not actual figures.

A

SETTLEMENT IN THE UK

Hierarchy	Distance apart (km)	Population size	Services (non-shopping)
One capital	—	Over 5 000 000	Government offices; several universities; main line railway stations; international airport; large, specialist hospitals; national events
Two or three conurbations		Up to 1 000 000	
Several cities	100	Up to 500 000	County hall; Cathedral; luxury hotel; university; many cinemas; theatres; hospitals; main railway station; several football teams
Many large towns	50	Up to 100 000	Small hospital; large restaurants; hotels; cinema and small theatre; several secondary schools; large bus and railway stations; large football team
Hundreds of small towns	20	Up to 20 000	Town hall; doctor; several churches/chapels; several public houses; cafes and restaurants; small secondary school; railway station; bus station; football team
Thousands of villages	7	Up to 1 000	Village hall; church; public house; small primary school
Several thousand hamlets	2	Up to 20	Public telephone

N.B. All places in the hierarchy have all the services of the settlements below them

Activities

B

1 Find the seven places named in table **B** on the OS map on pages 82 and 83. Using map evidence only, list the services found in each settlement. Complete table **B** (the first settlement has been done for you).

2 What other services may the settlements have which are not shown by symbols on the map?

Settlement	List of services provided	Total number	Type of settlement
Great Orton	Post office, public house	2	Village
Dalston			
Thursby			
Rockcliffe			
Wetheral			
Moorhouse			
Carlisle			

Is there a hierarchy of shopping centres of different sizes?

Shops can also be placed into a hierarchy based upon the services they provide. At the bottom of the hierarchy are small shops selling low order, convenience goods which are needed daily, such as food and newspapers. At the top are shops selling high order, specialist goods bought less frequently, such as furniture and video recorders. The same three methods used to produce the settlement hierarchy can also be applied to shops.

1 Population size – the larger the settlement the greater the number of high order shops.

2 Distance apart – the larger the shopping centre the further it will be to other large centres.

3 Range of services – the larger the shopping centre the more services it will provide.

These methods, and the shopping hierarchy, are summarised on diagram **C**.

C

SHOPPING IN THE UK				
Hierarchy	Distance apart (km)	Types of shop	Goods sold	Frequency of visits
Major shopping centre Several central covered centres Several suburban and edge-of-city centres		All major national and some international chain and department stores	Highest order, specialist, luxury and comparison goods (top furniture and fashions)	Yearly
One covered area in city centre Many shopping streets Several edge-of-city centres	100	Large national chain stores, department stores, several hypermarkets	High order, increasingly specialist (fashion, jewellery)	Monthly
Several shopping streets One or two edge-of-city centres	50	Large chain stores, hypermarkets	Middle order, some specialist and comparison shops (clothes, books)	Weekly
One main shopping street and market	20	Small chain stores, superstores	Mainly low order - more volume and a bigger range	Two or three times per week
One village shop	7	Village shop, post office	Low order, convenience (bread, newspapers)	Daily
None	2	(Mobile shop)	(Meat, fish, groceries)	Weekly

N.B. All shopping centres in hierarchy have all the services of the centres below them

3 a) What are the differences between low order and high order shopping centres?
  b) Why are there many more lower order shopping centres than higher order centres?
  c) Name the nearest low order and the nearest high order shopping centre to your school.

Summary

Settlements can be placed in order in a hierarchy based on their size and the services which they provide. The same concept can be applied to account for the distribution of shopping centres of different sizes.

What are the benefits and problems of urban growth?

Cities in developed countries

Many cities in North-west Europe and the north-east of North America grew as a result of the Industrial Revolution. Their attraction was the large number of jobs available in industries such as steel and textiles. The trend for these cities to grow continued until the late twentieth century when the problems of living there began to outweigh the earlier advantages.

What were the earlier advantages?

People moved into cities because they believed there were:

- more and better paid jobs, although many were unskilled;
- more and better quality housing, although much of it was very high density;
- better transport facilities, and a chance to live nearer to their place of work;
- better services available, such as education and health care;
- more reliable food supplies, and a greater range of shops;
- more social and cultural amenities, such as libraries, sporting events and concerts.

What are the present day problems: a case study of New York?

By the 1960s New York had become the largest city in the world. It attracted migrants from many parts of Europe as well as from less developed countries. Its tall office blocks, numerous and often expensive shops, and its glamorous night life made it seem a very prosperous place in which to live and work (photos **A** and **B**). But to most of its inhabitants, present day New York has a different side, a side of ghettos, poverty and violence. Those who can move out do. Those who cannot find themselves trapped in what has become known as the '**vicious circle of poverty**' (diagram **C**).

Housing and urban decay The inner city areas of New York were built over 100 years ago. These tall tenement blocks have suffered from years of neglect (photo **E**). Many still lack modern amenities such as hot water, individual toilets and garages. Most are rented, but as rents rise many become unoccupied and vandalised. Housing density is highest in the ghettos which are the homes for the poorest members of the community - single-parent

families, ethnic minorities, the unskilled and the unemployed. The number of people living in shelters for the homeless or living rough on the streets is far higher than in Britain. There is very little open space and many shops are barred up with iron shutters.

A New York skyline

B
World Trade
Tower, New York

Ethnic divisions According to US census categories there are two large groups ('White' and 'Black') and three smaller ones (American Indians, Asians and others). One large group, the Spanish speakers or Hispanics, is not listed as theirs is a language rather than a racial difference (graph **D**). While the mixture of ethnic groups can be seen as a positive feature, it often results in tension and injustice. There is a strong ethnic housing segregation with most Whites and a small but increasing number of African-Americans living in the suburbs, and most Hispanics and the majority of African-Americans living in inner city ghettos.

Unemployment and crime These are major problems in New York. There are over 1.5 million unemployed, mostly non-Whites living in ghettos. As the number of unskilled jobs becomes fewer, more people have to rely on 'public relief' which is a social security payment. New York has some of the highest crime rates in the world, with gang warfare, street violence, subway muggings, burglaries and drug peddling. There is, on average, one murder every five hours.

Traffic congestion Each day over 2 million commuters travel into and out of the city centre in Manhattan. As Manhattan is on an island there is considerable traffic congestion and delays as commuters are forced to use the relatively few bridges and ferries or the subway (underground). It is this congestion which is forcing more firms and industries away from places near to the city centre and into the suburbs which have modern freeways.

Pollution New York has a severe refuse collection and disposal problem. Cars cause air and noise pollution, the ghettos are full of litter and wrecked vehicles, and run-down houses and graffiti create visual eyesores (photo **F**).

C

Immigrants, e.g. Hispanics and African-Americans
↓
Areas of poor quality housing
→ Lower educational standards in under-staffed slum schools
→ Mainly unskilled jobs. High rates of unemployment, crime and drug abuse.
→ Lower than average income and high dependence on social security by the unemployed.

D Ethnic groups in New York

(American Indians, Asians, Pacific Islanders, etc.)
Others 7%
Hispanics (over half from Puerto Rico) 25%
Whites 43%
Blacks (African-Americans) 25%

E

F

Activities

1 Imagine you are a newly arrived migrant into New York. Write a letter to your former school friends telling them:
   a) Why you and your family wanted to go to New York to live.
   b) What your first impressions of the city were.

2 In a developed country, why are more people now moving out of big cities like New York than are moving in?

3 Divide your class into five groups. Each group should choose one of the five problems listed on these pages. Prepare a short report, to be read to the other groups, on how the problem you chose might be reduced.

Summary

The jobs and bright lights of big cities have always attracted large numbers of newcomers, but the continued growth has created many problems.

▶ What are the problems of urbanisation? ◀

Cities in developing countries

The term '**urbanisation**' means the increase in the proportion of the world's population who live in cities. Urbanisation has increased rapidly in developed countries since the mid-nineteenth century and in developing countries since the mid-twentieth century (table **A**). Between 1950 and 1990 the urban population in developing countries doubled (100 per cent increase). In developed countries the increase was less than half. Apart from urbanisation there have been two other rapid changes (map **B**).

1 The increase in **million cities**, i.e. places with over one million inhabitants. In 1850 the only two million cities in the world were London and Paris. By 1990 there were 286.

A

	1950	1990
World	30%	51%
Developed countries	53%	74%
Developing countries	17%	34%

2 The increase in million cities located in developing countries, especially within the tropics.

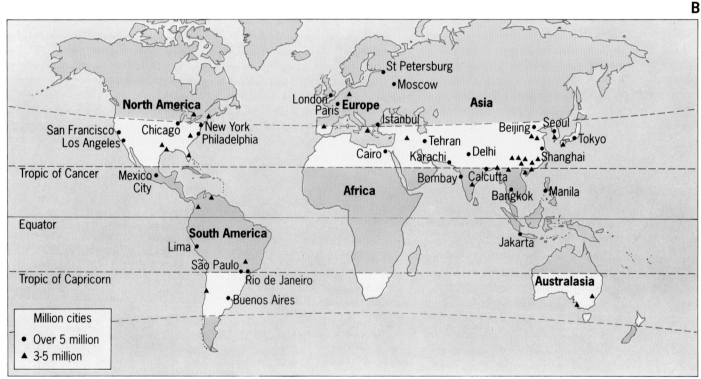

B

What are the problems of rapid urbanisation: a case study of Calcutta?

Calcutta is a good example of how problems are created when cities grow too quickly. The city is built on flat, swampy land alongside the River Hooghly which is part of the Ganges Delta. Its population is believed to have grown from 7 million in 1970 to over 9 million in 1990. As Calcutta has a high birth rate and receives many migrants from the surrounding rural areas, it is claimed that its population will exceed 16 million by the year 2000. The city authorities have no hope of providing enough new homes, jobs or services for the increasing population.

Housing Many families have no homes and have to live on pavements (photo **C**). Nearly half a million people are reported to sleep in the open, covered only by bamboo matting, sacking, polythene or newspaper. Many more live in shanty settlements called, in India, bustees. Bustee houses have mud floors, wattle or wooden walls, and tiled or corrugated iron roofs – materials which are not the best for giving protection against the heavy monsoon rains. The houses are packed closely together and are separated by narrow alleys (photo **D**). Inside each house there is probably only one small room, in which the whole family, perhaps up to ten in number, live, eat and sleep.

Services Houses lack electricity, running water and sewage disposal. There are very few schools and a lack of doctors and hospitals. Public transport is often absent or overcrowded.

C Pavement dwellers, Calcutta

D A lane in the bustees

Sanitation and health One water tap and one toilet in each alley may serve up to 50 people. Sewage often flows down the alley and may contaminate drinking water causing cholera, typhoid and dysentery. Rubbish, dumped in the streets, provides an ideal breeding ground for disease. Most children have worms and suffer from malnutrition.

Employment Those with jobs often use their homes as a place of work. The front of the house can be 'opened up' to allow the occupants to sell food, wood, clothes and household utensils (photo **E**). Few people in the bustees are totally unemployed, but most jobs only occupy a few hours a week.

Crime This is a major problem as people struggle to survive and as there is not enough money to try to prevent crime or catch criminals.

The Calcutta Metropolitan Development Agency, set up in 1970, has tried to make the bustees more habitable by paving alleys, digging drains, and providing more water taps and toilets. Pre-fabricated houses have been built and a better community atmosphere created. Even so, the lack of money has meant only relatively small areas have been improved.

E Spices stall in Calcutta bustee

Activities

1 a) What is meant by urbanisation?
   b) Give three points to describe the distribution of million cities.

2 a) Write a short article for a magazine describing the scenes in photos **C**, **D** and **E**. Include sketches and mention the houses, the alleys and jobs.
   b) What do you consider to be the worst problems of living in the bustees?

Summary

Urbanisation is the increase in the proportion of people living in cities. It is most rapid in cities in developing countries where it causes considerable problems.

Is there a typical land use pattern?

It has been suggested that towns and cities do not grow in a haphazard way but tend to develop recognisable shapes and patterns. Although each town is unique and will have developed its own distinctive pattern making it different from other towns, it will also show some characteristics shared by other urban settlements. Several people have offered theories as to how these characteristic patterns and shapes develop. These theories are illustrated as **urban land use models**. Remember a model is used to simplify complex real world situations and make them easier to explain and to understand. The two simplest models are shown in diagram **A**.

The Burgess model Burgess claimed that the focal point of a town was the **central business district** or **CBD**. As towns developed they grew outwards from the CBD. This means that buildings become increasingly more recent towards the city boundary. The outward growth is shown on the model by four circular zones. Apart from the transition zone next to the CBD, where Burgess suggested industry had replaced the oldest of houses, the resultant circular zones were based on the age of the houses and the wealth of their occupants.

The Hoyt model By the time Hoyt suggested his model, public transport had become much more important. Just as older factories grew up alongside canals and railways, so newer industries located along main roads leading out of cities. As a result Hoyt suggested that towns developed in sectors, or as wedge shapes, along main transport routes. Hoyt also claimed that if industry and low cost housing grew in one part of a town in the nineteenth century, then newer industries and modern low cost housing would also develop in that same sector.

Functional zones in a city

As towns continued to grow, each of the zones shown on diagram **A** developed its own special type of land use. Each type of land use performs a special **function** or purpose. The three major types of land use, or functions, in a town are shops and offices, industry, and housing (photo **B**). Other types of land use include parks, transport and services. It has already been pointed out that each city will develop its own pattern of land use, and that

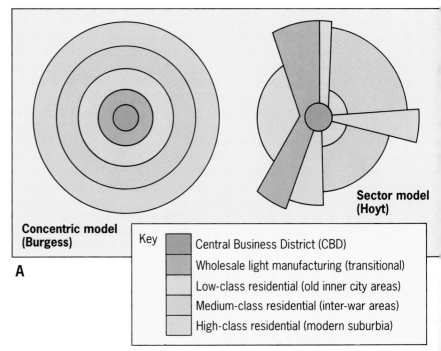

Concentric model (Burgess)

Sector model (Hoyt)

Key
- Central Business District (CBD)
- Wholesale light manufacturing (transitional)
- Low-class residential (old inner city areas)
- Medium-class residential (inter-war areas)
- High-class residential (modern suburbia)

A

B Land use zones in a city

each pattern will be more complex than that shown in the Burgess and Hoyt models. Diagram **C** is a more realistic map showing land use and functional zones in a city.

Land use and functional zones

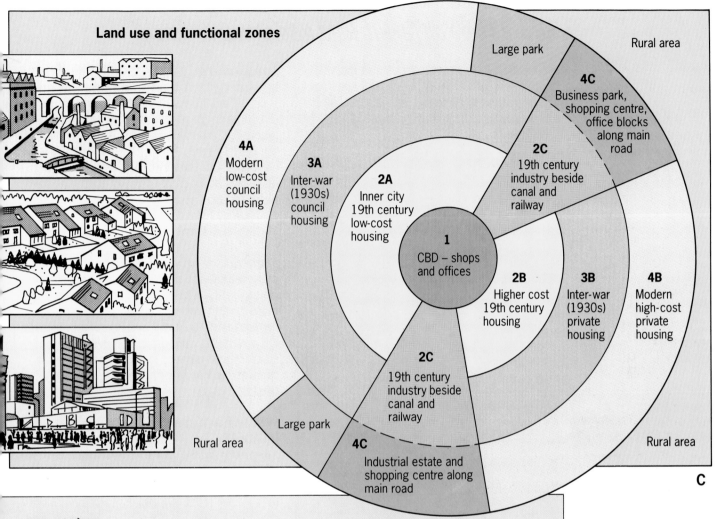

C

1 CBD – shops and offices

2A Inner city 19th century low-cost housing

3A Inter-war (1930s) council housing

4A Modern low-cost council housing

2B Higher cost 19th century housing

3B Inter-war (1930s) private housing

4B Modern high-cost private housing

2C 19th century industry beside canal and railway

4C Business park, shopping centre, office blocks along main road

4C Industrial estate and shopping centre along main road

Large park

Rural area

Activities

1 What are the advantages and disadvantages of using urban land use models?

2 a) Look at diagram **C**. How do you account for the differences in housing between zones 2A, 3A and 4A?

   b) Does this sequence of urban development suggest any similarity with either the Burgess or the Hoyt model?

   c) What do you notice about the location of the two areas of low cost housing and the two areas of high cost housing?

   d) Do these two locations suggest any similarity with either model?

   e) Which types of land use are found alongside the canals, railways and main roads?

   f) Does the location of these types of land use suggest any similarity with either model?

3 Match the three sketches in diagram **C** to their appropriate zones.

4 Sketch **D** has been drawn from photo **B**. Complete the sketch by labelling the type of land use in each zone.

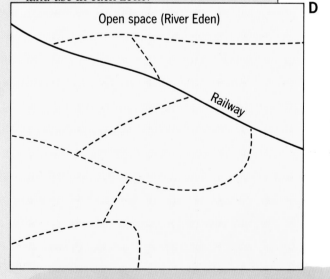

D

Open space (River Eden)

Railway

Summary It is possible to recognise patterns of land use and functional zones within a city. These patterns can be shown more simply as urban land use models.

Why are there different land use zones in a city?

The location of functional zones and the distribution of different types of land use in a city are related to three factors – accessibility, land values and the sequence of urban development.

Accessibility The CBD has traditionally been the easiest place in the city to reach. This is because most road and local rail routes meet here and so it is equally accessible to people from all over the city. Places on the edge of a city are accessible for local people but not to those who live on the opposite side of that urban area.

Land values As the CBD is the most accessible part of a city then several different types of land use will want to locate there. Competition for this prime site, especially as the amount of available space is limited, pushes up the price of land. This explains why land values are highest in the city centre. As competition decreases away from the CBD, then land values begin to fall. The concept of land values falling as distance from the city centre increases is known as **distance decay** (diagram **A**).

Sequence of urban development When many British towns began to expand last century, the main demand for land came from industry and low cost housing. Present day demand is for industry and housing in pleasant environments, shopping centres and open space. These have to locate on the edges of cities as land nearer the centre has already been used.

Where have the main types of land use located?

Shopping and offices These locate in the CBD because they need to be accessible to as many people as possible. They are often found in high rise buildings which gives them more space and helps to offset the high cost of land (photo **B**). Even so, it is only those shops and commercial companies making high profits which can afford to locate here. Recently many shops and some offices have moved to cheaper land on the edge of cities, especially if those sites have easy access to good roads and motorways.

Industry Until the growth of industry most cities did not extend beyond the limits of their present day CBD. When industry developed it located next to the city centre on the nearest available land. Being the first in the sequence of urban development, industry located on what was then the edge of the city. Nearby canals and railways gave accessibility to other parts of the country. Later urban growth has meant that what remains of this early industry finds itself in inner city areas where land is now expensive and where traffic congestion reduces accessibility (photo **C**). New industries seek edge-of-city locations (photo **D** and Unit 7).

A

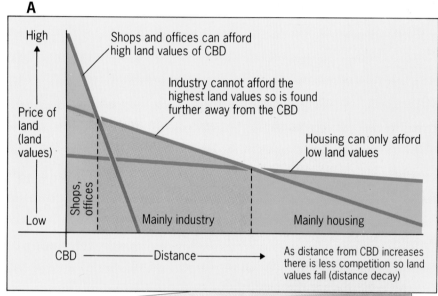

High

Shops and offices can afford high land values of CBD

Industry cannot afford the highest land values so is found further away from the CBD

Price of land (land values)

Housing can only afford low land values

Shops, offices

Low

Mainly industry

Mainly housing

CBD ——————— Distance ————————➤

As distance from CBD increases there is less competition so land values fall (distance decay)

B London's financial district

Housing In the last century people lived in tightly-packed houses within walking distance of their places of work, which were either in the city centre or the local factory (photo **E**). During this century a sequence of housing developments has taken place (photos **F** and **G**). Improved public and private transport has increased people's mobility. Recent housing developments have therefore taken place a long way from the city centre. As land values are lower here, many houses are large and have easy access to open space.

C

D

E

G

Activities

1 Table **H** lists the three main types of land use in a city. On an enlarged copy show how the location of these types of land use have been affected by accessibility, land values and the sequence of urban development.

H

Land use		Location	Accessibility	Land values	Sequence of urban development
Shops and offices					
Industry	19th century				
	Modern				
Housing	19th century				
	Recent				

2 The six photos (labelled **B** to **G**) show different types of land use in a city in Britain. Although the photos were not taken in Carlisle they do show the same type of land use as that found at the following map references on pages 82 and 83:
- 387592
- 395586
- 401559
- 398577
- 399553
- 408553

Complete table **I** by matching each map reference with the correct photo.

I

Photo	Map reference
B	
C	
D	
E	
F	
G	

Summary

The location of functional zones and the distribution of land use in a city is affected by accessibility, land values and the sequence of urban development.

► *Why does land use in a city change?* ◄

Settlements are constantly changing. As towns and cities develop, or decline, their layout, land use and functions are all likely to alter. These changes, the result of human actions and decisions, have various effects on different groups of people living in a town or city. Changes in land use can result from several processes. These include:

- the ageing of parts of the city;
- the decline of original economic activities and their replacement by newer economic activities;
- changes in people's needs and expectations, especially their attitudes to living conditions;
- increased concern for the environment.

How have processes of change affected land use in inner cities?

British towns first began to grow rapidly at the beginning of the Industrial Revolution in the early nineteenth century. The first developments took place in areas next to the city centre – places now referred to as inner city areas. Large factories were built and houses were built as close as possible to them (map **A** and photo **B**). This enabled the factory workers, who had no other form of transport in those days, to walk to work easily. As house builders were not subject to building regulations they tried to pack as many houses into as small an area as possible (photo **C**). It was usual for a factory to be found at one end of a street and either a corner shop or a public house at the other. Most factories were built beside canals or railways. No land was wasted, and was too valuable to be left as open space.

■	Terraced housing
■	Industry
■	Shops (corner)
■	Transport (railways and roads)
□	Waste land
■	River
■	Open space (none)

Housing
High density. No gardens or garages. Both terraces and back to back.

Roads
Grid-iron pattern. Narrow and still cobbled. Broken, uneven, poorly-lit pavements.

Environment
River polluted. Buildings covered in dirt from smoke. Air pollution from factories and houses. Areas of rubbish and waste/derelict land.

A

Goods depot

Shared back yards
Individual back yards

Textile mill

Furniture works

To CBD ½ km

Tyre depot

Textile works   Engineering works

Land use in an inner city area – 1970s

Box works

C Inner city housing, Bradford

B Leeds, 1885

Why did many inner cities decline?

Industry declined as old factories closed down either due to their age, competition from new products, congested sites with insufficient room to expand, poor transport facilities with canals and railways closed and roads narrow and congested, or because of the area's unattractive environment. Some factories remained empty and have decayed while others were pulled down and the land often left unused.

Housing in many cities had become slum-like by the 1960s, often through no fault of the occupants. Many houses were already a hundred years old and built before such amenities as electricity, running water, indoor toilets and damp courses were considered to be essential or had become available (photo **D** and graph **E**).

The **environment** was polluted and unattractive. Houses were blackened by smoke from factory and domestic chimneys and Clean Air Acts were still a thing of the future. Rivers and canals were a dumping ground for industrial and household waste. Empty buildings were vandalised while sites of demolished buildings became rubbish tips.

How did this decline affect people?

People living in inner city areas wanted:
- Jobs. The original factories employed hundreds of manual and unskilled workers. When these factories closed down there was little alternative work and much unemployment.
- Better housing with modern amenities.
- Things to do in their leisure time. A lack of indoor and outdoor recreational facilities increased boredom and is blamed for a rise in crime among the younger age group.
- A cleaner and a more attractive environment.

D

E

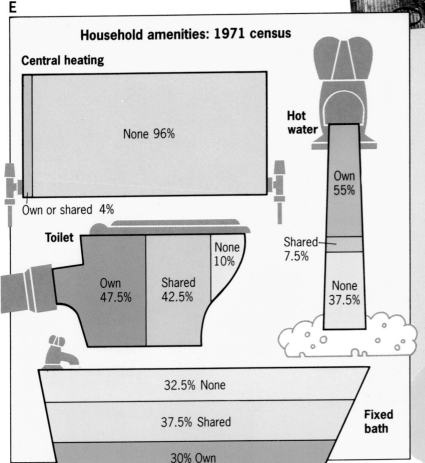

Household amenities: 1971 census

Central heating
None 96%
Own or shared 4%

Toilet
Own 47.5% Shared 42.5% None 10%

32.5% None
37.5% Shared
30% Own
Fixed bath

Hot water
Own 55%
Shared 7.5%
None 37.5%

Activities

1 a) What were the three major types of land use in an old inner city area?
  b) Which important type of land use was often absent in old inner city areas?

2 a) Describe the likely living conditions in areas such as those in photos **B**, **C** and **D**.
  b) List some ways in which you think these areas could have been improved.

3 Think of your local town or city. What changes have you seen take place:
  a) in the CBD (city centre);
  b) in inner city areas next to the CBD;
  c) on the edges of the town or city?

Summary

Land use and functions change as settlements get older and people develop different needs. One example is the inner city where changes in land use have affected different groups of people.

99

▶ *How has land use changed in London's Docklands?* ◀

During the nineteenth century the port of London was the busiest in the world. The docks were surrounded by warehouses storing goods being brought into or sent out of Britain, industries using imported goods and high density, poor quality housing (map **A**). After the 1950s the size of ships increased so much that they could no longer reach London's docks. By 1970 Docklands had become virtually derelict with few jobs, few amenities and poor living conditions for the local people (photo **B**). In 1981 the London Docklands Development Corporation (LDDC) was set up to try to improve the economic, social and environmental conditions of the area.

A What were conditions and land use like in 1981?

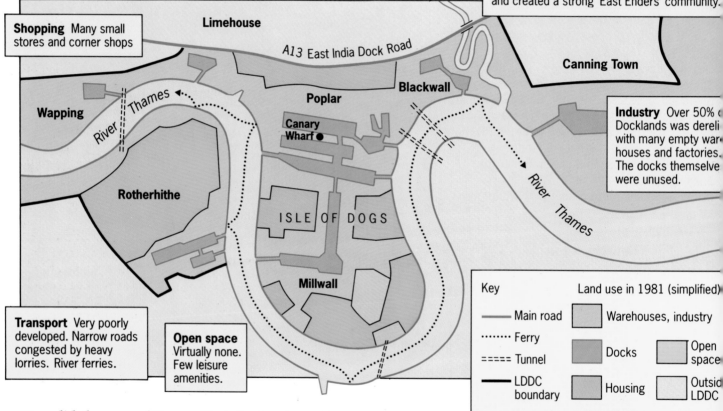

Housing High density housing covered most of the area not used by industry. Houses were small and lacked modern amenities but were cheap enough for poorly paid workers to afford and created a strong 'East Enders' community.

Shopping Many small stores and corner shops

Limehouse

A13 East India Dock Road

River Thames

Wapping

Canary Wharf ●

Poplar

Blackwall

Canning Town

Industry Over 50% of Docklands was derelict with many empty warehouses and factories. The docks themselves were unused.

Rotherhithe

River Thames

ISLE OF DOGS

Millwall

Transport Very poorly developed. Narrow roads congested by heavy lorries. River ferries.

Open space Virtually none. Few leisure amenities.

Key

—— Main road
········· Ferry
===== Tunnel
—— LDDC boundary

Land use in 1981 (simplified)

Warehouses, industry
Docks
Housing
Open space
Outside LDDC

How did these conditions affect the local people?

Traditional jobs in the docks and nearby industries had been manual, unskilled, unreliable and poorly paid. By 1981 large numbers of local people were unemployed and living in sub-standard housing in a poor quality environment. Many were forced to leave the area to look for work and a better quality of life elsewhere. These were the conditions when the LDDC was set up. It was given three main tasks:

1 To improve economic conditions by creating more jobs and improving the transport system both to and within the area.

2 To improve the environment by restoring derelict land, cleaning up the docks and creating areas of open space.

3 To improve social conditions by creating new housing and recreational amenities, and improving shopping facilities.

B
Derelict land in Docklands

How had land use changed by the early 1990s?

Industry Many new office blocks had been built including that at Canary Wharf (photo **C**). Financial businesses and high-tech firms were attracted by the low rates, and several large newspaper organisations moved here from their expensive sites in the centre of London. Over 10 000 jobs had been created before the recession of 1992.

Housing Approximately 20 000 new houses and flats had been built. Many old warehouses overlooking the River Thames had been converted into luxury flats. Elsewhere lower cost housing with modern amenities had replaced most of the older properties (photo **C**).

Transport Improved transport links have brought the Docklands within 10 minutes of central London. The City Airport, built between two docks, and the Dockland Light Railway both opened in 1987. Roads have been improved. The Jubilee underground line is being extended into the Docklands.

Shopping Improved shopping facilities include large superstores near to Canary Wharf and at Surrey Quays, and a luxury complex at Tobacco Wharf.

Environment and recreation facilities The environment has benefitted from Europe's largest urban tree planting scheme and the setting up of 17 conservation areas. Recreational additions include a national indoor sports centre and improved amenities for water sports.

How have people been affected by these changes?

Many of the new firms needed highly skilled people but in relatively few numbers. This

C Canary Wharf

meant that most new jobs went to people living outside of Docklands. As much of the new housing was expensive it was beyond the reach of local people. This led to well-off people moving in but they rarely mixed with the original 'East Enders'. Recently, more low cost housing has been built and more local people have been able to buy their own home. While wealthy newcomers have brought extra money and trade into the area, they have caused local shop and recreational prices to rise. Money has been spent on expensive office blocks and houses rather than on improving local services such as hospitals and care for the elderly. By 1990 it was believed that the economic and environmental conditions had improved but not the social conditions. The recession of the early 1990s has seen work stopped on Canary Wharf and a sharp increase in the numbers of unemployed and homeless people in the area.

Activities

1 Table **D** refers to London's Docklands. Copy and complete it to:
   a) summarise the changes in land use between 1981 and the early 1990s;
   b) show which groups of people benefitted or lost out as a result of the changes.

2 Why is it believed that since 1981 economic and environmental conditions have improved in this area but social conditions have not?

D

Land use 1981	Land use today	Groups in favour of change	Groups against the changes

Summary

The London Docklands is an example of how land use in an inner city area has changed. The changes have greatly affected the lives of people living there.

Who makes the decisions in urban planning?

Until fairly recently towns and cities grew in a haphazard way. Nowadays their growth is planned and controlled. No change is meant to take place unless planning permission has been given. Getting **planning permission** involves several groups of people. Some of these groups are likely to be in favour of the plan, and some will be against it. As each group has a role to play before the final decision is made, it can often take a long time before the plan is finally accepted or rejected.

A Who are the decision makers?

I am an entrepreneur. The new business I want to set up will be a big risk and will cost a lot of money, but I hope to make a big profit.

I work for a property developer who buys land and builds houses and shops. We then sell them hoping to make a large profit so that we can buy more land for development.

I am the Planning Officer for the local council. I collect information and get the opinions of different groups of people.

I sit on the local council's Planning Committee. We should make decisions which are in the best interests of the community but sometimes it depends on party politics.

I am chairperson of the local residents' association. We want to know if the plan will benefit us by creating more jobs and providing better services or if it will just cause extra noise and pollution.

I work for English Heritage. My job is to see that the plan does not spoil the environment.

I am Secretary of State for the Environment. If people do not like the Planning Committee's decision they can appeal to me and I can call a public enquiry.

B How is a planning decision made?

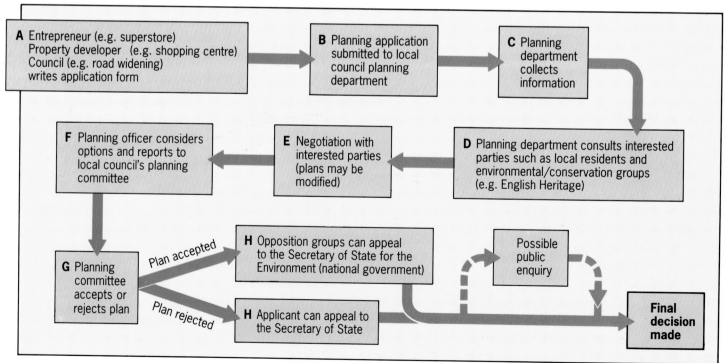

A Entrepreneur (e.g. superstore)
Property developer (e.g. shopping centre)
Council (e.g. road widening)
writes application form

B Planning application submitted to local council planning department

C Planning department collects information

D Planning department consults interested parties such as local residents and environmental/conservation groups (e.g. English Heritage)

E Negotiation with interested parties (plans may be modified)

F Planning officer considers options and reports to local council's planning committee

G Planning committee accepts or rejects plan

Plan accepted

Plan rejected

H Opposition groups can appeal to the Secretary of State for the Environment (national government)

H Applicant can appeal to the Secretary of State

Possible public enquiry

Final decision made

After the football disaster at Hillsborough the government decreed that all major stadiums had to become all-seater by 1994. Before building their new stadium one football club had to go through the planning procedures illustrated in diagram **B**.

C

Photos **C** and **E** were taken from the same place. Photo **C** shows what one football ground looked like in 1992. Photo **D** is the architect's model, showing how it might be developed. The main objections to the proposed development came from residents and others wishing to preserve the character of the Victorian houses seen in the background, behind what was then the all-standing area. The plan was accepted and the development completed by 1993 (photo **E**).

D

E

Activities

1. a) Why does any change in a town or city have to get planning permission?
   b) What is the role of these groups of people in the planning procedure?
   entrepreneurs – property developers –
   local community groups – local and central government

2. Choose a recent plan put forward in your nearest town or city. The plan might be for a shopping centre on farmland on the edge of the town or a housing development on land at present used as a play area.
   a) Which groups of people are likely to support the plan and which groups are likely to be against it.
   b) What your decision would be.

Summary

Various groups of people will have different opinions and will play different roles when making decisions which affect urban development and planning.

► What are transport networks? ◄

A transport **network**, or system, is when several places are joined together by a series of routes to form a pattern. Transport networks vary both within a country and between countries. A network consists of two elements:

1 **Links** are the routes between places.
2 **Nodes** are places where two or more routes meet (diagram **A**).

The transport pattern produced also shows the **accessibility** of a place and the **density** of the network. Accessibility is the ease by which one place may be reached from other places. On diagram **A**, place J has the greatest accessibility as it is connected to all of the other places. Place W is the least accessible as it is only directly connected to one other place. Density shows the number of routes and how closely packed together they are (diagram **B**). The network density is found by dividing the total length of the routes within an area by the size of area in which those routes are found. For example on diagram **B (ii)**:

$$\frac{\text{Total length of routes in the network (km)}}{\text{Area covered by the network (sq km)}} \quad \frac{5 \cdot 17 \text{ km}}{12 \text{ km}^2} = 0 \cdot 43$$

A

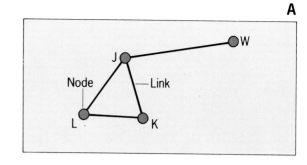

B

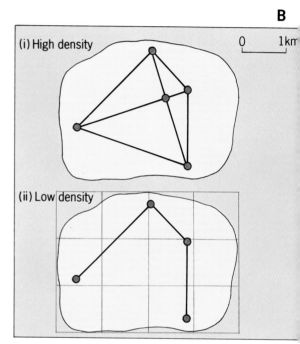

Notice that an area with a high density has more links and nodes and that places within the network are more accessible than those in an area which has a low density.

How do road and rail networks compare in Britain?

Diagram **C** is taken from the OS map on pages 82 and 83. It shows, in common with elsewhere in Britain, that:

- the road network has a higher density than the rail network;
- both networks have a higher density in the urban area than in the surrounding rural areas.

What the diagram does not show is that the highest densities in Britain are in the south and east where most people live, where there is more wealth to build routes, and where the land is flatter and more low-lying.

C

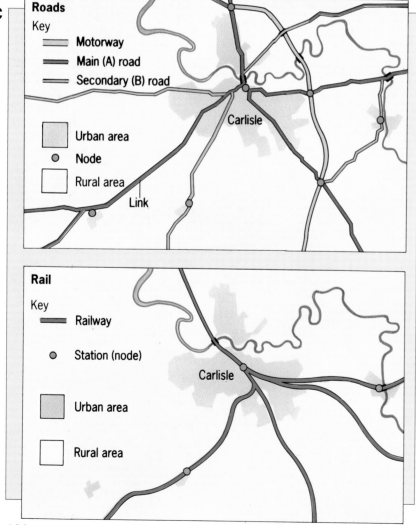

How can changes in transport networks affect people's lives?

By adding a new road (link) then the flow of traffic between two places (nodes) should be quicker and easier **but ...** as this is likely to increase the amount of traffic at the junction of the routes (node) then the result will be more congestion and pollution.

A **one–way system** allows traffic to flow more evenly and safely in one direction around the network **but ...** the new route will cause detours which will increase the distance of the journey.

When a new **bypass** (link) is built around a settlement (node) then one point (node) in the network will be eliminated making the journey for through traffic quicker and safer, and life in the settlement more peaceful **but ...** traders in the settlement will lose business (Activity **4**).

The closure of a railway line (link) or station (node) will make the rail network less dense **but ...** this will increase the number of people and vehicles using the road network.

Activities

1 What is the difference between a link and a node?

2 Using the OS map (pages 82 and 83) and diagram **B** compare the similarities and differences between the network density
 a) of roads and railways,
 b) in urban and rural areas.

3 Using an atlas compare
 a) the main road network and the rail network for England and Wales.

 b) the road network in an upland region like Wales or Scotland and a lowland region like South-east England.

4 The map below shows a new bypass. How has it affected the lives of the following groups of people:
 the petrol station owner – children attending the village school – the farmer – residents of the housing estate – the shop and cafe owners – elderly residents – a long distance lorry driver.

D

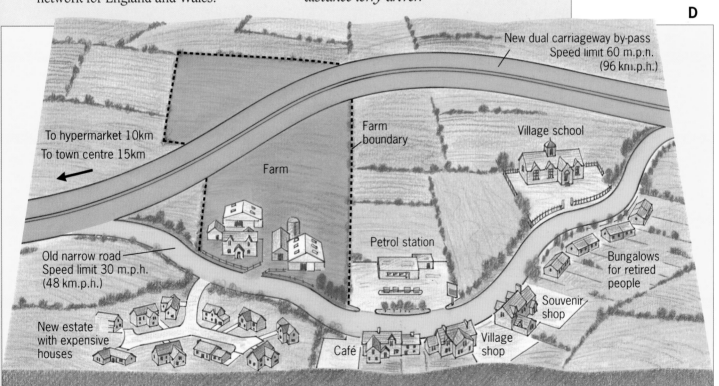

Summary There are different transport networks for road and rail. Any changes to the network will have an effect on people's lives.

► *Which is better – road or rail?* ◄

There are many different types of transport found across the world. Each type has its own advantages and disadvantages. Ideally a country needs several types of transport so that it can use the benefits of each. Britain has a wide choice, being an economically more developed country. Britain initially had the inventiveness and wealth to introduce new types of transport which have been continually modernised through new technological developments. Even so Britain is increasingly relying on just one type. By 1990 over 90 per cent of passenger journeys and over 80 per cent of goods (freight) moved were by road (diagram **A**).

A

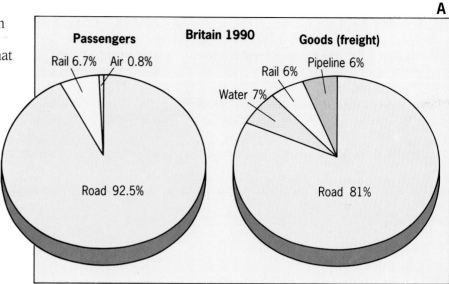

Britain 1990

Passengers
Rail 6.7%   Air 0.8%
Road 92.5%

Goods (freight)
Rail 6%   Pipeline 6%
Water 7%
Road 81%

B Advantages of road and rail

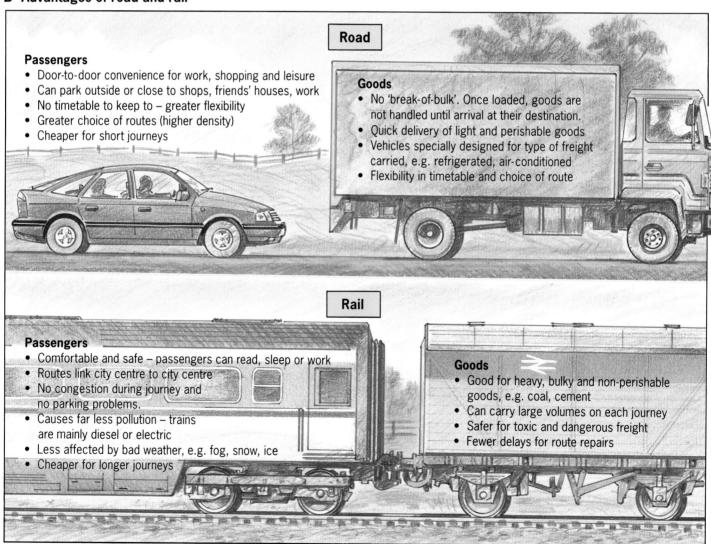

Road

Passengers
- Door-to-door convenience for work, shopping and leisure
- Can park outside or close to shops, friends' houses, work
- No timetable to keep to – greater flexibility
- Greater choice of routes (higher density)
- Cheaper for short journeys

Goods
- No 'break-of-bulk'. Once loaded, goods are not handled until arrival at their destination.
- Quick delivery of light and perishable goods
- Vehicles specially designed for type of freight carried, e.g. refrigerated, air-conditioned
- Flexibility in timetable and choice of route

Rail

Passengers
- Comfortable and safe – passengers can read, sleep or work
- Routes link city centre to city centre
- No congestion during journey and no parking problems.
- Causes far less pollution – trains are mainly diesel or electric
- Less affected by bad weather, e.g. fog, snow, ice
- Cheaper for longer journeys

Goods
- Good for heavy, bulky and non-perishable goods, e.g. coal, cement
- Can carry large volumes on each journey
- Safer for toxic and dangerous freight
- Fewer delays for route repairs

Changes due to technological developments – the TGV

The TGV (*Train à Grand Vitesse*) is the high speed French train (photo **C**). It operates at average speeds of 270 km/hour (170 miles/hour) and is the fastest train in service in the world (the new trial German ICE train will take this record when it starts to take passengers). When the first section was opened in 1983, travel times between Paris and Lyon were halved from four to two hours.

The high speeds and the good safety and punctuality records have been achieved through a series of technological developments. The TGV is computer-controlled and runs on new and specially designed track. This track has no level crossings and no tight curves. Slower trains carrying goods and local passengers run on adjacent updated lines.

Most French people are proud of their fast, safe and comfortable train. They appreciate its advanced technology and believe that the French rail system will become the centre of Europe's proposed high speed network (map **D**). Parisian tourists can now reach the Mediterranean coast in three hours, and people living in towns near to the railway have benefitted from an increase in the number of jobs available. But there is also growing opposition, especially from airlines and people living in the south-east of France. The Government wishes to build a second TGV link through Provence as the existing route to Nice is overcrowded. The proposed route would pass through several densely populated and forested areas and important vine growing districts. Local people believe that their environment has already been spoilt enough by 'tourists from the north'. Their protests, not always peaceful, have at times blocked roads and railways.

C French high-speed train – the TGV

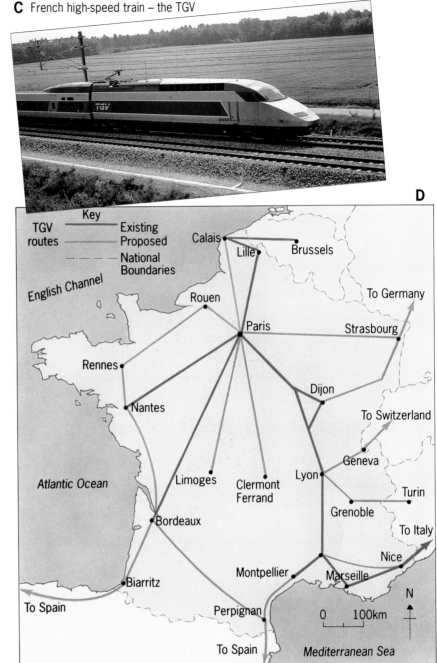

Summary

Different forms of transport each have their own advantages and disadvantages. These can change as a result of technological and other developments.

Activities

1 a) What percentage of British passenger journeys are made by road?
   b) What percentage of British goods are sent by road?

2 a) Copy out table **E**. Complete it by listing three advantages of road transport and three advantages of rail transport.
   b) If both types of transport have advantages, why is road used far more than rail?

3 Your company's head office is in Brussels. You have to travel to a meeting in Nice.
   a) What is the shortest TGV route for the journey?
   b) Which towns will you go through?

4 How has the French TGV benefitted from recent technological developments?

E

	Advantages: road	Advantages: rail
1		
2		
3		

How have transport developments affected economic activities?

Improvements to communications and changes in transport networks affect how people live. Transport and technological developments can affect a wide range of economic activities. The following examples illustrate some of these effects.

A Information Technology and where people work

Offices have always needed and used large amounts of information. In the past offices employed many typists and secretaries who often had to work in large rooms where information could easily be transferred. In turn these offices had to be near to other sources of information – libraries, commercial buildings such as banks, and other firms with whom they did business.

Modern offices are now increasingly relying on **Information Technology (IT)** to transfer ideas and knowledge. The introduction of computers, word processors and fax machines has reduced the number of employees needed, but has widened the choice of places where offices may locate and people can work. More people can work from home and send information by fax or on computer disc. Firms no longer have to locate in the expensive CBD (page 96), but can move to modern edge-of-city sites in a more pleasant environment. Likewise, firms can also move away from large urban areas to smaller towns in more rural parts of the country.

Above: New office location

Left: Bulk carrier

Below: Sullom Voe oil terminal, Shetland

B Bulk carriers and ports and port industries

Before the 1960s thousands of dockers were needed to load and unload ships. It was hard, tiring, unreliable and badly paid work. Since then Information Technology has been used to reduce both labour costs and the time a ship spends in port. One change has been the building of huge bulk carriers. These carriers are specifically designed not just to carry large quantities but also to transport just one special cargo by sea, e.g. oil or iron ore.

To be successful a modern port has to have a large deep water harbour capable of handling bulk carriers. Ships can reach ports located on the coast (e.g. Felixstowe) far more easily and quickly than ports situated up a river (e.g. London). New loading equipment has been introduced to handle specialist cargoes and large containers.

Whereas older ports had a range of industries, modern ones tend more to specialise in one or two main industries based upon a limited range of imports. For example, Milford Haven has refineries using oil and Port Talbot has steelworks using iron ore and coal. The surrounding environment may be put at risk from noise, fumes, spillage and explosions.

C Rapid air freight and market gardening

Air transport is usually better suited to carrying passengers rather than freight. However, certain goods can be carried if they are light in weight, are high in value and are **perishable**.

Perishable goods include **market garden produce** such as fruit, vegetables and flowers. These have a short life and decay rapidly. If a market garden lies close to an airport, especially an international airport, then its goods can be sent quickly to other parts of the world.

Kenya, an economically developing country, needs to increase its exports to earn more money. Until recently limited amounts of fruit and vegetables were canned before being exported. Now an increasing number of farms with good road access to Nairobi Airport are growing fresh produce, such as pineapples and French beans, for export by air. A recent welcomed money-earner for Kenya is the export of freshly cut flowers, mainly carnations and orchids. Fast transit lorries to the airport mean the flowers can reach European markets within twelve hours. Unfortunately even large planes can only carry small amounts and at a high cost.

Carnations being grown for export in Kenya

Activities

1 What is Information Technology?

2 Diagram **D** gives five newspaper headlines. How have the changes referred to in each headline resulted from developments in communications?

3 How has an economic activity in your home region been changed by developments in communications?

D

Fewer people needed to work in offices and docks

Port industries become more specialised

Offices move to new location

Increase in world trade of market garden produce

Changing location of ports

Summary

Economic activities can be changed by developments in communications. The effects of these developments may cause changes in locations, products and the workforce of the economic activities.

▶ *How do changing transport patterns affect settlements?* ◀

The volume of road traffic in 1990 was six times greater than in 1950. During that period the number of cars on the road rose from 2.5 million to 23.1 million (graph **A**), and the number of heavy goods vehicles (HGVs) and buses rose from 0.8 million to 3.2 million. It is predicted that this increase in cars and HGVs will continue. By 2025 the number of cars might double and the amount of freight carried could be three times greater than in 1990.

This increase in road usage has led to an extension of the road network. However, it is now an accepted fact that as the network improves the amount of traffic using it increases at an even faster rate (graph **B**). When the three-lane M25 was built it was predicted that it would carry 80 000 vehicles a day. Within months of opening it was attracting over 160 000 vehicles a day causing an increase in congestion and pollution. A fourth lane is now being added in some parts and up to 14 lanes are proposed for the busiest sections.

A

Growth of road traffic

Distance travelled (billion kms)

- Cars
- Light vans
- Heavy goods vehicles
- Buses and coaches
- Total vehicles

Million cars

23.1

17.4 (1985)

14.5 (1978)

5.5

2.5

B

Increase in road usage and road network 1980-1990

Increase in length of motorways

Increase in motorway use

Increase in length of all main roads

Increase in main road use

How does the traffic increase affect urban areas?

Problems created by extra traffic in cities are increasing. The average speed of traffic in London in 1992 was 20 km/hour – the same as in 1900. Other problems are summarised in figure **C**.

Buildings affected by
- noise
- vibrations

Land needed for
- larger, wider roads
- car parks, access roads

Urban motorways can cause
- visual pollution
- accidents
- delays at peak times
- split communities in half

Air pollution – total % from vehicles

- smoke   46%
- nitrogen oxide   51%
- carbon monoxide   90%
- carbon dioxide   21%
- sulphur dioxide   2%
- ground level ozone   9%

C

How can the damaging effects of transport be limited?

Transport planners have to try to improve:
- the network so that congestion and delays are reduced and traffic flows more quickly;
- safety for both drivers and pedestrians;
- the quality of the environment by reducing the various types of pollution.

How might this be achieved?

Table **D** lists some recent attempts by governments, car and petrol companies to reduce pollution.

D

Problem	Attempted solution
Air pollution	Catalytic converters added to all new cars from 1992
Lead pollution	Lead free petrol - unleaded petrol was used by 5% of car users in 1989 and by 45% in 1992
Noise	Directives on noise levels issued by the EC.

What else may be done?

The newspaper extracts in figure **E** describe attempts made in Manchester and Leeds to limit transport pollution.

E

Activities

1. a) Describe three changes in transport patterns shown on graph **A**.
   b) Why might the opening of a new motorway lead to an increase in congestion?
   c) How does an increase in road traffic affect large cities?
   d) What can different groups of people do to limit the damage resulting from an increase in traffic in cities?

2. With which of the two views expressed in figure **F** do you agree? Give reasons for your answer.

Manchester

Manchester's new metrolink system consists of lightweight electric 'supertrams'. The trams link suburban centres and surrounding towns with the city centre. Some routes use existing rail track, others have had to have new track laid along main roads leading into, and within, the city centre. Peak-time trams will carry 10 000 passengers an hour on a network designed to move 10 million people in a year. The supertrams share roads with cars and pedestrians.

LEEDS - March 1993

Leeds is to introduce a scheme, similar to ones in Essen (Germany) and Adelaide (Australia), to try to entice motorists to abandon their cars for buses. About 75 000 people commute, mainly by car, into Leeds city centre each day. By the year 2000 the present roads are expected to become totally blocked at peak times. Passengers will be picked up along non-congested roads by specially converted buses. The buses will then use 'corridors' down the middle of congested roads. Travel should be quicker, faster, safer, cheaper and cleaner.

F

Keep all traffic, or at least all cars, out of the city centre.

We should improve public transport either by having new supertrams, bus corridors or undergrounds.

A new by-pass would get rid of through traffic.

In suburban areas 'sleeping policemen' would reduce traffic speeds.

We want to use our car to get into the city centre – for work, for collecting shopping, for evening entertainment.

We do not want to pay higher taxes needed to build new undergrounds or supertrams, nor the high fares which would be charged.

Delivery vans and buses will still have to reach the city centre.

Summary

Changing patterns of transport, including the increase in the number of vehicles, effects cities. Planners have to try to limit the resulting damaging effects.

▶ *What do topological maps show?* ◀

Atlas maps try to show areas, distances and directions correctly. **Topological maps** are a simplified method of showing geographical data where one aspect of the map is correct while others, usually distance and direction, are distorted. The aim is, therefore, to highlight one main factor and to eliminate less relevant information. For example, the scale used to show the size of a country is usually based on area. However, alternative scales include those based upon:

- Population data – size, density (page 62), natural increase, birth and death rates;
- Economic data – wealth, trade, employment in economic activities;
- Transport data – networks, travel times and travel costs.

Topological maps are frequently used to show transport networks – for example, the London Underground and the Tyne and Wear Metro or routes operated by British Airways and British Rail. Rail passengers are more interested in the number of stops to their destination or the time the journey will take rather than how far or in which direction the train has to travel.

Map **A** is a topological map showing British Rail's network. Being a network the routes (links) are shown as straight lines. Major places (nodes) along the routes are shown in their correct order, but distances and directions are not accurate and travel times are not shown. In map **B** where only travel times are accurate the resultant coastline of Britain takes on a bizarre shape. Equally bizarre is map **C** which was based upon the cheapest airfares from London in 1992.

A

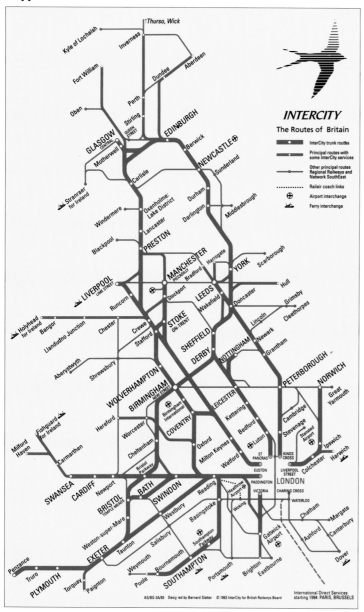

B

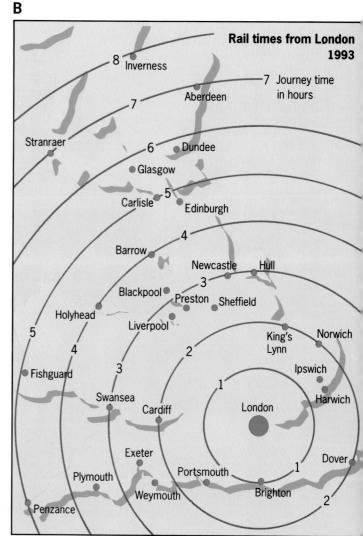

C

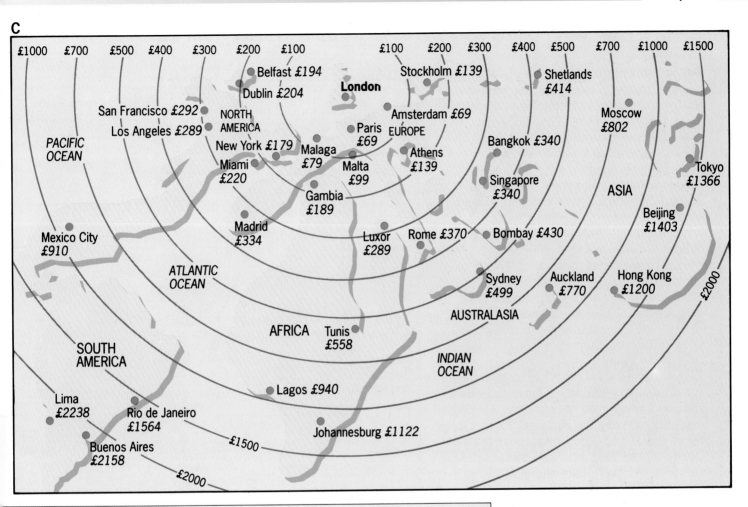

Activities

1 a) In what ways is a topological map different to an ordinary atlas map?

b) When are topological maps more appropriate to use than atlas maps?

2 a) On map **B** which of the following are accurate:
distances, directions, travel times, outline shape (of Britain), travel costs.

b) In the early 1990s the east coast mainline route was improved and electrified. What evidence is there on the map to show this improvement?

c) How will the building of the Channel Tunnel Link affect map **B**?

3 a) Table **D** ranks ten places in the world according to the cost of airfares from London (map **C**). Complete the table by ranking the same cities according to their distance from London.

b) It is cheaper to fly on charter flights to major holiday resorts than it is by ordinary economy flights to business centres. Explain whether your completed table supports this statement or not.

D

Cost of air fare from London		Distance from London
New York	1	
Belfast	2	
Luxor (Egypt)	3	
San Francisco	4	
Madrid	5	
Singapore	6	
Rome	7	
Sydney	8	
Hong Kong	9	
Tokyo	10	

Summary Topological maps highlight one aspect of geographical data which is drawn accurately while other information, which is less relevant, is left distorted.

113

► How can transport patterns be interpreted from OS maps? ◄

Topographical maps show the physical features (relief and landforms) and human features (settlements and communications) of a place. While these features can be seen on atlas maps, they are shown in far greater detail and accuracy on Ordnance Survey maps.

Ordnance Survey maps show considerable amounts of information on topics such as relief, land forms, land use, settlement and communications. With so much detail, it can be difficult to isolate and to identify patterns relating to just one of these topics. The OS map on pages 82 and 83 shows, amongst other detail, transport patterns in the Carlisle area. Map **A** has simplified the OS map by removing all detail not relevant in trying to recognise possible transport patterns.

Two reasons why Carlisle offered a good site for a settlement were that several routes met here and that it was a good place to cross, or bridge, the river (page 85). Carlisle is still a route centre with a **radial** transport network (map **B**). It is called radial because roads and railways radiate outwards, in all directions, like spokes in a bicycle wheel. Map **B** and the OS map show that the courses followed by these routes are determined by the relief of the land.

- They try to keep to low-lying land near to the coast.
- They take advantage of river valleys to pass through the many surrounding highland areas.
- They try to avoid being too close to rivers which may flood. This is especially true in Carlisle where the River Eden still floods most winters.

In mid-1993, the Department of Transport (DoT) announced their proposed route for a 9.4 km southern by-pass of Carlisle. The aim would be to link the A595, the main road to West Cumbria, and the M6 (OS map pages 82-83 and 115). At present traffic, including heavy lorries, has either to pass through the centre of Carlisle or travel along minor roads and through the villages of Dalston and Durdar. The DoT claim that a southern by-pass would 'remove through traffic from the city and the pleasant rural settlements and improve links between existing radial routes'.

A Carlisle – a route centre

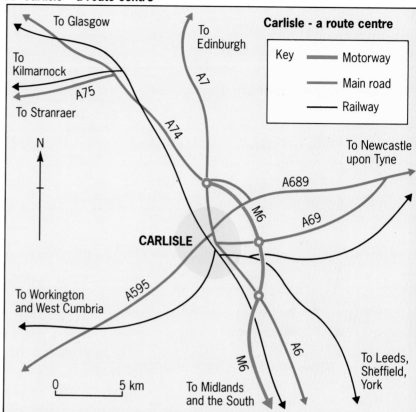

B Carlisle – transport and relief

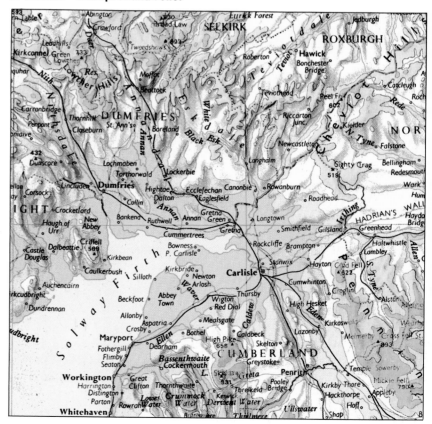

Activities

1 Name the type of communication found at the following grid squares (pages 82 and 83):
   a) 431570   e) 409567
   b) 363527   f) 365565
   c) 379571   g) 463535
   d) 25525   h) 362542.

2 Map **C** shows the main relief features found on the OS map (pages 82 and 83).
   a) Make a copy of map **C** and add to it:
      i) the main roads and the M6
      ii) the railways.
   b) Describe the routes taken by the roads and railways in relation to the main relief features.
   c) Attempt the same two exercises using the OS map of your local area.

3 a) What do you think the traffic conditions were like in Carlisle before the M6 was built?
   b) Using the OS map (pages 82 and 83) and map **B** describe the course of the M6 in relation to:
      i) settlements
      ii) relief features.

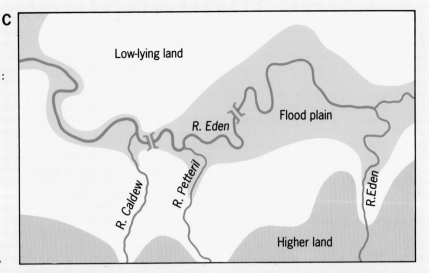

C

4 Map **D** shows four routes considered by the DoT for a southern by-pass of Carlisle. They recommended route A/B. They rejected routes:
   ● C1/D/E1 and C2/D/E1 on environmental and economic grounds;
   ● E1 because of damage to residential areas (property demolition, dividing a community, noise);
   ● C1/D/E2 and C2/D/E2 on environmental and economic grounds.
   Using map evidence, suggest why the DoT
   a) recommended route AB;
   b) rejected each of the other three routes (i.e. effect on the environment; effect on residential areas; cost; etc.)

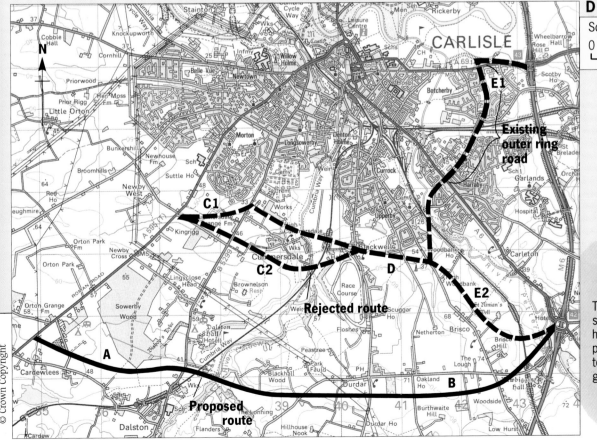

D

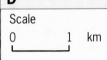

Summary

Topographical maps show the physical and human features of a place. They can be used to identify and interpret geographical patterns.

▶ What are employment structures? ◀

A

1790

10%
15%
75%

Primary —

1890

15%
30%
55%

Secondary —

1990

3%
28%
69%

Tertiary —

The different types of jobs which people can do can be divided into three groups – **primary**, **secondary** and **tertiary**.

Primary jobs are activities which involve the collection and use of natural resources, for example farming, fishing, forestry and mining. Secondary industries are those which process, manufacture and assemble the primary resources into usable goods, for example steelmaking, house construction and car assembly plants. Tertiary industries provide a service for people, for example health, education, retailing and transport.

The proportion of people working in primary, secondary and tertiary activities in any place is called the **employment structure**. One method of illustrating the proportion of people employed in each group is by a pie graph (graph **A**). Employment structures can:

* Change over a period of time (graph **A**)
* Vary from place to place - i.e. between different towns or regions in Britain (map **B**) and between different countries (map **C**).

Changes over time – the UK (graph A)

Before 1800 most people living in Britain earned a living from the land. The majority were farmers while many of the remainder made things either for use in farming (e.g. scythes) or from items produced by farmers (e.g. bread).

During the nineteenth century the main types of job changed dramatically, mainly as a result of the Industrial Revolution. Fewer people worked on the land and many moved to towns to find work. Many mined coal or worked in heavy industries making things like steel, ships and machinery.

Further changes have occurred in the twentieth century. Farming and industry have become more mechanised and need fewer workers. Coal and other natural resources are running out, while industry is faced with increasing competition from other countries. However, there are now many more hospitals, schools and shops. Transport has also provided numerous jobs.

All industrialised, developed countries have experienced these same changes.

Changes between places – within Britain

Map **B** shows employment structures in Britain. Every region has fewest workers in the primary sector and most in the tertiary. However, the proportion in each region varies considerably, for example compare South-east England and the West Midlands. Also within each region there may be big differences between types of town. For example, one may be a market town, one an industrial centre and one a holiday resort.

B Employment structures in Britain, 1990

Employment in the UK, 1990

UK average

Primary 3.3%
Secondary 28.0%
Tertiary 68.7%

Figures give percentage of total employed population in each division

8 million
5m
1m
0.5m

Area of circle proportional to total employed population in each region

Scotland

Northern Ireland

North

North-west

Yorkshire and Humberside

West Midlands

East Midlands

Wales

East Anglia

South-east

South-west

N

0   200 km

Changes – between countries

Map **C** shows the employment structures for 16 countries which are at different stages of economic development. It also divides the world into two economic parts. Countries to the north and east of the dividing line are the 'rich' countries and those to the south and west are the 'poor' countries. (See if you can suggest exceptions to this statement.)

In most of the rich, or economically more developed countries, there are relatively few people employed in the primary sector, a higher proportion in the secondary sector and most in the tertiary sector.

By contrast in the poorer, or economically less developed countries, most people find jobs in the primary sector, and relatively few are employed in the secondary and tertiary sectors. Usually it is the primary jobs which are the most poorly paid.

C World employment structures

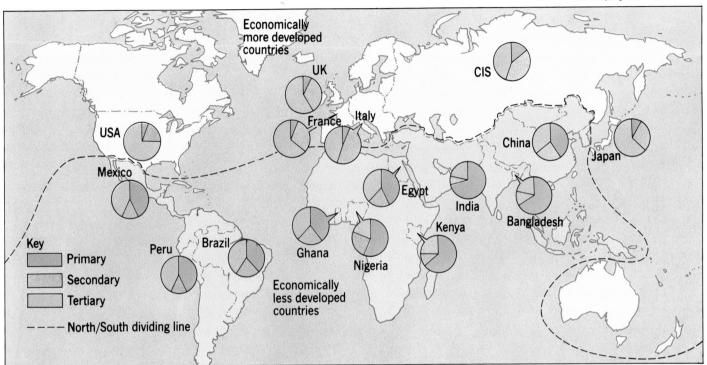

Activities

1 In your own words give the definitions for primary, secondary and tertiary activities, and employment structures.

2 a) List the following jobs under the three headings of **Primary, Secondary** and **Tertiary:**
   teacher – doctor – police officer – bus-driver – farmer – bricklayer – steelworker – nurse – ambulance driver – shopkeeper – pop singer – bank manager – plumber – quarry worker – forestry worker – shop assistant.
   b) Copy and complete table **D**.

3 a) Using map **C** list those countries with over:
   i) 50 per cent employed in the primary sector
   ii) 50 per cent employed in the tertiary sector.
   b) Describe the
   i) location of economic development,
   ii) level of economic development of the countries which you named in part a).
   c) Is graph **E** for a developed or a developing country? Give three reasons for your answer.

D

Primary	Secondary	Tertiary
Lumberjack	Sawmill operator	Furniture shop assistant
Dairy farmer		
North Sea oil rig worker		
	Bricklayer	
		Car sales person

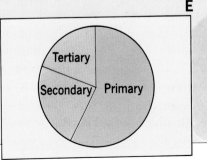

E

Summary

The proportion of people employed in primary, secondary and tertiary industries changes over time and differs between places.

How do employment structures show levels of development?

The proportion of people working in primary, secondary and tertiary industries changes over time, especially as individual countries develop economically. India, Brazil and the USA are three countries at different stages of economic development. Their employment structures are given in graph **A**. India, the least economically developed, has by far the greatest proportion of its workforce employed in primary activities. The USA, the most economically developed, by contrast has most of its workforce employed in the tertiary sector. Two hundred years ago countries like the USA and the UK had employment structures similar to that of present day India. Diagrams **B** and **C** explain how employment structures alter as a country reaches different levels of economic development.

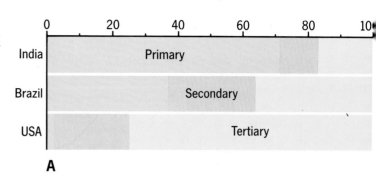

A

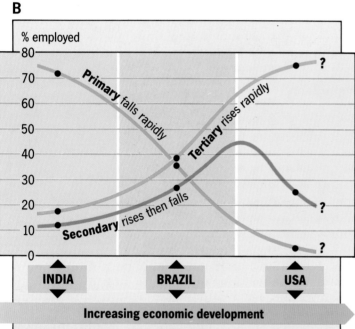

B

INDIA

BRAZIL

USA

Increasing economic development

Mainly hand labour	More mechanised	Machines, robots, computers
Providing raw materials	Providing some raw materials and some processed goods	Providing manufactured goods
Limited education, health, commerce	Improving	High levels of education, health, commerce
Poor transport systems	Improving	Good transport systems
Limited capital/wealth, much borrowing	Slightly more capital/wealth **or** debt	Considerable capital/wealth

C

Our country is in the early stages of development. We are still poor and have a low standard of living. Most of our labour force works in **primary** activities like farming, forestry and mining. Farming is very important because we have to try to produce enough food for our own people. We sell primary products like iron ore, timber and tea to rich countries. However, we rarely earn enough money from them to be able to buy many goods or much machinery in return.

Our country is continuing to develop. We still produce much of our own food but the use of machines has reduced the number of people needed to work on farms. Many of these people have now moved to towns and cities where they find jobs in **secondary** activities working in new factories. We are richer than before and our transport systems, health care and education have all improved. This is leading to an increase in tertiary industry jobs.

We live in one of the more economically developed countries. Many people are employed in **tertiary** activities. They work in hospitals, schools, offices, banks and in the leisure industry. We still have many secondary industries but these need fewer workers because we use machines, robots and computers in factories. Very few people work in primary industries since we are rich enough to buy most of our raw materials from other countries. This helps us to conserve our resources and to protect our environment.

Location Quotients

The **Location Quotient (LQ)** is used to measure the concentration of a specific industry. It shows whether the industry is spread out evenly across a country or region or whether it is concentrated within a few parts of that country or region. The LQ is found by comparing the proportion of the industry within a given area (%P) with the proportion of the industry found in the total area (%A). This is explained in diagram **D**.

D

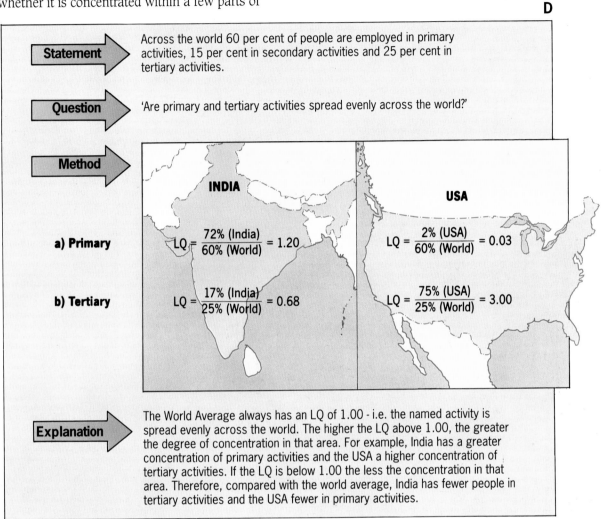

Statement ▶ Across the world 60 per cent of people are employed in primary activities, 15 per cent in secondary activities and 25 per cent in tertiary activities.

Question ▶ 'Are primary and tertiary activities spread evenly across the world?'

Method ▶

INDIA **USA**

a) **Primary** $LQ = \dfrac{72\% \text{ (India)}}{60\% \text{ (World)}} = 1.20$ $LQ = \dfrac{2\% \text{ (USA)}}{60\% \text{ (World)}} = 0.03$

b) **Tertiary** $LQ = \dfrac{17\% \text{ (India)}}{25\% \text{ (World)}} = 0.68$ $LQ = \dfrac{75\% \text{ (USA)}}{25\% \text{ (World)}} = 3.00$

Explanation ▶ The World Average always has an LQ of 1.00 - i.e. the named activity is spread evenly across the world. The higher the LQ above 1.00, the greater the degree of concentration in that area. For example, India has a greater concentration of primary activities and the USA a higher concentration of tertiary activities. If the LQ is below 1.00 the less the concentration in that area. Therefore, compared with the world average, India has fewer people in tertiary activities and the USA fewer in primary activities.

Activities

1 Copy and complete table **E** by giving the employment structures for India, Brazil and the USA.

E

	Primary (%)	Secondary(%)	Tertiary(%)
India	72		
Brazil			
USA			75

2 As a country becomes economically more developed why do the numbers in
a) primary activities decrease;
b) secondary activities increase and then decrease;
c) tertiary activities increase?

3 Copy and complete table **F** by adding the missing Location Quotients (LQ).

F

	Primary	Secondary	Tertiary
India	1.20		0.68
Brazil			
USA	0.03		3.00

Summary

There is a link between the employment structure of a country and its level of development. Location Quotients show the degree of concentration of an industry in a given area.

▶ How are different types of farming distributed in the UK? ◀

There are three main types of farming.

- **Arable** is the ploughing of the land and the growing of crops.
- **Pastoral** is leaving the land under grass and the rearing of animals.
- **Mixed** is when crops are grown and animals are reared in the same area.

Farming, especially in Britain, is a big business. Farmers must choose carefully the best type of farming for the place where they farm.

Farming is a system which has inputs into the farm, processes on the farm and outputs from the farm (diagram **A**). Deciding which type of farming is best depends upon several physical and human inputs (diagram **B**). To be successful and to make a profit, the outputs from a farm must be worth more than the inputs. In many parts of the world where the outputs are less than the inputs the farmer is struggling to survive.

A

Inputs (Physical/natural environment, human/economic factors)	Processes (Methods of farming)	Outputs (Produce, e.g. crops, animals)

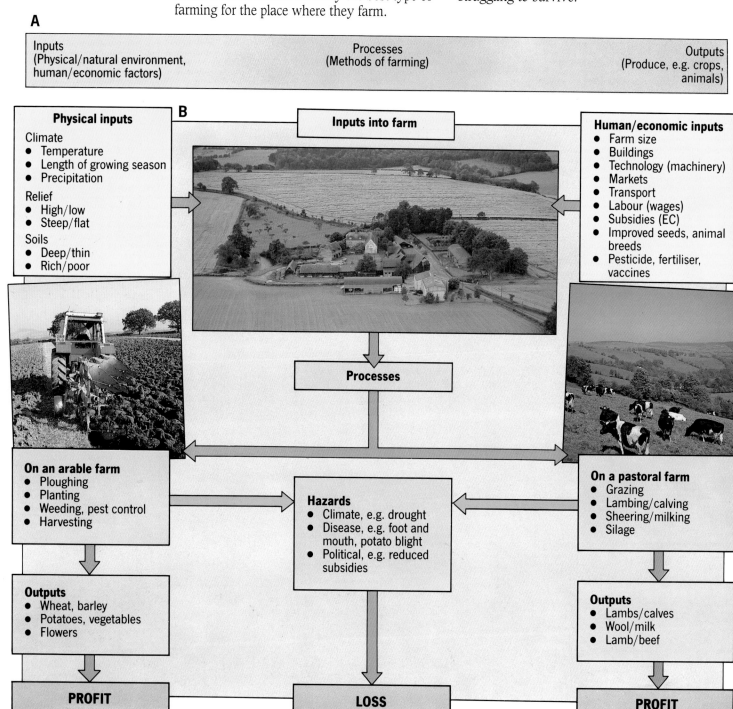

B

Physical inputs

Climate
- Temperature
- Length of growing season
- Precipitation

Relief
- High/low
- Steep/flat

Soils
- Deep/thin
- Rich/poor

Inputs into farm

Human/economic inputs
- Farm size
- Buildings
- Technology (machinery)
- Markets
- Transport
- Labour (wages)
- Subsidies (EC)
- Improved seeds, animal breeds
- Pesticide, fertiliser, vaccines

Processes

On an arable farm
- Ploughing
- Planting
- Weeding, pest control
- Harvesting

Hazards
- Climate, e.g. drought
- Disease, e.g. foot and mouth, potato blight
- Political, e.g. reduced subsidies

On a pastoral farm
- Grazing
- Lambing/calving
- Sheering/milking
- Silage

Outputs
- Wheat, barley
- Potatoes, vegetables
- Flowers

Outputs
- Lambs/calves
- Wool/milk
- Lamb/beef

PROFIT

LOSS

PROFIT

It is essential, if a British farmer is to make a profit and a livelihood, that farming is as efficient as possible. This means that certain areas will be better suited to one type of farming. Groups of farmers in this area will therefore tend to specialise in that one type. However, there are likely to be local variations within each specialist area creating some local diversification. Map **C** shows the major areas of specialised farming in Britain. It is a generalised map and as such it has been simplified to make its interpretation easier. This means that any local variations are hidden because the generalised map lacks detail. The map shows how physical and human inputs into the farming system in places situated towards the north and west of Britain differ to places in the south and east. Taking these factors into consideration most farms in the north and west of Britain will be pastoral with individual farmers having decided to rear animals. In contrast farms in the south and east are more likely to be arable.

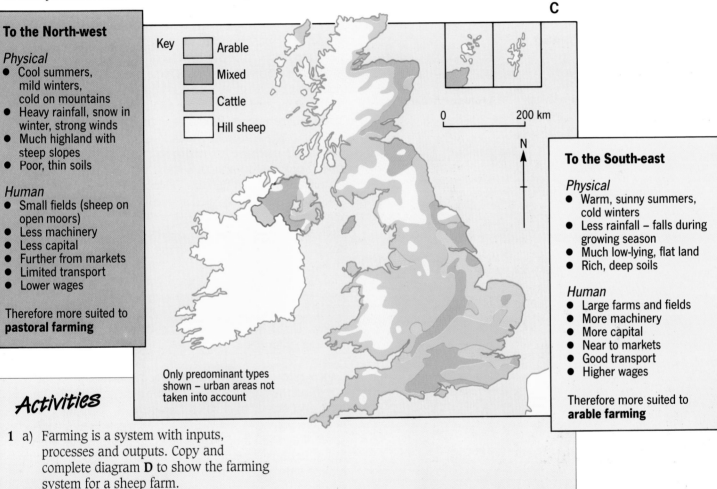

C

To the North-west

Physical
- Cool summers, mild winters, cold on mountains
- Heavy rainfall, snow in winter, strong winds
- Much highland with steep slopes
- Poor, thin soils

Human
- Small fields (sheep on open moors)
- Less machinery
- Less capital
- Further from markets
- Limited transport
- Lower wages

Therefore more suited to **pastoral farming**

Key
	Arable
	Mixed
	Cattle
	Hill sheep

0   200 km

N

Only predominant types shown – urban areas not taken into account

To the South-east

Physical
- Warm, sunny summers, cold winters
- Less rainfall – falls during growing season
- Much low-lying, flat land
- Rich, deep soils

Human
- Large farms and fields
- More machinery
- More capital
- Near to markets
- Good transport
- Higher wages

Therefore more suited to **arable farming**

Activities

1 a) Farming is a system with inputs, processes and outputs. Copy and complete diagram **D** to show the farming system for a sheep farm.

Physical inputs				
	Processes	Hazards	Outputs	**D**
Human inputs				

b) Choose a farm in your home region and then:
   i) name its main type of farming;
   ii) draw its likely farming system;
   iii) explain why you consider the more important inputs into the farm were either the physical or the human.

2 a) What is the difference between an arable farm and a pastoral farm?
   b) Why are most arable farms in Britain found in the south and east?
   c) Why are most pastoral farms in Britain found in the north and west?

Summary

Farming is a system with inputs, processes and outputs. A farmer has to consider the different inputs before deciding which type of farming is best suited to the area where he farms. It is possible to recognise a generalised distribution pattern of farming types on a map of Britain.

Why do certain areas specialise in one type of farming?

A

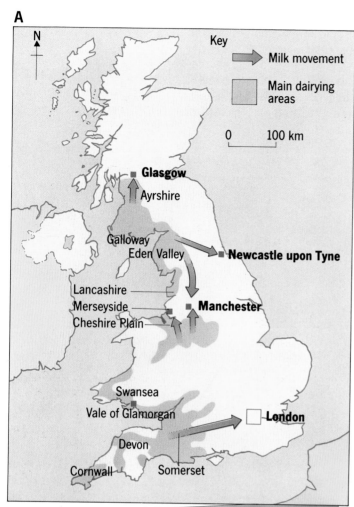

It is hard to imagine a day in which you do not consume milk in one form or another. It may be as a liquid poured onto your breakfast cereal or added to your cup of tea or coffee, or it may be once it has been processed into cheese or butter. Multiply your daily requirements by Britain's 58 million people and you can see the great demand for fresh dairy produce.

Dairy cows cannot, despite this demand, be reared just anywhere in Britain. Dairy cows need certain conditions if they are to give high yields of top quality milk and if the farmer is to make a profit. The physical conditions of the Cheshire Plain make this area ideal (map **A**). The land here is low-lying and relatively flat (photo **B**). Soils are deep and rich allowing the growth of good quality grass. The quality is further improved by a reliable rainfall which is spread evenly throughout the year. Winters are quite mild. This gives the grass a longer season in which to grow and means that farmers do not have to provide so much winter fodder for the cows. As summers are not usually very warm then the grass is unlikely to wither and die. Of course these ideal climatic conditions are not expected to occur every year and when they do not the farmer is faced with short term problems such as summer drought caused by unexpected heatwaves. Animals are also vulnerable to disease.

The Cheshire Plain is not the only place in Britain where these ideal conditions for dairy farming occur. They are also found in the south-western parts of Scotland, England and Wales. That is why those areas also specialise in dairy farming (map **A**).

Gilbert Hitchen's family have farmed 450 hectares (200 acres) on the Cheshire Plain for five generations. The family were encouraged to build up their herd of 100 dairy cows after the Second World War at a time when Britain was very short of agricultural products. Encouragement came initially from the British government and later from the EC which offered **subsidies** on milk production. This meant dairy farmers were guaranteed a fixed price for the milk produced on their farm. They would be given this agreed price even if there was a glut of milk and the market price for the product fell. The government also made efforts to stop other countries 'dumping' their own cheaper dairy products into Britain. The Hitchens were also encouraged by their bank to increase their herd to 190 cows. The bank assumed that the cost of buying extra cows and building accommodation for them would soon be repaid by the expected increase in income. The family were unlucky in the 1960s. They were one of many whose herd had to be destroyed after it fell victim to foot and mouth disease. The herd was insured but, with so many other farmers also having to rebuild their stock, it had to be replaced with animals costing high prices and which were not always of top quality.

B The Cheshire Plain

During the 1970s and 1980s dairy farmers were helped by improvements in **accessibility** and **technology**. The Hitchens were helped by the building of the M6 and the improvements in local roads. The improvements in accessibility enabled them to get their milk to the urban markets of Manchester and Merseyside quickly and easily. The transport of fresh milk was made easier by the introduction of the refrigerated lorry (photo **C**) and its twice daily collection of milk from the farm. Most milk is bought by the Milk Marketing Board (renamed Milking Mart in 1994). Another important technological improvement has been the introduction of computers. Amongst other advantages the computer controls the amount and quality of food given to each cow (photo **D**) and punches out cards to record the daily milk yields of each animal. Gilbert Hitchen has invested a lot of money into his farm by increasing his herd to 160 cows, building new barns and introducing computers and modern machinery.

Yet recent changes in dairy farming have meant that Gilbert is no longer making the profits which he had hoped for and expected. Indeed, as will be seen in the next section, Gilbert is wondering, like many other dairy farmers, how he can manage to continue farming.

D Computerised dairy farming

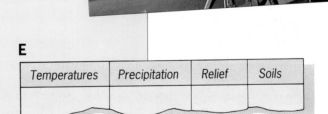

C Refrigerated milk lorry

Activities

1 With reference to map **A**, describe the distribution of dairy farming in Britain.

2 a) Copy and complete table **E** to show the ideal physical conditions for rearing dairy cows.

   b) Why were dairy farmers encouraged to produce more milk after the Second World War?

   c) Name two groups of people who have helped dairy farmers to produce more milk.

   d) How have the following helped Britain's dairy farmers?
   • Improvements in accessibility
   • Developments in technology

E

Temperatures	Precipitation	Relief	Soils

Summary

Certain areas have advantages which enable them to specialise in one type of farming. Farming can be affected by improvements in accessibility and technology.

▶ *Why is agricultural land use changing?* ◀

Despite the efforts of Mr Hitchen and other dairy farmers to produce more milk, Britain is still not self-sufficient in dairy produce. However, Britain is no longer in isolation but is part of the European Community. One outcome of this is that British farmers are subject to decisions made under the EC's **Common Agricultural Policy (CAP)**. There are several other areas within the EC which are very important for dairy farming, notably Denmark and the Netherlands. Taken as a group, EC farmers, including dairy farmers, have overproduced certain commodities. This has created the so-called 'mountains and lakes' surpluses (diagram **A**), which include milk and butter. The surplus products are stored, at a high cost, because they are not needed by EC countries. Nor can they be sold to the many countries with food shortages either because they are too poor to be able to buy the produce or because of existing trade restrictions. The EC has been under increasing pressure to try to reduce its farm surpluses. It is claimed that 70 per cent of the EC's money goes on helping farmers produce food which we often do not need, while agriculture, in return, only provides about 5 per cent of the total income of the EC.

How do changing EC farm policies affect dairying?
The EC has made major changes to the CAP in an attempt to reduce its 'mountains and lakes' and the money which it spends on agriculture.

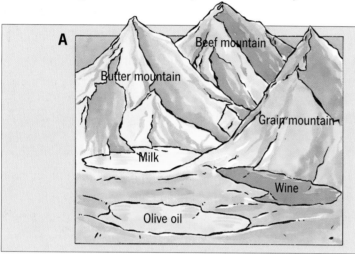

A (Butter mountain, Beef mountain, Grain mountain, Milk, Wine, Olive oil)

Dairy farmers:
- Can no longer produce as much milk as they wish but are given a **quota** which they must not exceed. They still receive the subsidy for their quota but they can be fined if they try to exceed it. The quota is for less milk than was previously produced.
- Are encouraged to **'set-aside'** part of their farm and are paid if they do **not** produce food on up to 15 per cent of their land. The payment is made on the understanding that the land will not be used for food production for a minimum of five years. Farmers have the option of leaving it fallow or using it for non-agricultural purposes (table **D**).

B Kilnsey Park Trout Farm, Yorkshire

What are the options available to Mr. Hitchen?
Mr Hitchen's quota has meant that he has had to reduce his herd from 160 cows (page 123) to 100. Even with the guaranteed subsidy his income is no longer enough for his farm to remain profitable. If he is to continue farming, which he wants to do, then he is going to have to make changes. He has several options. These are summarised in diagram **D**.

C Farmland converted into a wetland wildlife site

	SCHEME	ADVANTAGES	DISADVANTAGES
1 Within farming	a) Diversify farming	Grow some cereals, e.g. barley Less reliance on milk quotas	Cereals not suited to the climate of Cheshire
	b) Improve milk quality	Higher quality milk receives higher subsidies. (i.e. fewer bacteria to treat)	Only a limit to improvement and increase in subsidy.
	c) Increase quota	Done by buying a neighbouring farm and using its quota	Very expensive to buy another farm. Puts another farmer out of business. Will EC reduce quotas again?
2 Set-aside	d) Leave fallow (under grass)	Most popular option with farmers. Costs no money. Receives a payment - about £200 a hectare. Land use not changed.	No big improvement in income, possibly only a short term solution
3 Alter land use	e) Woodland	Management scheme. Given grants for up to £190 per hectare to plant trees. Higher grants for deciduous trees than for coniferous	Slow growing No income for many years
	f) Wildlife scheme	Re-creation of a pond/wetland site. Re-planting hedgerows Small grants from conservation agencies	No real income even though it would improve the environment.
	g) Recreation	E.g. golf course, trout farm, scrambling, riding stables, camp site, education visits Widens chance of income.	Often involves a lot of initial investment which farmer is unlikely to have. Some threaten the natural environment.

Activities

1. a) What is the Common Agricultural Policy?
   b) Why is there a surplus of dairy produce in the EC?
   c) There should be five newspaper headlines in diagram **E**, but each has been torn into two.
      i) Match up the ten torn pieces to give the five original correct headlines.
      ii) Explain how two of these headlines refer to attempts by the EC to reduce its 'milk lake' and 'butter mountain'.
      iii) How do the remaining headlines suggest other ways by which the EC could reduce its surplus even further?

2. Mr Hitchen is going to have to find an extra source of income. This will probably mean changing the land use of part of his farm. A change in land use will also affect the environment. Look at the schemes in diagram **D**.
   a) Which do you think is his most attractive option
      i) economically,
      ii) environmentally?
   b) Which do you think is his least attractive option
      i) economically,
      ii) environmentally?

E

Poorer communities cannot afford the price EC produces food

EC produces food at high cost

Farmers to be paid to take land out of production

Less milk will be produced

Trade agreement stops EC food going to developing countries

Food surplus in EC

EC to cut quotas

EC introduces set-aside land scheme

African countries have little money to buy food

Famine in Africa gets worse

Summary

By subsidising farmers the EC has built up a large food surplus in several products. As the EC changes its policies to reduce the surplus, it means some farmers are having to change the land use on their farms or go out of business.

How has farming affected the environment?

A Open fields where hedges have been removed

Developments in farming, as in other economic activities, lead to changes in the environment. Farmers are continually trying to make their farms more efficient and to improve the quality of their produce. To achieve this there must be careful planning and management. Until recently, improvements to farming were often made with little or no consideration for the management of the environment. It was not realised that developments such as the removal of hedgerows and the increasing use of fertiliser would have such an unintended, adverse effect upon the environment. Today it is a top priority that the costs of developments in farming are balanced against the costs to the environment.

Hedges provide a home for wildlife – birds, animals, insects and plants

Hedges reduce wind speed

Well looked after hedges are attractive

Hedge roots hold the soil together and reduce erosion

B

Cutting hedges costs the farmer time and money. A hedgecutter costs over £7000

Hedges get in the way of big machinery in fields

Hedges take up space which could be used for farmland

Hedges harbour insect and animal pests as well as weeds

The removal of hedgerows

Although most of Britain's hedgerows were only planted by farming communities in the eighteenth century, they are now often considered to be part of our natural environment. Modern farming, especially in arable areas, uses large machines which are easier to work in large fields. The result was that between 1945 and 1990 over 25 per cent of Britain's hedges were cleared (in parts of East Anglia the figure was over 60 per cent) in order to have larger fields (photo **A**). Diagram **B** shows some of the arguments for and against the clearing of hedges. Apart from the loss of a habitat for wildlife, the major and often unintended problem has been the increased risk of **soil erosion**. The leaves and branches of hedges break the fall of heavy rain (page 16), reducing its force before it hits the ground. Roots bind the soil together and slow down the flow of water. Where hedges are removed and the soil is left exposed, then erosion can result either from the soil being washed away during times of heavy rainfall or being blown away by the wind under drier conditions (photo **C**).

C Soil erosion caused by rain water run-off

The use of fertiliser and farm waste

Fertiliser contains nutrients which are necessary for plant growth. Although it is expensive to use, chemical fertiliser replaces nutrients which may have been removed from the soil. This helps to give healthy crops and increasingly higher yields. Farmers also spread slurry, which is animal waste, over their fields. This, being a natural fertiliser, is cheaper to use than bought chemical fertiliser and is just as effective. Both chemical fertiliser and slurry contain nitrate. If the amount of nitrate released into the soil becomes too great for the plants to use, then the excess will find its way into underground water supplies or surface rivers. Excessive nitrate in water supplies can be harmful to human health. Excessive nitrate in rivers acts as a fertiliser and results in the rapid growth of algae and other plants (photo **D**). Algae and plants use up large amounts of oxygen leaving too little for fish life.

Farming has also affected the environment by:
- Using pesticides to kill insect pests but this has also reduced numbers of harmless insects such as bees.

D Algal growth caused by excess nitrate in the water

- Burning straw which releases carbon dioxide into the air and reduces the amounts of nutrient being put back into the soil. This was banned in 1993.
- Draining **wetland** wildlife habitats.

Activities

1 a) Why have some farmers removed hedgerows?
  b) Why do conservationists object to the removal of hedgerows?

2 a) Why do farmers use chemical fertiliser and farm slurry?
  b) How can the use of chemical fertiliser and farm slurry affect the environment?
  c) Copy and complete the flow chart from diagram **E** to show how the use of chemical fertiliser and slurry can kill fish life in rivers. Choose your answers from the following list.
  - Algae and plants use up oxygen
  - Nitrate and slurry reach rivers
  - Fish die due to lack of oxygen
  - Fertiliser and slurry added to field
  - Nitrate makes algae and plants grow
  - Fertiliser and slurry contain nitrate.

E

1   2   3   4   5   6

Summary

Developments in farming need careful planning and management otherwise they can have unintentional adverse effects upon the environment.

▶ *What are the main sources of energy?* ◀

The sun is the sole source of all the earth's energy. We have to rely on green plants to convert this energy, through a process called photosynthesis, into forms which are usable by people. The resultant forms of energy, like other natural resources, can be divided into two groups - **renewable** and **non-renewable** (table **A**). Up to now most of the countries which have developed large industries and modern transport systems have mainly relied upon non-renewable sources as these have been easier and cheaper to use (graph **B**). However, these types of energy often pollute the environment and some are beginning to run out. This means that countries are going to have to develop new technologies which will allow them to use more of the renewable sources of energy.

A

Non-renewable resources		Renewable resources	
These resources can be used only once		These resources will not run out and so they can be used over and over again. The majority are forces within nature.	
75% of energy comes from fossil fuels.They are called 'fossil' because they are the remains of plants and animals.	Uranium is a mineral not a fossil fuel	From forces of nature	From living plants, and animal waste
Coal, fuelwood, oil, natural gas	Nuclear	Tidal waves, wind, solar, geothermal, hydro-electricity	Biomass, biogas
89% world's energy	6% world's energy	Hydro-electricity - 5%	Rest total under 1%
Relatively cheap and easy to convert into energy - but they can only be used once and they can cause much pollution and destruction to the environment.		Of the natural forces only hydro-electricity is relatively cheap and easy to use. The technology needed to make the rest economically usable has not yet been developed. They cause very little pollution.	

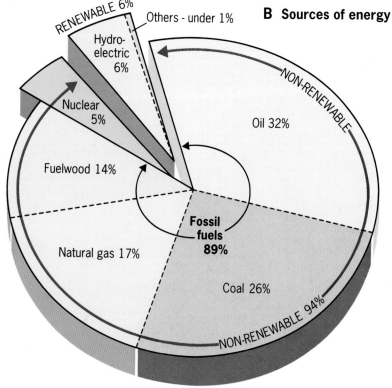

B Sources of energy

RENEWABLE 6%
Others - under 1%
Hydro-electric 6%
Nuclear 5%
Fuelwood 14%
Natural gas 17%
Oil 32%
Fossil fuels **89%**
Coal 26%
NON-RENEWABLE
NON-RENEWABLE 94%

Energy and development

Although only a quarter of the world's population live in industrialised countries, they use over three-quarters of the world's energy. As graph **C** shows, there is a close link between the wealth of a country and the amount of energy which it uses. The relatively few countries with a high standard of living consume large amounts of energy to operate machines in industry, transport and the home. The first countries to become industrialised were those which had large amounts of their own easily accessible fossil fuels. Today some of these countries no longer have sufficient energy resources of their own but they usually have enough money to import what they need.

Economically less developed countries, especially those in sub-Saharan Africa, rarely have any fossil fuels of their own, and are even less likely to have the wealth to buy their basic requirements. Several did borrow money, which they have been unable to repay, to build prestigious hydro-electric schemes. The remainder, as do many non-industrialised countries, have to rely upon fuelwood as their major source of energy.

Fuelwood can account for up to 90 per cent of the energy consumed by some of the world's poorest countries (photo **D**). The balance may be made up from animal dung which would be of greater value to the local people if it was spread on the land as a fertiliser. Although fuelwood comes from trees which could be renewed, in reality there is rarely the money to replace many and those which are planted are likely to be used long before they grow to more than bush height. Not only is the supply of fuelwood not being replaced, but the rapid growth in population in these countries means that existing reserves are being used up at an even faster rate.

C

Energy consumption per capita (person) 1990

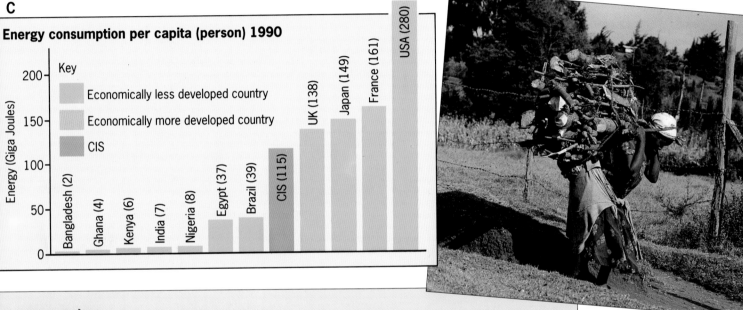

Key
- Economically less developed country
- Economically more developed country
- CIS

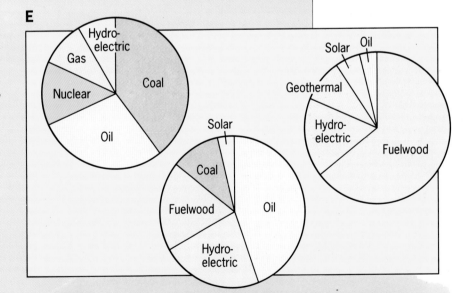

D Collecting fuelwood

Activities

1 a) What is meant by the following terms?
   i) Renewable resources
   ii) Non-renewable resources
   iii) Fossil fuels
  b) What are the following types of energy?
- nuclear
- hydro-electricity
- solar
- geothermal
- tidal
- biomass
- biogas

2 The three graphs on the right show the sources of energy for Kenya, the UK and Brazil (but not necessarily in that order). For each graph:
a) Name which country it represents.
b) Give two reasons for your answer.
c) Draw a graph to show any likely changes in energy sources by the year 2025.
d) Give reasons for the changes which you have shown in part c).

E

Summary

Most industrialised countries consume large amounts of non-renewable sources of energy, especially fossil fuels. Although these are cheaper and easier to use than renewable sources, they are responsible for high levels of pollution.

The exploitation of oil - new technology and the environment

A

New techniques to exploit North Sea oil	New techniques to protect the environment from oil
• Large concrete platforms needed to withstand severe storms and waves. Need for stability. • Platforms had to be large enough to accommodate drilling rig, process plant, power plant, helicopter landing pad, living and sleeping quarters for the crew. • Newly designed oil pipe-laying barge which welds pipe before laying it on the uneven sea bed. • Improved lines for supplies and medical care. • Computers to control operations. • Double-hulled tankers to remove oil from Sullom Voe terminal (Shetland).	• Mechanical booms to spread across estuaries. • Oil skimmers and vacuums to clean up oil spills. • Planes and spray dispersants. • Better trained staff and emergency planning between oil companies and environmental groups. • Tanks on heated ground to prevent freezing and surrounded by concrete in case of spillage. • Oil equipment in Southampton ready for world-wide use.

Oil companies were faced with many new and complex problems when they began a search for oil in the North Sea in the 1960s. The weather was worse and the sea deeper and rougher than they had previously experienced. Following the discovery of oil in 1970, new technology was needed (table **A**) to:

- bring the oil to land;
- protect the environment.

Shetland

Shetland is a group of islands off the north coast of Scotland. It is noted for its wildlife and coastal scenery (map **B**). It is also the nearest land to the more northerly of the North Sea oilfields. Oil companies decided that, in the long term, it would be safer, easier and cheaper to transport oil by two underwater pipelines to a terminal at Sullom Voe in the north of Shetland. Sullom Voe is a deep and sheltered natural harbour capable of taking large oil tankers. Oil arriving at the Sullom Voe terminal is stored until it can be taken by tanker to refineries on the British mainland.

Since the oil began coming ashore there had always been fears of a major disaster, either an:

- explosion or fire on an oil-rig (e.g. Piper Alpha in 1988) or at the terminal;
- oil spillage from a broken pipeline or a tanker running aground (e.g. Exxon Valdez in Alaska in 1989).

These worst fears were realised on 5 January 1993, although the cause of the disaster had nothing to do with the British oil industry. The tanker *Braer* was on its way from Norway to North America full of light crude oil. It was taking an accepted short cut through the relatively narrow, but dangerous, 35km wide channel between Fair Isle and the south of Shetland when its engines broke down. The weather conditions at the time were:

Wind:
South; storm force 10; gusting - hurricane force 12 (135 km/hour or 85 m/p/h).

Sea conditions:
Average wave height 8 m. Extreme height estimated at 30 m.

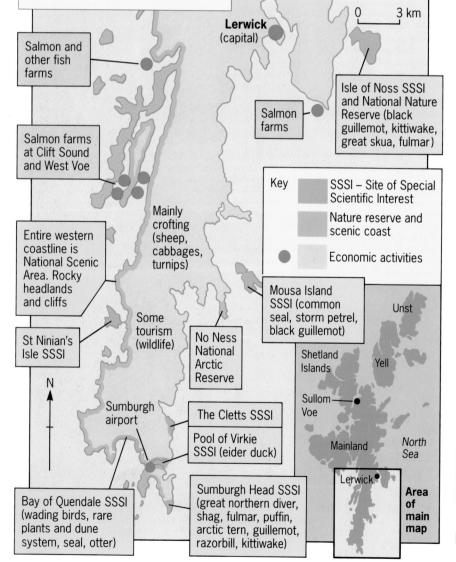

Salmon and other fish farms

Lerwick (capital)

0   3 km

Isle of Noss SSSI and National Nature Reserve (black guillemot, kittiwake, great skua, fulmar)

Salmon farms

Salmon farms at Clift Sound and West Voe

Mainly crofting (sheep, cabbages, turnips)

Key

SSSI – Site of Special Scientific Interest

Nature reserve and scenic coast

Economic activities

Entire western coastline is National Scenic Area. Rocky headlands and cliffs

St Ninian's Isle SSSI

Some tourism (wildlife)

No Ness National Arctic Reserve

Mousa Island SSSI (common seal, storm petrel, black guillemot)

N

Sumburgh airport

The Cletts SSSI

Pool of Virkie SSSI (eider duck)

Bay of Quendale SSSI (wading birds, rare plants and dune system, seal, otter)

Sumburgh Head SSSI (great northern diver, shag, fulmar, puffin, arctic tern, guillemot, razorbill, kittiwake)

Unst

Shetland Islands

Yell

Sullom Voe

Mainland

North Sea

Lerwick

Area of main map

B Shetland Islands – economy and environment

The Braer was driven onto rocks (photo **C**). The resultant release of oil affected both the environment and the economy of Shetland (map **D**).

Environment The spillage affected seabirds, seals, otters and fish. Beaches were covered in brown oil. At first the wind was too strong for spray dispersant planes to fly or for the chemicals to be used accurately. Later there were complaints that the sprays were getting into the food chain and that, being toxic, they were highly dangerous to sea life. Some conservation groups claimed that the chemicals were far more dangerous to wildlife than the oil.

People Toxic fumes were blown inland. These gave people headaches, sore throats and a feeling of nausea.

C The *Braer* aground, January 1993

Economy Local salmon farms, which provided Shetland with 20 per cent of its income, were contaminated. The fish were declared to be unfit for human consumption.

Storms made the disaster much worse, with the wind carrying the oil inland. It was deposited on fields, sheep and vegetables (cabbages and turnips). No one knows what long term effect this dispersal will have upon soils and grazing land.

Fortunately, because of the severe seas and the oil being light crude, the oil dispersed naturally far faster than people had thought and with less impact than had originally been feared. Even so, there may be as yet unnoticed long term effects.

Activities

1 How did improvements in technology help in the:
   a) exploitation of North Sea oil,
   b) protection of the environment from oil?

2 According to map **B** what
   a) types of wildlife are found on Shetland;
   b) occupations are available other than in the oil industry?

3 a) What physical conditions contributed to the *Braer* disaster?
   b) Using map **D** and other information on these pages explain what effect the disaster had on the:
   i)   environment,
   ii) people,
   iii) economy.

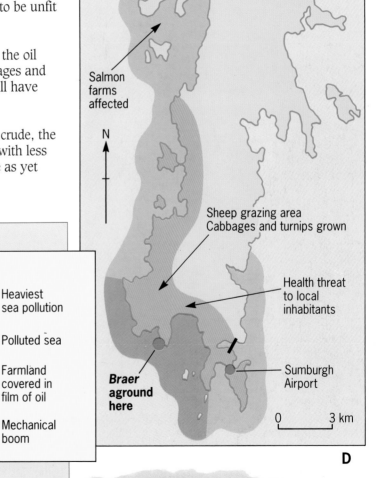

Salmon farms affected

N

Sheep grazing area
Cabbages and turnips grown

Health threat to local inhabitants

Braer aground here

Sumburgh Airport

0   3 km

D

Key

Heaviest sea pollution

Polluted sea

Farmland covered in film of oil

Mechanical boom

Summary

Technological developments have helped in the exploitation of natural resources such as oil. The exploitation of energy resources can have an important effect upon the environment.

How can the production of electricity affect the environment?

In Britain our way of life seems to depend upon electricity. Whether at work, play or at home, it is usually taken for granted. All it needs is the touch of a switch. Yet in many parts of the world, electricity is either unavailable or its provision is unreliable. Places without electricity often tend to remain economically less developed and their people are likely to have a poorer quality of life.

There are many different sources of energy (page 128). All have advantages for the economy and people of a place. They all affect the environment in one way or another.

Non-renewable types of energy are used mainly in industrialised countries. These resources are usually very efficient but they create considerable environmental problems. Renewable resources cause fewer environmental problems but often still lack the technology needed for their economic development. Most of Britain's electricity is produced in **thermal power stations** using coal, oil or natural gas. The remainder comes either from **nuclear** or **hydro-electric power stations**. Fact files **A**, **B** and **C** explain how each of these three types of power station affect the environment:

Fact file A: thermal (coal-fired)

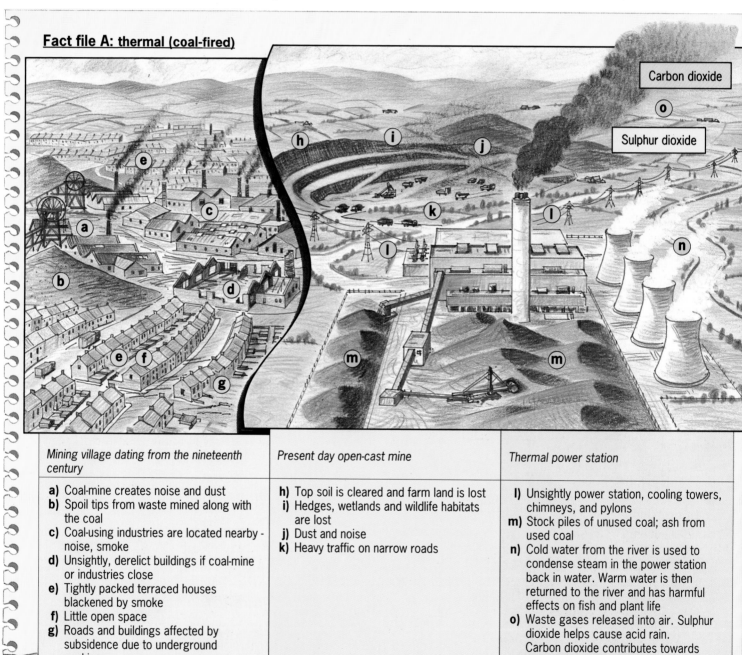

Mining village dating from the nineteenth century	Present day open-cast mine	Thermal power station
a) Coal-mine creates noise and dust **b)** Spoil tips from waste mined along with the coal **c)** Coal-using industries are located nearby - noise, smoke **d)** Unsightly, derelict buildings if coal-mine or industries close **e)** Tightly packed terraced houses blackened by smoke **f)** Little open space **g)** Roads and buildings affected by subsidence due to underground workings	**h)** Top soil is cleared and farm land is lost **i)** Hedges, wetlands and wildlife habitats are lost **j)** Dust and noise **k)** Heavy traffic on narrow roads	**l)** Unsightly power station, cooling towers, chimneys, and pylons **m)** Stock piles of unused coal; ash from used coal **n)** Cold water from the river is used to condense steam in the power station back in water. Warm water is then returned to the river and has harmful effects on fish and plant life **o)** Waste gases released into air. Sulphur dioxide helps cause acid rain. Carbon dioxide contributes towards greenhouse effect and global warming.

Fact file B: nuclear

Advantages
- Very little natural resource (uranium) is needed
- Nuclear waste is limited and can be stored underground
- Cleaner than fossil fuels. There is less air pollution and it is not a major contributor to acid rain or global warming.

Disadvantages
- Safety risk. It is feared that an accident at a power station could kill many people.
- Accidental releases of radio-active material can contaminate land and sea areas
- Health risk, e.g. possible links with leukaemia and other serious illnesses
- Nuclear waste is dangerous and can remain radioactive for a long time
- Safety fears in transporting and storing nuclear waste

Nuclear power station

Fact file C: hydro-electricity

Advantages
- Very clean form of energy. No contamination of the air, land or water.
- A renewable form of energy so it is not using up the earth's resources.
- Usually produced in highland areas that have heavy, reliable rainfall. These places rarely have high population densities.
- Dams built to store water also reduce the risks of flooding and water shortages.

Disadvantages
- Where storage lakes (reservoirs) have formed behind dams, large areas of farmland and wildlife habitats may have been flooded.
- People and animals are forced to move as lake levels rise.
- Unsightly pylons take electricity from power station.
- Silt previously spread over farmland is now deposited in the lake.

Hydro-electric dam, Scotland

Activities

1. How has the environment been affected by the:
   a) mining of coal in the nineteenth century;
   b) present day open-cast mining?

2. a) How can the environment be affected by the production of electricity in:
   i) thermal power stations,
   ii) nuclear power stations,
   iii) hydro-electric power stations?

b) In groups of two or three compile a newspaper report describing which of the three methods of producing electricity has the
   i) most harmful effect
   ii) least harmful effect
   upon the environment. Give reasons for your opinions.

Summary

Electricity can be produced from a wide range of energy sources. While all these sources affect the environment, some have a much more harmful effect than others.

Overuse of energy resources - causes and effects

There are two main causes of the overuse of energy and other natural resources. As to which cause is the more important depends upon whether you live in the richer 'North' or the poorer 'South' (diagram **A**).

1 The 'North' blames the rapid rise in population in the economically less developed countries which form the 'South' (page 68). As the number of births increase then more parts of the world are likely to become overpopulated (page 74), with the number of people living there outweighing the resources available to them.

2 The 'South' blames the wasteful use of resources in the economically more developed countries (diagram **B**). On average the amount of energy used by each person in the USA could sustain over 500 people living in poorer countries like India and Ethiopia.

A

The **USA** has only 5% of the world's population yet it consumes 35% of the world's resources including:

42% of the aluminium
33% of the copper
44% of the coal
33% of the oil
63% of the natural gas

all of which are **non-renewable**.

The North has 25% of the world's population. It consumes 75% of natural resources including 80% of energy resources. Slow population growth apart from the proportion of elderly who use human resources (pensions, retirement homes and health care).

North

South

The South has 75% of the world's population but only consumes 25% of its natural resources. Rapid population growth, especially of younger people. They need natural resources - food, energy, wood, etc.

Energy and other natural resources are not spread evenly across the world. This has led to differences in supply and demand, and to uneven economic growth between countries (diagram **B**). We have already seen that, so far as energy is concerned, it is the non-renewable resources which are in biggest demand. The two major effects of using non-renewable energy resources are:

1 Some energy supplies are beginning to **run out**. This means that those reserves still left are becoming harder and more expensive to obtain. The increase in cost will affect the poorer countries more than the richer ones. The world must make a greater effort to **conserve** more of its resources or to find alternative solutions.

2 Non-renewable resources, especially those used in industry and thermal power stations, are the major **polluters** of the environment (page 133) by contributing to acid rain and global warming. Once pollutants get into the atmosphere they are blown across national frontiers and so become an international problem. These problems can only be reduced by **international agreement** and **management**.

B

Some developing countries have virtually no energy resources	Some have limited resources or one main resource	Others have a wider range of resources	Developed countries usually have a wide range of resources
Not enough capital to import . . . . . . or technology to develop resources	Rely on multinationals to provide capital . . . and technology. Profits go overseas	More capital . . . . . . and improved technology to develop resources	Plenty of capital . . . . . . and technology to buy and develop resources
They remain very poor	They remain poor	They have higher levels of wealth and development	They are wealthy and economically developed

Energy = Tonnes of coal equivalent per person per year

e.g. **Ethiopia**
Energy 0.02
GNP 120

e.g. **Nigeria**
Energy 0.14
GNP 250

e.g. **Brazil**
Energy 0.8
GNP 2550

e.g. **USA**
Energy 10.13
GNP 21 000

GNP = Annual income per person ($ US)

The value of fuelwood in Kenya

Fuelwood, like any natural resource, is considered to be very important within an economically less developed country like Kenya. Today only 6.4 per cent of Kenya is forested – a much lower figure than a century ago. Forests have been cleared for:

- small shambas (farms) where farmers grow just sufficient food for their own needs;
- plantations where multinational companies grow commercial crops including Kenya's two largest money earning exports of tea and coffee;
- fuelwood which is needed by local people for cooking and heating.

Attempts are being made, with the help of an organisation called Intermediate Technology, to use less fuelwood and to develop equipment which will help Kenyans to become more self-sufficient and, hopefully, less poor (diagram **C**).

C

Improved cooking stoves in Kenya

Kenyan women are almost entirely dependent on wood as fuel for cooking. In the cities women must buy wood or charcoal (transported from rural areas) to use on their traditional stoves, while rural women spend long hours gathering the fuel they need. At the same time, Kenyan resources of wood are decreasing.

An improved cooking stove (jiko) has been developed which drastically reduces the use of charcoal in urban households. The stove is based on a traditional design and is made by local metal workers from scrap metal (photo **B**, page 143). It incorporates a ceramic lining which is produced by local potters.

This development has had an impact on large numbers of people.
- More than 40 000 households are now making sizeable savings in their fuel costs. In many homes the new stove pays for itself in about a month. Moreover, the improved stove reduces smoke and fumes in the kitchen and contributes to improving women's health.
- Large numbers of small-scale metal workers and potters are now involved in making the jiko and have found new support from the government which makes their businesses more stable.

Widespread use of the stove also has a potential impact on the environment, as any saving in urban fuel consumption helps relieve the pressure on rural wood resources.   *Source:* Intermediate Technology

Activities

1 a) Draw two pie charts. On the first show the proportion of the world's people living in the rich 'North' and the poor 'South'. On the second show the proportion of energy reserves used by the 'North' and the 'South'.
   b) Give reasons for the differences between the two graphs and the comments made in diagram **D**.
   c) Why does the average American use about the same amount of energy per day as 500 people living in many parts of India or Africa?

2 How has population growth and economic development put increasing pressure on each of the following natural resources?
   - Vegetation (forests)
   - Wildlife
   - Open space
   - Soil
   - Water supply
   - Minerals.

3 Why has the introduction of improved cooking stoves been important to Kenya?

D

NORTH

The rapid growth of your population in the South is using up the earth's resources.

People in the North use most of the world's resources. You leave hardly any for us.

SOUTH

Summary The growth of both populations and economies increases pressure on natural resources. This calls for international co-operation of resource and environmental management. The protection of their limited resources is even more important to economically less developed countries.

▶ Where did industry grow and how is it distributed in the UK? ◀

Activities

1 The following is a list of factors which affect the location of industry:
Markets - Raw materials - Transport - Labour supply (workers) - Sources of energy(power) - Land (site) - Government policies
   a) Explain the importance of each factor in the list.
   b) Complete table **A** by listing the factors under physical or human and economic.
   c) Were the physical factors or the human and economic factors the more important in:
      i) the nineteenth century
      ii) the early 1990s?

A

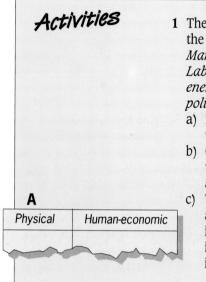

Physical	Human-economic

2 Industry is a system with inputs, processes and outputs (table **B**).
   a) Draw a system for the steel industry using the following:
   iron ore - production of pig iron - coking coal - sheet steel - girders - manufacture of steel - limestone
   b) Draw a system for the textile industry using the following:
   wool - cotton shirts - spinning - cotton - woollen jumpers - weaving

B

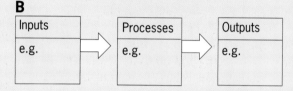

Inputs		Processes		Outputs
e.g.	⟹	e.g.	⟹	e.g.

The first 'industries' in Britain used charcoal to smelt ores such as iron. The iron was turned into agricultural equipment (e.g. scythes) and weapons (e.g. spears). These early industries located in forested areas and where iron ore was easily obtainable.

By the eighteenth century, power to turn machinery was obtained from fast-flowing rivers. Textile mills and iron forges grew up along the banks of rivers flowing from the Pennines in Yorkshire and Lancashire.

The rapid growth of industry in Britain came in the early nineteenth century with the introduction of steam power. As coal was needed to heat water to produce steam, and as coal was heavy and bulky to move, then coalfields became the ideal location for industry (map **C**). Map **D** shows the distribution and the location of the main traditional industrial areas in Britain in 1945. Notice how:
- most industrial regions were located on coalfields;
- each region tended to specialise in one or two types of industry.

C Britain's coalfields, 1800-1945

D The major industrial regions in Britain, 1945

Recently the location of the main centres of industry have again changed. As the amount of coal produced in Britain has declined rapidly and as electricity (power) can now be transmitted through the National Grid to virtually every part of the country, a raw material (coalfield) location has become less important. Although some industry still exists on the former coalfields, the present distribution pattern shows two major changes (map **E**).

Firstly, there has been a shift from inland coalfields to coastal estuaries. Ports have long been important places for industries, especially those involved with the processing of imported raw materials, e.g. sugar refining and flour milling. Since the Second World War, ships have increased in size, they have become more specialised in what they carry, and they need specialist loading and unloading facilities. At the same time, as Britain's raw materials have begun to run out, more have to be imported. The advantage of a sheltered, deep water location is shown by the increase in industrial development along coastal estuaries (e.g. the Humber and Thames) and the location of oil refineries (e.g. Teesside, the Solent and Milford Haven).

Secondly, there has been a movement from the more northerly parts of England to the south. This has partly been due to modern industry becoming 'footloose'. Footloose refers to those industries which are not tied to raw materials. As a result many new industries, a large number of which are high-tech, seek a location in an attractive environment and as close as possible to their market.

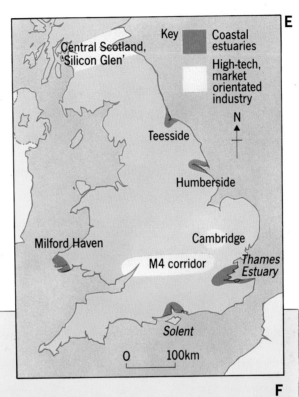

E Distribution of industry in the 1990s

Activities

1 Sixteen industrial towns have been numbered on map **F**.
   a) Use an atlas to identify each place.
   b) Complete the table below the map to give the main reason why each place became an important centre for industry. The first one has been done for you. Maps **C**, **D** and **E** will help you to answer this question.

2 Choose any industry which grew up in your home region in the nineteenth century.
   a) What factors favoured its original location?
   b) **Either:**
      i) If the industry is still there today, give reasons why it is still operating.
      or
      ii) If it has closed, give reasons why it did so.

3 Choose an industry or firm which has recently located in your home region. What advantages attracted it to this location?

Summary

Both physical and human–economic factors affect the location of industry. As the relative importance of these factors changes over a period of time, then the distribution and location of industrial areas changes.

Number	Place	Water route	Coalfields	Coastal estuaries	Near market, high-tech
1	Birmingham				✓

► *Why do some industries group together?* ◄

A

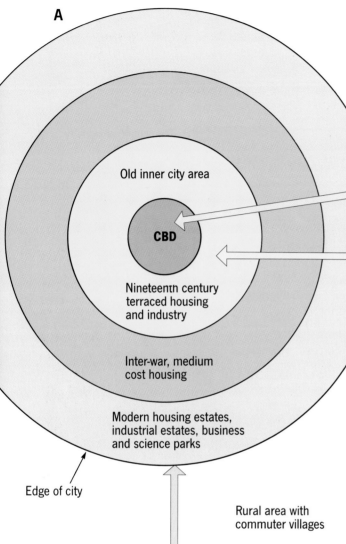

Old inner city area

CBD

Nineteenth century terraced housing and industry

Inter-war, medium cost housing

Modern housing estates, industrial estates, business and science parks

Edge of city

Rural area with commuter villages

When looking at a simple urban land use model (diagram **A**, page 94), it can be seen that certain types of economic activity group together. Shops and offices group together in the CBD. Older nineteenth century industries located in today's inner city areas. Firms wishing to locate on modern industrial estates or on science parks group together on the outskirts of urban areas. There have always been advantages for similar types of firms and industries to group together in particular locations (diagram **A**).

Concentration of shops and offices (page 144).

Inner city

Concentration of industries, many of which developed in the nineteenth century. The area may still include old mills and factories, or it may have been redeveloped with smaller units and DIY shops.

Advantages of inner cities:
- near commercial centre (CBD)
- near main roads leading into city centre
- next to railways and canals
- near to workforce living in low-cost, terraced housing
- at time of development this location was on the edge of the urban area
- small firms making component parts for larger, nearby assembly companies

Edge-of-city

Concentration of modern firms on industrial estates and science parks.

Advantages of edge-of-city locations:
- cheaper sites as land values decrease away from the CBD
- need large areas of land for car parking and possible future expansion
- near to main roads and motorway interchanges
- near skilled and mainly female workforce in modern private housing estates and commuter villages
- easier to exchange information with similar types of firm
- attractive layout (diagram **B**) with 70 per cent of science parks left as open space

Science and business parks

Both **science** and **business parks** are located on edge-of-city greenfield sites. They have attractive lay-outs (diagram **B**) with grassy areas, ornamental gardens and ponds, and buildings screened by trees. The modern buildings have central heating, air conditioning and large windows allowing in the maximum amount of light. Each unit has plenty of space for car parking. Many of the firms are connected with the information, **high-technology**, and electronics industries. Whereas science parks have direct links with universities for research, business parks may also include superstores, hotels and leisure centres.

What are the disadvantages of similar firms concentrating together?

If all firms in a given area require the same levels of skill, some may find difficulty in recruiting the right type of workforce. It is possible that too many similar industries might produce too many goods for people in the local area to buy. If a town relies too much on a particular type of industry it is more likely to experience unemployment if that industry is hit by a recession.

Activities

1 Diagram **B** shows the layout of Cambridge Science Park.
   a) What is a science park?
   b) Name three types of companies found on the Cambridge Science Park.
   c) What are the advantages of locating on this particular site?
   d) What are the advantages to the companies of concentrating together on the same site?
   e) What are the disadvantages to the companies of concentrating together on the same site?
   f) Describe the layout of the Cambridge Science Park under these headings.
      • Buildings
      • Road pattern
      • Landscaped areas

2 Diagram **C** shows three possible locations for a new science park.
   a) Which of the three locations would you choose? Give reasons for your choice.
   b) Why would you reject the other two sites?

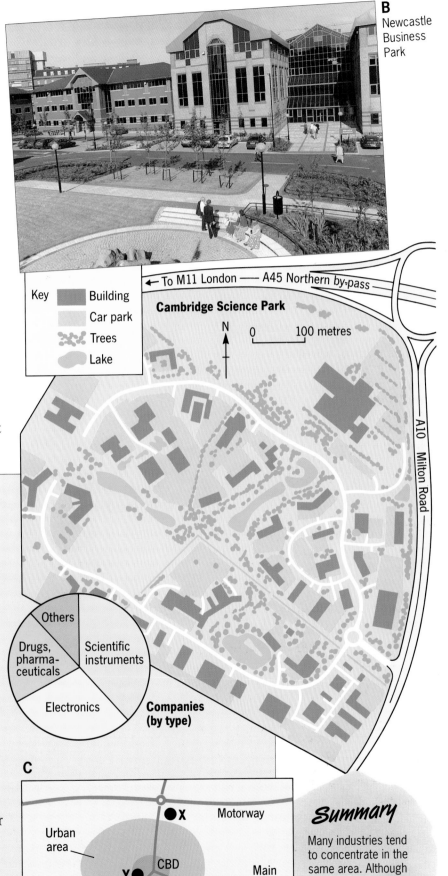

B Newcastle Business Park

Key — Building, Car park, Trees, Lake

Cambridge Science Park

← To M11 London — A45 Northern by-pass

A10 Milton Road

N   0   100 metres

Drugs, pharmaceuticals / Others / Scientific instruments / Electronics — **Companies (by type)**

C

Urban area — Motorway — ●X — CBD — ●Y — Main road — ●Z

Summary

Many industries tend to concentrate in the same area. Although this provides many advantages, there are disadvantages too.

The relocation of industry in the UK since 1945

We have already seen how the UK's industry was distributed in 1945 (map **D**, page 136). Since then significant changes have taken place. These include towns where industry has moved from inner city areas to edge-of-city locations (page 138). Also industry has moved away from inland areas where raw materials used to be found, to either coastal estuaries or nearer to large markets (page 137). There has been a more general movement from the north and west of Britain to South-east England. Diagram **A** shows some of the factors which have caused these changes.

The recession of the early 1990s has upset this trend. This time it is the South-east of England, not northern Britain, which has experienced more job losses and falling house prices.

A Changes in industrial location

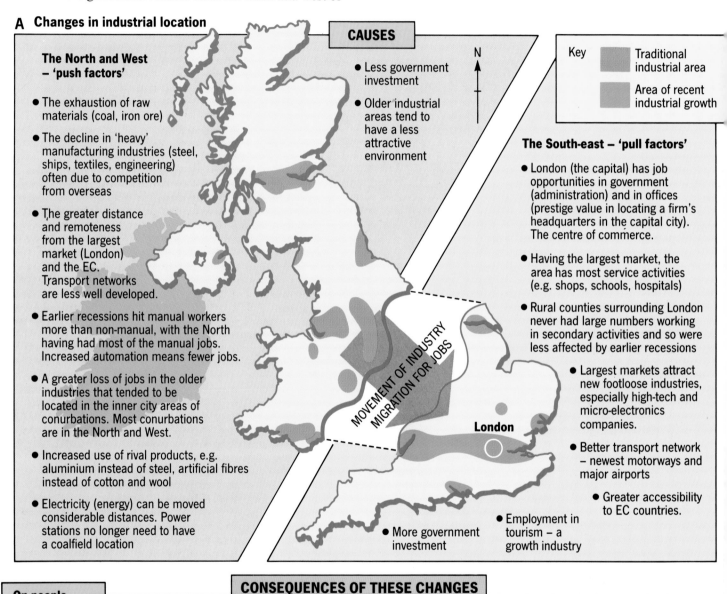

CAUSES

Key — Traditional industrial area / Area of recent industrial growth

The North and West – 'push factors'

- The exhaustion of raw materials (coal, iron ore)

- The decline in 'heavy' manufacturing industries (steel, ships, textiles, engineering) often due to competition from overseas

- The greater distance and remoteness from the largest market (London) and the EC. Transport networks are less well developed.

- Earlier recessions hit manual workers more than non-manual, with the North having had most of the manual jobs. Increased automation means fewer jobs.

- A greater loss of jobs in the older industries that tended to be located in the inner city areas of conurbations. Most conurbations are in the North and West.

- Increased use of rival products, e.g. aluminium instead of steel, artificial fibres instead of cotton and wool

- Electricity (energy) can be moved considerable distances. Power stations no longer need to have a coalfield location

- Less government investment
- Older industrial areas tend to have a less attractive environment

MOVEMENT OF INDUSTRY MIGRATION FOR JOBS

London

- More government investment
- Employment in tourism – a growth industry

The South-east – 'pull factors'

- London (the capital) has job opportunities in government (administration) and in offices (prestige value in locating a firm's headquarters in the capital city). The centre of commerce.

- Having the largest market, the area has most service activities (e.g. shops, schools, hospitals)

- Rural counties surrounding London never had large numbers working in secondary activities and so were less affected by earlier recessions

- Largest markets attract new footloose industries, especially high-tech and micro-electronics companies.

- Better transport network – newest motorways and major airports

- Greater accessibility to EC countries.

CONSEQUENCES OF THESE CHANGES

On people

Many job losses. Higher level of unemployment and fewer career opportunities. People move out of the region.

Increase in number of jobs. Lower level of unemployment and more career opportunities. People move into the region.

On settlements

Unsightly and depressing appearance of disused mills, factories, mines and waste land. Fewer new industries. Lack of money to maintain services so shops may close and schools may have more vacant places. Lower land and house prices. Fewer road improvements.

As many industries are new, they are in modern buildings on attractive, well-planned industrial estates or business and science parks. Many services with newer schools, shops and hospitals. Rapid growth of smaller towns and commuter villages. Rising land and house prices. More road improvements, e.g. by-passes.

Changes in the location of the iron and steel industry

The nineteenth century iron industry was concentrated upon coalfields which also contained bands of iron ore. The major producing centres were in the South Wales Valleys, North-east England, parts of the Central Valley of Scotland and around Sheffield. Although, later technological developments enabled steel rather than iron to be manufactured, there was no need to change the location of the new steelworks and the distribution pattern remained the same (map **C**). When a method of smelting low grade iron ore was discovered, two new steelworks were opened near to the ore deposits at Scunthorpe and Corby (map **B**). Since then much of Britain's most accessible coal, as with iron ore, has been used up. As imports of these two raw materials increased, then Britain's latest steelworks were built on the coast (map **C**). By 1993 only four integrated steelworks remained open.

B Iron and steelworks, before 1960

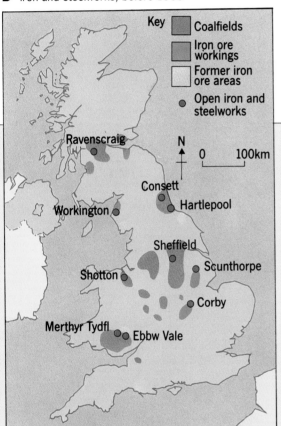

C Integrated steelworks, 1993

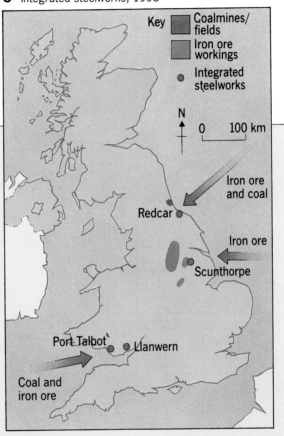

Activities

1 a) Why have the main centres of UK industry moved from the north and west (push factors) to the South-east (pull factors)?
  b) Using diagram **A** explain what effect this has had upon:
    i) people living in the north and west,
    ii) settlements in the north and west,
    iii) people living in the south-east,
    iv) settlements in the south-east.

2 Using maps **B** and **C**:
  a) Describe the distribution of steelworks in 1960. How do you account for this distribution pattern?
  b) Describe the distribution pattern of steelworks in 1993. Why has the pattern changed between 1960 and 1993?

Summary

As the distribution of industry in the UK has changed from coalfield locations towards coastal estuaries and the south, it has affected people and settlements. Likewise, whereas Britain's iron industry grew up near to raw materials, today's depleted steel industry is located near to coastal ports.

▶ *What affects the economic development*

One important factor affecting the economic growth of a country is the nature of, and the value placed upon, natural resources. Often natural resources, such as mineral wealth or the potential to produce high yielding foods, are limited. When resources, especially minerals, are available economically developing countries often lack the capital and the technology to develop them. As a result most of the available resources are bought, at as low a price as possible, by the richer and already industrialised economically more developed countries. Having traded their natural resources at a low price, developing countries have then to buy back these materials in a processed (manufactured) form at a much higher price. The resultant trade deficit means even less money is available to try to develop their own resources.

A

Bamburi Portland Cement Company, Mombasa	
Type of industry	**Formal**, i.e. it is organised, so workers have contracts, work fixed hours and receive a regular, but low, wage. A raw material location.
Raw materials	Built on coral limestone which provides the lime for the cement. Adequate supply of water from rivers and boreholes. Some coal (to heat furnaces) has to be imported.
Energy	Electricity from National Grid. Uses 5 per cent of Kenya's total electricity.
Technology	Advanced methods to compete with other world producers. Production is capital intensive.
Investment	A multinational. Parent company is International Cementia of Switzerland. Also has links with Blue Circle (UK). Overseas companies provide the high level of investment needed.
Trade	Up to 35 per cent of cement is exported, mainly to neighbouring Somalia, Tanzania and the Indian Ocean islands. About 65 per cent is used internally in Kenya for new buildings. Specialised machinery, lorries and spare parts for both have to be imported for quarrying the coral, and producing and transporting the cement.
Workforce	European managers. There are 850 permanent Kenyan workers, many of whom have had training. Not large numbers since production is capital intensive.
Advantages to Kenya	High level of taxes paid to the Government for land rates, using water and electricity, etc. Helps trade balance as value of export of cement is greater than costs of imports. Provides employment and improves skills of local people. Paid for the building of a local school.

Activities

The Bamburi Portland Cement Company is a formal industry developed by a multi-national company. Jua Kali are groups of informal industries which have grown spontaneously.
  a) What is the difference between a formal and an informal industry?
  b) What effect does the development of industries like the Bamburi Portland Cement Company and small scale Jua Kali enterprises have on the economic development of an economically

# of an economically developing country? ◄

Industrial development is also affected by the amounts and type of inward investment from the government within a country, or through foreign investment, loans and development assistance programmes. These, and other factors, may provide opportunities for the economic development of a country, but more often put constraints upon it.

Two extreme examples, taken from Kenya, have been selected to try to show how the factors listed earlier can affect economic growth. They are the large Bamburi Portland Cement Company near Mombasa (table **A**) and the Jua Kali metal workshops in Nairobi (table **B**).

B

Jua Kali metal workshops, Nairobi

Type of industry	**Informal**, i.e. spontaneous jobs, often small scale family enterprises. Long and irregular hours, low and uncertain wages. A market location.
Raw materials	Cheap scrap metal is recycled by melting it down and hammering it into various shapes, e.g. locks, boxes, cooking utensils, water barrels. Charcoal is used to heat the scrap metal.
Energy	Manual labour.
Technology	Appropriate technology which is sustainable and suited to the skills of the people, the availability of raw materials and capital. Labour intensive.
Investment	Very limited. The Government (inward investment) has supported this Jua Kali scheme by providing roofs to protect the workers from the weather (Jua Kali means 'under the hot sun'). There are many types of Jua Kali in Nairobi.
Trade	All the products are sold and used locally.
Workforce	Over 1000 workers in an area about 300m x 100m. Workers have had to develop their own skills. Large numbers since production is labour intensive.
Advantages to Kenya	Estimates suggest 600 000 people are employed in 350 000 small scale Jua Kali enterprises in Kenya. Enterprising spirit. Firms need little capital, recycle materials which otherwise would be wasted, provide low cost training, and can react quickly to market changes. They provide the backbone for Kenya's industrial development.

developing country like Kenya? Give your answer under the following headings:
- Use of natural resources
- Technology
- Trade
- Inward (internal) investment
- Foreign investment.

Summary

Several factors including the nature and value of natural resources, the level and development of technology, the balance of trade, the amount and type of inward investment, and the significance of foreign investments, can all affect the economic growth of economically developing countries.

Shopping in British towns in the 1960s and 1970s

The concept of a **shopping hierarchy**, ranging from large regional shopping centres down to the village or corner shop, has already been described (page 89). During the 1960s and 1970s, four main types of shop and shopping centres could be identified in British towns and cities. Diagram **A** shows how the four types fit into an urban hierarchy. Diagram **B** shows, by means of a simplified transect, their generalised location.

A

| CBD | **High order centre** (usually only one) Sells: comparison, luxury and specialist goods |

| Secondary centres and suburban parades | **Middle order centres** (usually several) Sell: a mixture of convenience and specialist goods |

| Corner shops | **Low order centres** (many) Sell: convenience goods |

C

The city centre (CBD)

- Commercial and shopping centre. Accessible as most main roads meet here.
- Area of largest number of shops, biggest shops, and most shoppers.
- Large department stores and superstores which can afford the high land values.
- Comparison shops (e.g. clothes, shoes) where style and prices can be compared.
- Specialist shops (e.g. jewellery, furniture, electrical goods).
- Small food shops (e.g. bakers, grocers, butchers and fishmongers).
- Some out-of-door pedestrian precincts, but most streets shared between cars, buses, delivery lorries and shoppers.

D

Secondary shopping centres

- Usually a line of shops extending alongside main roads leading into the city centre.
- Take advantage of cheaper land values, easier parking facilities, passing traffic and good accessibility.
- Many shops rely on impulse buying.
- Includes car show rooms and petrol stations.
- Some specialist shops (e.g. florists, food take-aways, off-licenses).
- Some convenience shops (e.g. newsagents).

Activities

1 What is the difference between
  a) low order and high order goods;
  b) convenience and specialist goods?

2 Look at diagram **B**. Which part of the shopping transect does your local area fall into? Draw a plan of your local area and label the types of shops in it.

3 How have **a)** accessibility and **b)** land values affected the type of shops found in:
  i)   the city centre (CBD)
  ii) a secondary shopping centre
  iii) an inner city housing area
  iv) a suburban parade?

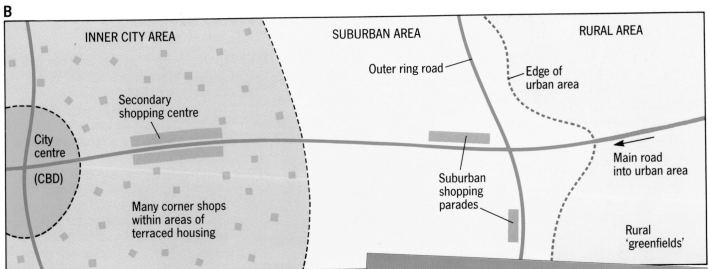

B

INNER CITY AREA

SUBURBAN AREA

RURAL AREA

Outer ring road

Edge of urban area

Secondary shopping centre

City centre (CBD)

Many corner shops within areas of terraced housing

Suburban shopping parades

Main road into urban area

Rural 'greenfields'

F

E

Corner shops

- Date from the nineteenth century and before the time of cars and public transport. Had to be easily accessible as people had to walk to them.
- Sell convenience goods - items people need daily but are not necessarily prepared to travel long distances to buy (e.g. milk, bread, newspapers, sweets).
- Open long and irregular hours for locals who might work late, receive unexpected guests or who have forgotten odd items.
- Friendly atmosphere. Social meeting place especially for elderly people living alone.

Suburban shopping parades

- Found in the suburbs either alongside main roads leading into the city centre or within large, modern housing estates. In both cases they provide easy access for local people.
- Saves people living near the edge of the urban area from having to travel into the city centre.
- Usually have limited space for car parking.
- Mainly convenience shops and small chain stores (e.g. Spar, VG).
- A few specialist shops (e.g. chemist, baker, post office).

Summary

Different types of shopping centres can be placed into a hierarchy based upon their size and the services which they provide. It is possible to identify a pattern showing the distribution of these various shopping centres within an urban area. This pattern is affected by accessibility, land values and the sequence of urban development.

Why have shopping habits and patterns changed?

Today's shoppers are more discerning in their choice of goods and the places where they shop. They are increasingly better educated and more aware through travel and television, and require sophistication and convenience in the shopping environment. Increased car ownership, more working women and greater demands on leisure time have resulted in less frequent food shopping. Bulk buying and late night shopping are now commonplace.

Source: GeoActive, Spring 1993, 'Recent trends in Retailing in the UK'

Increased mobility Due to the increase in car ownership, and two-car families, people can travel further to shops, visit shops with a wider range and volume of stock, and buy in bulk.

Accessibility Improved urban roads and national motorways enable shoppers, and delivery lorries, to travel more easily and more quickly to new shopping centres. Many of these new centres have an edge-of-city location.

Bulk buying Many shoppers now buy in bulk either once a week or once a month. This is a result of more people being paid monthly, having less free time, owning a deep freezer, and being able to park their cars near to the shop exit. Bulk buying is also cheaper.

Space Many new superstores and hypermarkets have been built on edge-of-city locations (pages 147 to 149). They need large areas of space for their buildings, car parks and quality environment, land which is relatively cheap to buy, room for expansion and good access by road.

Population movement The location of shops has altered as an increasing number of people move out of urban areas, especially the inner city and conurbations, into suburban areas and smaller rural towns.

Shopping hours Partly due to the increasing number of women in paid employment, a greater number of shops open later on many evenings and, more recently, on Sundays.

A

Left: Queensgate Shopping Centre, Peterborough
Below: Union Street, Bath

Changes in the CBD

- An increase in both pedestrianised precincts and covered shopping centres. Covered shopping malls shield shoppers from the weather and shorten the distances between shops.
- An increase in the number of food supermarkets which has resulted in the closure of specialist shops such as butchers, fishmongers and small grocers.
- Many large furniture and carpet stores have moved out of the city centre.
- The spaces created were filled by building societies, estate agents, small restaurants and cafés, and even more clothes shops.

B

Changes in the inner city

- Many corner shops have been pulled down during redevelopment schemes.
- Others have closed either because their goods were too expensive and limited in choice compared with city centre supermarkets, or because of people moving out of the area.
- Some corner shops now specialise in ethnic foods.
- DIY, furniture and carpet discount warehouses have opened along main roads leading into the city centre or on sites previously occupied by factories and terraced housing.

C

Changes on the edges of urban areas

- Major developments on cheaper, unused land on an edge-of-city, greenfield location.
- Developments include superstores (over 2 500m²) of selling space, car parking and quality environment), hypermarkets (over 4 500m²), regional shopping centres (over 45 000m²) and retail parks (pages 148 and 149).
- Smaller developments may only have foodhalls. Larger ones are likely to contain DIY and garden centres, furniture and car salesrooms, and leisure facilities.

Activities

1 Photographs **D**, **E** and **F** (pages 144-145), **A**, **B** and **C** (pages 146-147) all show different types of shop. Similar types of shop are found in most urban areas in Britain. Copy out and complete table **D** by answering a) and b).
   a) Match up the following map references, taken from the OS map of Carlisle on pages 82 and 83, with the type of shop that might be found there.
      401559 • 408551 • 398554 • 393559 • 393596 • 422545
   b) Name a place in your home town or nearest urban area where that type of shop might be found.
   c) Give reasons for your answers to part b).

2 With reference to changes in shopping patterns in your nearest urban area:
   a) Are most shops still found in the city centre?

D

Shopping centre	OS reference on Carlisle map	Example from your nearest urban area
Secondary shopping centre		
Corner shop		
Suburban parade		
City centre (CBD)		
New redevelopment in inner city		
Edge-of-city hypermarket		

b) Are the largest shops still found in the city centre?
c) Do most people still shop in the city centre?
d) What changes have taken place in the city centre in the last two years?
e) What changes have taken place in inner city areas?
f) Has much edge-of-city shopping development taken place?

Summary

Factors such as the mobility of shoppers, the accessibility of shopping areas, bulk buying, the need for more space, and urban development schemes have all affected the pattern showing the location of shopping centres in British towns and cities.

▶ Why have large shopping centres developed on the edges of cities? ◀

The most important change in retailing in Britain since 1980 has been the rapid growth of edge-of-city shopping centres. It has been estimated that during this time four-fifths of all new shopping floor-space has been on out-of-town sites. Hypermarkets were the first to react to people's changing shopping habits (page 146). More recently, larger regional shopping centres have developed, based on the MetroCentre in Gateshead. Since then three other centres have opened (map **A**), including that at Meadowhall in Sheffield (photo **B** and plan **D**).

A UK regional shopping centres

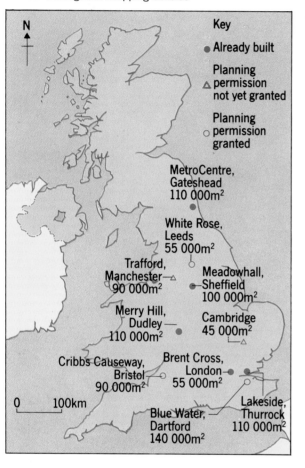

B Meadowhall shopping centre

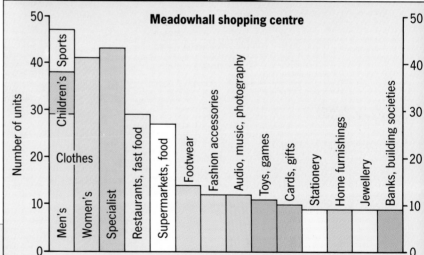

C

Advantages of an edge-of-city location

- They are near main roads and, ideally, a motorway interchange which makes the delivery of goods easier and gives access for shoppers from several large urban areas. Allows closer links with retailers selling similar goods.
- There is plenty of space for large car parks as hypermarkets and regional centres aim to attract motorists (over 12 000 parking places at the MetroCentre). No parking problems or traffic congestion as there is in the city centre.
- As land values are lower than those in the CBD, then so too are the rates and rent which shop-owners have to pay. This allows individual shops to use large areas of floor-space and to keep the prices of their goods down. Being so large, shops can stock a large volume and a wide range of goods.
- Unlike the city centre, there is plenty of space for possible future expansion.
- They are near to suburban housing estates which provide a workforce, especially as many employees are female, work part-time, and have to work late most evenings.

The majority of shoppers are relatively young, are car owners, are prepared to travel considerable distances, buy in bulk, and shop relatively infrequently.

The larger regional centre developments provide a wide range of associated facilities such as petrol stations, restaurants and leisure facilities. Sir John Hall, who pioneered this type of shopping at the Metro Centre, has said, 'The emphasis has to be laid on family shopping and associated leisure activities. In other words, it is to provide a day out for the whole family'. Plan **D** shows the layout for the two shopping malls in Sheffield's Meadowhall Centre, and graph **C** the number and types of shops and amenities available in the centre.

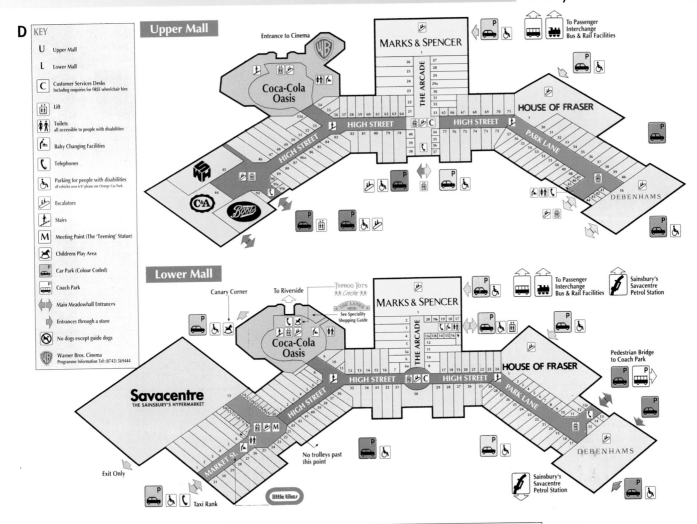

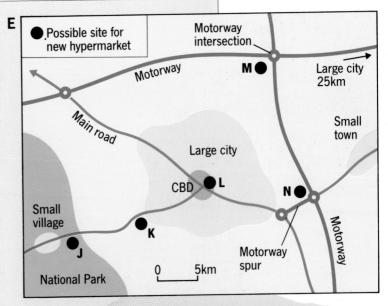

Activities

1 A large national supermarket chain wishes to build a hypermarket in the area shown on map **E**. Five available sites have been shown as **J** to **N**. Some sites will not be acceptable to the supermarket chain, other sites will not be acceptable to local people and the planners.
  a) Rank the five sites in the order which you think that the supermarket chain will prefer. Give reasons for your answer.
  b) Which of the sites do you think will:
   i) cause most opposition from local people;
   ii) be rejected by the planners?
   Give reasons for your answer.
  c) On which site do you think the hypermarket will eventually be built?

2 a) Give five advantages of building a regional shopping centre at Meadowhall, on the edge of Sheffield.
  b) According to graph **C**, what are the three major users of the units in the centre?
  c) Why is the centre a good place
   i) for family shopping;
   ii) for a day out for the whole family?

Summary

As city centres have become more crowded and expensive, and as people's mobility and shopping preferences change, a large number of new shops have chosen an edge-of-city location.

149

How can tourism change the environment?

Many tourists are attracted to areas of great scenic beauty or where there is abundant wildlife. Many of these environments are fragile, and can easily be changed and damaged by the large number of tourists they will attract. Therefore, it is essential that such environments are protected. To do this needs careful planning and management. One example which illustrate these points is the east coast of Kenya (transect **A**).

A Transect across the east coast of Kenya, near Mombasa

Bamburi Portland Cement Company (page 142)

Baobab Farm

Quarry being reclaimed

Main east coast road. Heavy local and tourist traffic

Wildlife disappeared

Natural vegetation cleared for large tourist hotels and expensive houses

Extensive sandy beaches with palm trees

Safe, shallow sheltered lagoon

Living coral reef extends parallel to coast, about 1km offshore. Fragile ecosystem exposed at low tide

Indian Ocean (sharks)

Sea level

Dead coral limestone

Transect across the east coast of Kenya, near Mombasa

The coral reef – a fragile environment

Coral is an organism which can only live in very warm, clear and clean seas. It produces attractive shapes and colours and provides a habitat for an abundance of marine life.

C Hotels near Mombasa

B Coral reef, Kenya

Unfortunately it can easily be damaged or destroyed by even the lightest contact, and suffocated if covered by sand or silt. The reef off the coast of Kenya is uncovered at low tide (photo **B**). In places it is possible either to wade out across the shallow lagoon, sheltered from large waves and shark attack, or take a boat to reach the reef. The reef is destroyed when these boats drop anchor, or when tourists trample over the living coral. Swimmers and snorklers disturb sand on the lagoon floor and this, together with increased pollution from the tourist resorts, suffocates the coral. Several marine parks and reserves have been created where it is illegal to spear fish, to collect coral and cowrie shells, or to disturb the highly sensitive ecosystem. It is still possible, for a small fee, to scuba dive to see underwater coral.

The beach hotels – tourism changing the natural environment

The coast is, arguably, Kenya's most important natural resource. Lying on the Equator, temperatures on the Kenyan coast reach 30°C every day. There is plenty of sunshine for most of the year and there are only two short rainy seasons. The beaches are long, clean and sandy. The coral reef extends along the whole of the Kenyan coast apart from a gap at Mombasa, Kenya's only port. Behind the coral reef the shallow lagoon is warm and sheltered making it safe for swimming and other water sports. The result has been the construction of an almost unbroken line of holiday hotels and beach complexes extending for many kilometres either side of the port of Mombasa (photo **C**). The building of these hotels has led to the removal of any remaining natural vegetation, the disappearance of wildlife, and the pushing inland of local farmers. The result has been a complete change in the local landscape and habitat.

Baobab Farm – restoring a damaged environment and creating a wildlife habitat

Behind the coastal hotels, the Bamburi Portland Cement Company quarries coral limestone (page 142). By 1971, 25 million tonnes of coral limestone had been removed leaving only a huge scar. The environment had been totally damaged – there was no soil, no vegetation and no wildlife. The Swiss multinational cement company then appointed Dr Haller to try to restore the environment from what he himself called 'a lunar landscape filled with saline ponds'. He found that one species of tree, Casaurina, could grow in the coral rubble, the saline soil and in temperatures reaching 40°C. The Casaurina trees (photo **D**) grew by three metres a year. Thousands of red millipedes were then added to break down the large number of fallen leaves to produce humus. Earthworms and indigenous grasses and trees were added, but no chemicals were used. Within twenty years 15 cms of soil had formed and a tropical rainforest environment had been created (photo **E**). The ecosystem was completed by the addition of insects, birds, and herbivores.

Yet the project is not just an environmental success. It has become a sustainable commercial venture with income from 46 enterprises including a fish farm, a crocodile hatchery and the sale of fruit and rice. The Baobab Farm, the name of the restored area, is open to school parties every morning, while in the afternoon it attracts other visitors. The near 100 000 visitors in 1992 made it the largest tourist attraction in the Mombasa area.

D Casaurina trees planted by the Bamburi Portland Cement Company

E Baobab Farm restored environment

Activities

1. a) Why do coral reefs form a 'fragile environment'?
   b) How is tourism affecting this fragile environment?
   c) What has been done to try to protect this fragile environment?
   d) How has tourism changed the coastal landscape of Kenya?

2. The Baobab Farm has become one of the largest and most successful environmental reclamation schemes in the world. Copy out and complete flow chart **F** by putting the correct phrases from the list opposite into the appropriate box.

A Thousands of red millipedes added
B Insects, birds and herbivores added
C Indigenous grasses and trees planted
D Bare lunar landscape
E Tropical rainforest ecosystem
F No soil, vegetation or wildlife
G Humus produced and 15 cms soil formed
H Casaurina trees planted

F

| D Bare lunar landscape | → | | → | | → | | → | | → | | → | | → | |

Summary

Many environments in the world are fragile and can easily be damaged or changed by human activities such as tourism. It is important to try to protect, plan and manage those environments that have not yet been damaged, and to restore those which have.

How can conflicting demands arise in National Parks?

A

Ten National Parks in England and Wales were set up by an Act of Parliament in 1949. The National Parks, which cover nearly 10 per cent of the two countries, were chosen because of their great natural beauty and scenic attraction (map **A**). They contain some of the most diverse upland and/or coastal scenery in England and Wales. The Act also created National Park Authorities whose task it was to look after the Parks. Each National Park Authority has to:

- protect and enhance the landscape;
- help the public to relax, and encourage them to participate in outdoor recreational activities.

To these can be added another duty:

- to protect the social and economic well-being of people who live and/or work in the National Park.

The term 'National Park' can be misleading. They are not 'parks' in the sense of an urban park. The public do not have complete freedom to wander where they would like. They are not 'national' in the sense that they are not owned by the nation - unlike most National Parks in Europe and America. Yet they are considered to be 'national' because their beauty and leisure opportunities are vital to the country. These two misconceptions can lead to conflicts between different land owners and different land users.

Figure **B** shows who owns the land in the National Parks.

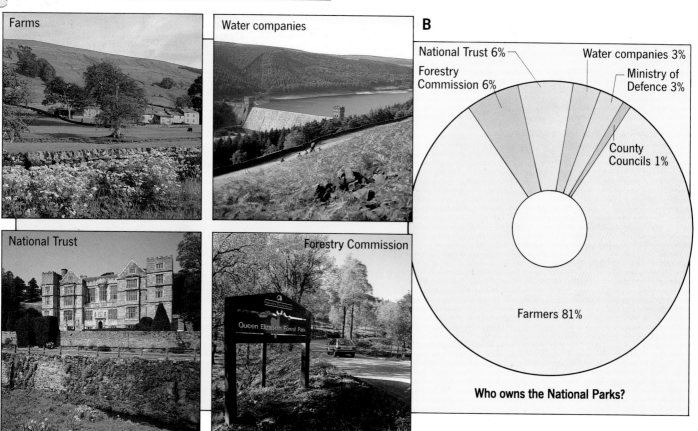

Who owns the National Parks?

How can conflicts occur?

Between different land users Farmers may want more land; the Forestry Commission may want to plant more trees; water companies may want to build another reservoir; the Ministry of Defence want to keep people off their land; property developers want to build holiday homes; tourists want to have free access to all types of land.

Between local residents and tourists Farmers do not want tourists on their land; a new reservoir may flood farmland and people's homes; tourists want to use reservoirs for recreation and they want souvenir shops while residents need convenience shops; quarries provide work for locals but spoil the views for tourists; tourists want wider roads while residents want less traffic; there is not enough room for quarry traffic and coaches on narrow roads.

Between different groups of tourists Water skiers disturb people who want to fish; large groups of ramblers disturb bird-watchers; conservation groups conflict with visitors causing pollution and damage.

Should quarrying be allowed in National Parks?

Benefits Quarries provide an important source of employment and income. Better roads have to be built to accommodate large lorries. Local councils benefit from rates paid by the quarrying firms. Slate quarries provide roofing material, limestone quarries give lime for fertiliser and cement (photo **C**) – both create wealth for the local community and the nation.

Problems Quarries cause considerable pollution and damage the environment. Dust is created during blasting operations. Noise is caused by both blasting and heavy lorries. Visual pollution results from ugly buildings, spoil heaps and scarred hillsides (photo **D**). Traffic congestion can be caused by heavy lorries using roads that are too narrow.

National Park Authorities try to ensure that working quarries are landscaped and screened, while old quarries are restored, whenever possible, to their pre-quarry appearance after the mineral has been extracted.

D Visual pollution caused by quarrying

C

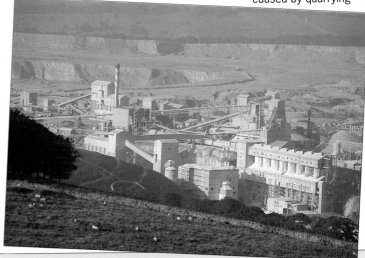

Activities

1 a) Why were National Parks set up?
   b) What are the main tasks of the National Park Authorities?
   c) How can conflicts occur in National Parks between:
       i)   different land users;
       ii) residents and tourists;
       iii) different groups of tourists?

2 For any one economic activity found in a National Park
   a) describe how it benefits the local community;
   b) describe how it can harm the environment.

3 Copy and complete diagram **E** by adding labels to show how quarries can reduce damage to the environment:
   a) when they are working,
   b) after quarrying has finished.

E

| Whilst the quarry is in operation | After quarrying has finished |

Summary

Conflicting demands can occur in National Parks and other areas of considerable scenic attraction.

How can tourists spoil the environment?

A Bowness, 1832

By providing leisure amenities for tourists visiting areas of outstanding scenic attraction, it is possible to damage the environment which first attracted people to it. For example:

- the building of tall hotel blocks in Mediterranean coastal areas has hidden the spectacular views of mountains which rise behind many of the resorts;
- the construction of ski lifts has damaged mountainous areas;
- the addition of tourist facilities and leisure amenities has affected the English Lake District.

Bowness is located on Lake Windermere. Its scenic environment has attracted visitors for many generations (photo **A**). The first tourists enjoyed mainly **passive activities** such as relaxing and admiring the views of the lake and the mountains. There was plenty of opportunity to wander through unspoilt woodland and to observe local wildlife. As time progressed visitors turned increasingly to more **active pursuits** such as water sports, fell walking and rock climbing. Even although more amenities were added for the comfort and enjoyment of the tourist, Bowness continued to maintain its attractive environment. Consequently it became an increasingly popular place to visit. Some of the reasons for this increased popularity are given in diagram **B**. Today, especially at weekends in summer, Bowness has become a '**honeypot**' (photos **C** and **D**). A honeypot is a place of attractive scenery, or of historic interest, to which tourists swarm in large numbers. The problem is, 'How can the honeypot's natural beauty, the reason for it attracting so many people, be preserved while providing facilities for the numerous peak time visitors?'. If the environment becomes too overcrowded or damaged, people will turn away and visit other places.

B

Improved access by M6 and local road improvements

More people have longer and paid holidays

More leisure time due to shorter working weeks, part-time jobs and earlier retirement

Greater mobility, more people own cars. Twenty three million people live within 3 hours drive of Bowness

Advertising on TV and in magazines. Emphasis on need to relax, health and exercise

Bowness – a Lake District honeypot

Self-catering holidays, camping and caravanning

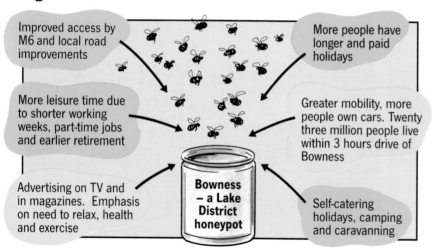

C Lake Windermere

D Bowness, 1993

Threats to the environment – especially at certain times of the week and year.

- Any large increase in numbers of tourists will reduce the peacefulness of the area, and is likely to increase the problems of litter and vandalism.
- An increase in the numbers of cars and tourist coaches means congestion on narrow roads leading into Bowness, congestion where several roads meet in the centre of Bowness, a bottleneck at the ferry, problems of car parking, and an increase in noise and fumes from traffic.
- Lake Windermere is becoming overused. As there is freedom of navigation on the lake, some 1500 vessels may use it on a summer Bank Holiday weekend. There is competition between people wanting to use canoes, yachts, speedboats and lake steamers, and those wanting to windsurf, water-ski, fish or just enjoy the wildlife.
- Bowness itself becomes overcrowded. Cafés and car parks fill up, and local shops either have to put up prices or become souvenir shops.
- Views of the lake and mountains are spoilt by increased house building and enlarged caravan parks and camp sites.
- In winter hotels, cafés, and souvenir shops may have to close and second homes are left unoccupied.

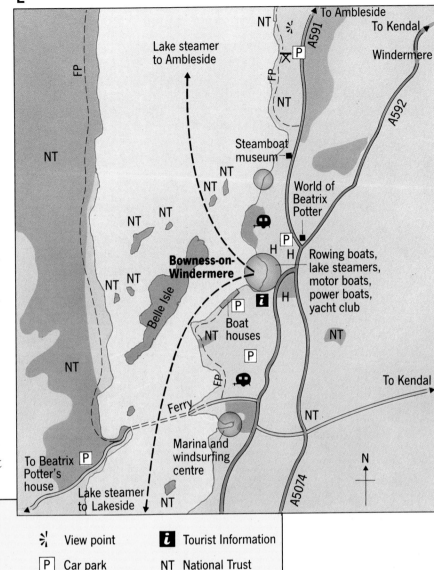

E

Key

═══ A Road	☀ View point	*i* Tourist Information
══ B Road	P Car park	NT National Trust
– FP – Footpath	✕ Picnic site	◯ Major water activity centre
Woodland	🚐 Caravan site	H Hotel
Scale 1:25 000		0 1 km

Activities

1 a) Why is the Lake District environment a source of attraction?

   b) Why are visitors to Bowness, on Lake Windermere, increasing in number?

   c) Refer to map **E**. What leisure amenities have been added to help visitors enjoy:
      i) the lake,
      ii) the lakeside,
      iii) the views,
      iv) a wet day?

2 a) In what ways has the increase in leisure activities harmed the very environment which was the source of their attraction?

   b) Table **F** is the result of a survey of tourists who were making a return visit to Bowness. Do you think Bowness has been completely spoilt or not? Give reasons for your opinion.

F

74% still liked Bowness	10.2% thought it had become too commercialised
26% didn't like it as much	15.3% thought it had become too crowded

Summary

Tourists often go to places of great scenic beauty, such as snow-covered mountains, sandy beaches with warm seas, and lakes in mountainous areas, to join in leisure activities. Without care and planning, these leisure activities can damage the environment which was the original source of their attraction.

How can tourism increase soil erosion?

Human activities can speed up the rate of several natural processes. In the case of tourism, this is most likely in areas of considerable scenic beauty and at honeypots. In both cases the large number of visitors can accelerate the rate of **soil erosion**. The most vulnerable places include mountains, where people can walk or ski, by lakes and along coastal cliffs.

Mountains

Footpaths Walking is the most popular active pastime in Britain. The most energetic walkers are those who climb mountains or use long distance footpaths. Many of the most favoured walks are in fragile environments. Walkers on grassy paths, however careful they might be, trample and kill vegetation, and compress the underlying soil. When it rains the water cannot sink into the hardened ground. Where footpaths are on level ground, they will become boggy. Where they are on steeper slopes, water will drain into them forming small streams. As these small streams flow downhill they will carry soil with them. In both cases walkers will make detours to find drier ground. In doing so they will either create new routes or widen existing ones (photo **A**). In some parts of the North Yorkshire Moors, the peat has been compressed from two and a half metres deep to under half a metre. Parts of the Pennine Way long distance footpath have been so badly eroded that suggestions have been made to pave parts of it, even if that would spoil its natural appearance.

A Footpath erosion on the Pennine Way

B Damage caused by ski runs

Skiing There are now over 40 000 ski runs and 15 000 ski lifts in Europe. Tracts of forest have often been cleared to create new, longer and more challenging ski runs. These cleared paths form natural routes for avalanches and snow meltwater in spring, and for rainwater following storms in summer. Rocks and stones are carried downhill creating large gullies. Where skiing takes place on thin snow, the underlying vegetation dies, and there will be no roots to bind the soil together. As ski runs are on steep slopes, the downhill movement of material can be significant (photo **B**).

Lakesides

Less energetic walkers like to walk along the banks of lakes enjoying either the views or the wildlife. Here too grass becomes trampled and dies leaving the roots of trees and the soil exposed. Meanwhile, waves are created on the lake, especially where there are fast power boats or large pleasure boats. These waves travel towards the land, breaking as they reach the shore. The waves will erode and undercut the bank causing it to collapse and retreat (photo **C**).

C

D Hollbeck Hall Hotel, Scarborough

Coasts

The best views looking along the coast or out to sea are obtained from vantage points on the top of sea cliffs. Hotels have often been built on top of cliffs so that their owners can attract visitors by advertising 'a room with a sea view'. The weight of a hotel, however, adds pressure to a cliff, and some cliffs are not as stable as people sometimes imagine them to be. Following several dry summers, the early months of 1993 were very wet. As the top layer of part of a cliff at Scarborough became saturated it began to move, under gravity, downhill. One large hotel on the cliff top collapsed and also slid downhill (photo **D**).

Activities

1 How can tourists increase the rate of soil erosion in:
   a) mountainous parts of Britain in summer;
   b) mountainous parts of Scotland in winter;
   c) along the sides of lakes in the Lake District;
   d) on coastal cliffs around Britain?

2 Choose phrases from the following list and place them in the appropriate boxes in flow graph **E**.
   wear away grass - undercut banks - cause waves - walkers - snow and rain channelled down paths - pleasure boat operator - rock and soil carried downhill - bank collapses - ski resort owner - path cleared through trees - soil exposed - rain flows down footpaths

3 a) Choose one of the four examples given in activity **1**. Describe carefully the methods you might use to try to reduce the damage and the rate of soil erosion caused by tourists visiting the area you have chosen.
   b) Give four other examples of how human activities may speed up natural processes.

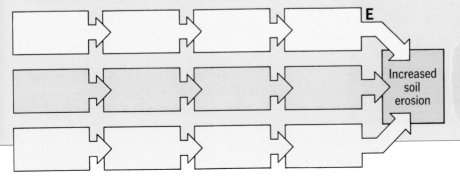

E

Increased soil erosion

Summary

Leisure activities can harm the environment by significantly speeding up natural processes. One example is the increased rate of soil erosion caused by tourists visiting areas of considerable scenic attraction.

157

How do growing populations put pressure on natural resources?

Each environment is considered to have a saturation point where the total population equals its **carrying capacity**. The carrying capacity is the total population, which can be wildlife as well as people, which can be supported by the natural resources of that environment. As populations increase, there will be extra pressure put upon the existing resources.

Kenya has one of the highest birth rates in the world. As its population increases so too does the need to produce more food. Two of Kenya's most valuable resources are its varied, attractive landscapes and its wildlife. Both resources attract tourists from overseas, and tourists spend money. But there is a conflict of interest. As Kenya tries to increase the amount of land under crops, then farming encroaches upon the landscape and wildlife habitats. Caught up in this conflict is the elephant. The elephant is considered to be essential for the tourist industry (a natural resource) but its existence and the recent increase in numbers (population) threaten Kenya's farmers.

A Elephants at Tsavo National Park

The elephant as an important natural resource

Tourism is Kenya's main source of overseas income. Over 50 per cent of tourists spend their whole holiday in beach resorts. The remainder travel inland, usually on safaris, hoping to see as much wildlife as possible. One of the greatest expectations on a safari is to see elephants. The most popular National Parks and Game Reserves are those where sightings of elephants can be guaranteed (photo **A**). But elephants are also essential to the ecosystem. They can 'smell' underground water during dry seasons and in times of drought. By digging with their feet and trunks (photo **B**) they create water holes which attract, and keep alive, many other types of wildlife.

The elephant as a threat

To many African farmers, elephants are animals to be feared. Feared partly because they do occasionally kill people, but feared mainly because of the damage they do to crops. Much of southern Kenya is intensively cultivated with individual shambas (farms) which are often only one or two hectares in size (photo **D**). The shambas may be surrounded by small thicket fences, but these are no protection against a herd of elephants – and a herd trampling across a shamba will flatten and ruin any crop. Farmers also need water for their own needs and their cattle. One large bull elephant can drink 100 litres at a time and 200 litres in a day – another source of conflict between farmer and animal. Elephants also eat for 19 hours a day. In the rainy season they eat leaves. As it gets increasingly drier and there are fewer leaves, they first eat the stems and finally the roots of plants. To obtain roots elephants have to uproot whole trees. The result is a short term destruction of the environment.

B Elephants creating a waterhole

The elephant under threat

During the early 1970s relatively large numbers of elephants died due to a severe drought. During the 1980s eight out of every ten elephants in Kenya were killed by poachers wanting ivory. In October 1989 CITES (the Convention on International Trade in Endangered Species) managed to get a global agreement which outlawed the trafficking of ivory (photo **C**). The elephant population is slowly beginning to rise again - although it still remains well below its carrying capacity. The same cannot be said for Kenya's human population. Kenya has one of the highest birth rates in the world, and its population is increasing at a rapid rate. More people means more crops, and more crops means less land for elephants and other wildlife. Slowly the natural habitats for wildlife are being destroyed.

Elephants under control

Attempts are being made to erect electric fences around farming areas to try to segregate elephants from farmland. Corridors are left through farming areas to allow elephants to migrate. Farmers are being encouraged to view elephants as an important resource. In return they are now beginning to receive some of the income obtained through tourism (previously local people did not benefit financially from tourists). Now that poaching seems defeated, elephants are being encouraged to spread out. This is widening the viewing areas for tourists and is enabling more local communities to benefit. Elephant numbers are now growing sufficiently rapidly for wildlife workers to be investigating methods of contraception among females in the herd. Such a policy is preferential to the alternative of possible future cullings as a means of controlling numbers.

C Burning confiscated ivory, Kenya

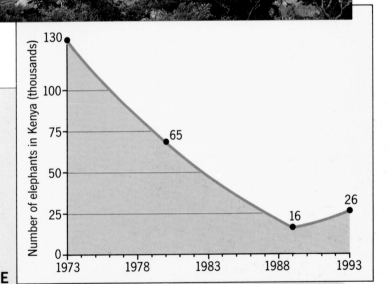

D Shambas in southern Kenya

Activities

1 Look at graph **E**.
   a) Why did the elephant population decrease in the
      i) early 1970s,
      ii) the 1980s?
   b) Why did the elephant population begin to increase after October 1989?

2 Why are elephants important to Kenya's:
   a) economy,
   b) natural environment?

3 a) Why is there conflict between farmers and elephants?
   b) How is this conflict being resolved?

E Graph: Number of elephants in Kenya (thousands)

130 (1973), 65 (c.1980), 16 (c.1989), 26 (1993)

Years: 1973, 1978, 1983, 1988, 1993

Summary In those parts of the world where there is a rapid growth in population, there is usually an equally rapid increase in pressure on natural resources.

HAMILTON COLLEGE

Index

accessibility 96, 104, 123
Amazon, River 5, 8
arêtes 40, 41

Bangladesh 11, 16, 29, 64
bars 27
bays 22, 48
beaches 24-5, 26, 27, 150
birth rates 66-9, 70, 74, 134, 158, 159
Bowness, Lake District 154-5
Brazil 4, 63, 68, 71, 118-19, 129
business parks 95, 138, 139

Calcutta 74, 92-3
caves 23, 45, 48
CBD (central business district) 94-5, 138, 144-6
chemical weathering 44
cliffs 22, 24, 25, 48, 157
coal and coalfields 108, 116, 128, 132, 136-7, 141
coasts 22-31, 157
Common Agricultural Policy (CAP) 124, 125
corries 38-9, 40, 41

death rates 66-7, 68-9, 70
deltas 10, 11, 31, 61
demographic transition model 66, 70
deposition 9-11, 26-7, 42-3

earthquakes 50, 51, 52-5, 56, 58-9, 60-1, 64
EC 36, 122, 124-5
economic development 108-9, 112, 117, 118, 132, 134-5, 142-3
electricity 132-3, 137, 140
employment structures 93, 116-19
energy sources 128-35
erosion 6-8, 22-3, 26, 31, 38-41, 43, 48
erratics 42
ethnic groups 78-9, 90, 91
evapotranspiration 14

farming 11, 116, 120-7; farming systems 120-1;
farm pollution 32, 34-5, 127
fertiliser 32, 126, 127, 153
fjords 30
flood hydrographs 14-15, 17
flood plains 10, 11, 18, 19
floods 8, 10-11, 12, 15, 16-21, 28-9, 114
France 63, 68, 71, 107
freeze-thaw 38
functional zones 94-5

Ganges, River 33
Germany 68, 107
glacial troughs 30, 40, 41, 42
glaciation 30, 38-43
global warming 31, 57, 132, 133, 134
government policies 100-1, 122-3

hanging valleys 41
headlands 22, 48
hedgerows 126

hierarchies 88-9, 144
honeypots 46, 154
housing 86, 90, 92, 94-5, 97, 98, 99, 100, 101, 138
hydro-electricity 20, 21, 128, 129, 132, 133
hydrological (water) cycle 12-13, 38

India 29, 63, 68, 69, 70-1, 118-19, 134
industrial pollution 32, 33, 34-5, 36, 37
industry 64, 65, 73, 96, 99, 100, 101, 108, 116, 136-41; see also employment
infant mortality 68
Information Technology (IT) 108
inner cities 95, 98-101, 138, 145, 147
iron and steel industry 108, 136, 141
Isle of Purbeck 48, 49
Israel 76-7

Japan 50, 63, 68, 74, 75

Kenya 10, 63, 68, 109, 129, 135, 142-3, 150-1, 158-9

land use 16, 94-101, 124-5, 138
land values 96, 138, 147
levees 10, 18, 19, 20
life expectancy 68
limestone (karst) 16, 44-7, 48, 49, 153
Location Quotient 119
London's Docklands 100-1
longshore drift 24, 26

map skills 80-3
meanders 8-9, 20
migration 70, 76-7, 78
mining 116, 132
Mississippi, River 5, 8, 10, 11, 18-19, 20
Missouri, River 5, 18, 20
models 66-7, 86, 94-5, 138
moraine 38, 39, 42

National Parks 152-3
natural resources 128-9, 142-3, 150, 158
networks 104-5
New York 90-1
Nile, River 5, 10, 11
North Sea 34, 35, 36-7, 130
nuclear power 128, 132, 133

offices 95, 96, 97, 108, 138
oil 34, 35, 36, 108, 128, 130-1, 137
Ordnance Survey maps 11, 80, 82-3, 85, 87, 104, 114-15
overpopulation 74-5, 134
oxbow lakes 8-9

planning 100-3, 111, 150-2, 159
plates and plate boundaries 53, 54-5, 56, 58, 61
pollution 32-7, 91, 98, 99, 106, 110-11, 127, 128, 130-1, 134, 150, 153
population 62-79, 112, 129, 134-5, 158-9
population pyramids 70-1, 73
ports 108, 137

power stations 32, 132, 134, 140
precipitation 12, 13, 14-15, 16, 38
pyramidal peak 40, 41

quarrying 153

reservoirs 13, 18, 20, 21, 133
Rhine, River 33, 34, 36
rias 30
ribbon lakes 42, 43
ridge and vale 44, 48, 49
river (drainage) basins 4-5, 12-13, 16, 18, 20
rivers 4-21, 45
rocks 7, 16, 22-3, 44, 48-9; see also limestone
run-off 12, 14-15, 16, 19, 20

science parks 138, 139
sea-level changes 28, 30-1
settlements 64, 80-93, 98-9, 110-11; location factors 84-5, 114
sewage 32, 33, 34-5, 36, 37, 74, 93
shanty settlements 79, 92-3
Shetland 130-1
shops and shopping 89, 94-7, 100, 101, 138, 144-9
soil erosion 21, 74, 126, 156-7
soils 11, 16, 65, 74, 120, 121, 122
South Africa 78-9
spits 26, 27
stacks 23, 48
storm surges 28-9
suburbanised (commuter) villages 86-7

technological development 107-9, 123, 130, 135, 139, 142-3
thermal power stations 132
Tokyo 51, 58-9, 60-1, 75
topographical maps 114-15
topological maps 112-13
tourism 107, 140, 150-1, 153, 154-7, 158, 159
transport 65, 74, 86, 90, 91, 94, 96, 98, 100, 101, 103-15, 116, 123, 128, 140
transportation 6, 8-9, 24-5, 38, 42
tsunamis 58, 59

urban growth 16, 86-7, 90-1, 96
urbanisation 92-3, 94-103, 110-11, 138
urban planning 102-3
urban population 62-3, 74
USA 63, 68, 118-19, 134

volcanoes 50, 51, 52-7, 60, 61, 64, 65
V-shaped valleys 6, 7

waterfalls and gorges 6, 7, 41
water pollution 32-7
watershed 4, 5, 40, 41
wave-cut platforms 22, 26
waves 22-3, 24-5, 26-7
weathering 38, 44
wildlife habitats 150-1, 158-9